D1264849

# THE STATE AS A FIRM

# STUDIES IN PUBLIC CHOICE 3

Gordon Tullock, *Editor*
*Virginia Polytechnic Institute and State University*

**Other volumes in the series:**
Buchanan, J., Wagner, R.E., *Fiscal Responsibility in Constitutional Democracy,* 1978, Number 1
McKenzie, R.E.; *The Political Economy of the Educational Process,* 1979, Number 2

This series, STUDIES IN PUBLIC CHOICE, like the journal *Public Choice,* is devoted to an important aspect of the interaction between the disciplines of economics and political science; it uses economic methods of analysis on matters which are traditionally political.

These publications are attempting to further the growth of knowledge in this intersection of the social sciences.

# THE STATE AS A FIRM
## *Economic Forces in Political Development*

RICHARD D. AUSTER
*University of Arizona*

MORRIS SILVER
*The City College
of the City University, New York*

*Martinus Nijhoff Publishing*
*Boston/The Hague/London*

Distributors for North America:
Martinus Nijhoff Publishing
Kluwer Boston, Inc.
160 Old Derby Street
Hingham, Massachusetts 02043

Distributors outside North America:
Kluwer Academic Publishers Group
Distribution Centre
P.O. Box 322
3300 AH Dordrecht, The Netherlands

**Library of Congress Cataloging in Publication Data**

Auster, Richard D
  The State as a firm.

  (Studies in public choice ; v. 3)
  Bibliography: p.
  Includes index.
  1. State, The—Economic aspects. I. Silver,
Morris, joint author. II. Title. III. Series.
JA77.A94     320.1     79–11950
ISBN 0–89838–000–6

Printed in the United States of America.

*To Morris' wife Sondra for her patience and encourage-
ment and to our parents for wisdom and compassion*

# PREFACE

We seem to be witnessing the rebirth of the concept of an integrated social science, a complete theory of human action and interaction in all its ramifications and complications. What we call society is simply the totality of human exchange. Economics is a theory of human exchange of certain types. Although the qualities of what is being exchanged as well as the conditions of exchange may vary, economic theory has recently broadened its scope sufficiently to begin to be general enough to handle these problems as well. In the present work we attempt to see what insights are revealed by the application of economic categories to political history. We feel there are many. At this point Silver stops.[1] Auster continues. A quick spin around the "policy" block in the new model so to speak, hence Chapter 8. For the rest, however, this is truly a joint work. The authors' names appear in alphabetical order. After 12 years of professional association, claims to precedence in origination could too clearly be self-deception.

---

[1] Silver is even more pessimistic than Auster, in particular about which types of reforms will be accepted. With the rise to affluence of most members of our society the mass itself has become concerned with political reform as almost a new form of entertainment. Unfortunately, they have no idea how to improve matters. In a sense, then, Auster hopes they will learn from the reforms suggested in this book while Silver sees that as unlikely.

Our early work was on the theory of the internal nature of the firm. Then we became interested in the issues raised by the existence of collective (or public) goods. Soon thereafter these two areas of interest, together with our belief that economic theory provides a basis for the understanding of all social behavior, merged to produce the research presented here.

We are indebted to numerous fellow workers in the renaissance field of public choice. They have both inspired us with their own work and been generous enough to devote their time to providing us with comments on earlier drafts. We have learned much from professional interaction. In particular we would like to thank Bairey, Buchanan, Denzau, Galatin, Horn, Niskanen, McCain, Murphy, Smith, Tullock, and Thurow. We would also like to thank the various somewhat underpaid secretaries in the University of Arizona's Department of Economics and its Division of Economic and Business Research, who have put up with our typing and retyping requests. We also wish to express our gratitude to Brooke Cadwallader whose generosity funded the opening phases of our work on this problem. Finally, B. Sears is to be especially thanked for her editorial efforts on behalf of whatever technical writing finesse appears.

# CONTENTS

Preface                                                                    vii

Introduction                                                                 1

Part I    A MULTIDIMENSIONAL ECONOMIC THEORY
          OF GOVERNMENTS

   1   The State as a Service Firm, the Production of Order      5
   2   Theories of the Emergence of States                     15
   3   The Sizes of States                                     27
   4   The Qualities of State Activity                          43

Part II   THE PROBLEM OF GOVERNMENT

   5   The Monopoly State                                      55

                                                                            ix

6    Democracy, the Corporate State                                  69

7    Democracy as a Consumer Good                                    89

8    Experimental Remedies: Some Preposterous
     Proposals                                                       96

**Appendixes**

I    Entrepreneurship, Profit, and Limits on Firm Size             111

II   Political Revolution and Repression: An Economic
     Approach                                                       116

III  The GPITPC and Institutional Entropy                          127

     **List of References**                                         135

     **Notes**                                                      150

     **Indexes**                                                    174

# THE STATE AS A FIRM

# INTRODUCTION

Scholars have been concerned with the design of an optimal political structure for thousands of years, so it is hardly surprising that the question continues to be at least implicit in much of modern social science. The present work is an attempt to approach this issue from the perspective of the positivist. Thus we are initially concerned with "will,"[1] not "should," with predicting the course of political history (or development) rather than prescribing an optimal political structure. Then, based on an understanding of "will," tentative "shoulds" are advanced. Proceeding in this order seems absolutely essential. Political structures are not static. Unlike the monuments they leave behind, they are constantly transforming themselves in response to pressures for which they themselves are partly, although indirectly, responsible. Unless one understands the underlying forces which govern political institutions, one cannot hope to reform them. Only from the vantage point of a positive theory of political structure does it make any sense to prescribe norms.

Our approach to the construction of the requisite theory is quite simple. The central element of a formal political structure is the state, or government, and so we focus on that. We take the view that states are simply firms, although admittedly ones that produce primarily public goods. "Firm" is the economist's word for the micro-decision unit for production. It is the institution by means

1

of which the various factors of production, labor, land, capital (to use the traditional triumvirate) are combined to produce the levels and qualities of outputs that "society decides" to produce. From the perspective on society that all exchanges are subject to the same underlying laws, states are simply service firms. They make decisions regarding certain services used by society: police protection, protection against foreign invasion, sanitation, and so on. While it is true that states typically are larger than other firms, the large firms of some societies are larger than the states of some small societies. Firms come in many sizes.

Just like other firms, states are, of course, owned in a variety of ways. Democracy is one form of ownership. The variety of forms of ownership of states has close parallels in the business world, where one finds not only single proprietorships and partnerships (analogous to monarchies and oligarchies) but also closely and widely held corporations. Democracy, as we argue in Chapter 6, is in essence a widely held corporation.

In the first five chapters we are concerned with developing the elements of a theory of the state based on the State as a Firm hypothesis and comparing its implications with what we find in the historical record. We begin with an examination of the two primal outputs of states: *protection* against internal and external threats to the current distribution of the ownership of resources, and *punishment* for attempts to violate the "rules." The pattern of the evolution of punishment through time is shown to fit quite nicely into a simple economic framework.

Next we look at the theory relevant for predicting the presence or absence of states in societies and for changes in the sizes of states in several dimensions: population, level of activity, and resource use. The comparative statics of a relatively simple theory of state size in these dimensions is developed and then confronted with a variety of historical, anthropological, archeological, and even some standard statistical evidence in Chapters 2, 3, and 4. On the whole, the evidence is not inconsistent with the implications of the theory. These chapters conclude with some brief words about the forces presently influencing the future of state size. We conclude that major opposing currents are at work and that the outcome, therefore, is not clear.

The world's system of states is viewed as an example of monopolistic competition in both quantity (population, land mass) and quality (level of order and so forth) dimensions. The latter are, of course, public goods.[2] In quantity space, the theory employed is essentially the familiar competitive model. The theory of quality employed relates to the optimum level of public good where we present some new results. The optimality assumption is somewhat justified in Chapter 5, where the behavior of a public goods monopolist is considered. Ideally, of course, both sets of dimensions should be analyzed simultaneously; that, however, is deferred for a future work.

A few words about our reliance on qualitative historical, anthropological, and archeological data are probably in order. Their use by economists is somewhat unusual but in our case is quite natural. People do not change their behavior with every minor shift in the world around them. Quite often, habits are strong and behavior is modified only slowly. Some changes require lengthy "gestation periods."[3] This consideration, relevant to many products and market structures, is especially so for the primarily public goods we consider and the political structures that control their production. As a consequence, exceptionally long periods of time are needed to observe the types of shifts predicted by any theory of the state. Quantitative data on time series, however, are generally not available over sufficiently long periods. Quantitative cross-sectional data usually do not exhibit sufficient variation relative to the underlying unspecifiable differences across samples. Our use of qualitative historical data in this study does, however, raise some issues which, in the interests of scientific objectivity, must be mentioned at the outset.

Ideally, one performs an experiment to test the validity of a theory. While we are aware of the recent breakthroughs in experimental techniques in laboratory economics, just like most of our profession we rely on history. The only difference is that we do not restrict ourselves to recent history. In our case, the theory was developed before the evidence was gathered, as often happens. We then began reading history, tentatively at first and later more systematically, with a view to gathering evidence relevant to the theory. Self-interest could have operated against the discovery of contradictory evidence; we trust it did not.

All the usual objections to simple *ad hoc ergo propter hoc* inferences of the types we necessarily employ may, of course, also be made: omitted variables, simultaneous determination of results, and so on. The list is well known and we plead guilty. This study is not meant as a final word on the subject. Indeed, we hope that future research follows up on our own tentative explorations.

There are, however, some advantages to qualitative historical evidence such as we employ. These should also be noted. When an economic series indicates that expenditures have risen, they may in fact not have done so. Measurement error is a persistent problem with the usual economic data, and when it is large (with "large" being only a maximum absolute error of less than 3.5%), econometric analysis may be in vain.[4] Little can be learned from the simple regression of noise on noise. When history records the fall of a state, there can be some question about the precise date; there is much less question about whether the state fell. Similarly, broad qualitative changes in population, in its dispersion, or in changes in the degree of urbanization are capable of more accurate observation than typical economic variables. While the inference patterns we use are less "reliable," the data are in a sense much more "reliable." Which way the advantage lies remains for future research to determine.

Having developed and presented evidence for the theory, we then turn to the problems posed by states for their citizens. In simplest terms, these problems arise because states are relative monopolists in their primal industries: collective protection and punishment. The state itself is a prime source of exploitation. This view of the state and the related exploitation issue are developed in Chapter 5. Evidence on the consistency of our theory with the outbreak and success of revolutions and other reactions to exploitation are considered at the same time.

The final chapters look at remedies for the problems with which states tend to confront their citizens. First, democracy is examined. It is found to create some tendency to overdevote resources to state services and, in general, to lead to the intensification of all sorts of efficiency problems inherent in all institutions[5] and in states in particular. Rather than being a way to make things better, democracy — without federalism — may simply be an expensive consumer good, that is, something desired for itself despite its costs. Some evidence for this view of democracy is presented in Chapter 7. The final chapter then provides a menu of experimental amelioratives for the problems of government, in the United States in particular but with occasional reference to the world as a whole. These are advanced in a very tentative fashion. The present system, after all, works neither as badly nor as well as it might, and since we do not claim to understand society fully as yet, it behooves us to be cautious. Social science is still in its relative infancy, a fact which policy advocates too often seem to ignore — when it is to their advantage to do so. In our experience one of the most important sources of many of our most pressing social problems has been our precipitous haste to try to make things better. The effects of this phenomenon are exacerbated by our continued substitution of dogma for scientific investigation of the fundamental issues in this area. At present, creative but cautious experimentation coupled with objective observation appears to be our most pressing social need.

# 1 THE STATE AS A SERVICE FIRM, THE PRODUCTION OF ORDER

We begin with a brief examination of the production of order, which was the original function of governments, and remains the primary objective of much state activity. Beginning in this way will allow us to develop *en passant* the economists' traditional view of the proper role of government in society. Our focus on the production of order should not be misconstrued, however. We do not wish to deny that modern states produce many other outputs, although in some sense, all of these may be considered to affect the level of order, if only because the latter will depend on the totality of society. It is clear that many people desire outputs other than order as ends in and of themselves. Consider equity, for example. There may be people who derive satisfaction from their perceptions of society as equitable, or who simply wish to insure themselves against possible losses in the economic game. In the case of state schooling, people may desire schooling for themselves and for their children (and wish others to pay for it), or they may desire to live in an educated society. Perhaps they believe that democracy works better with an educated population, and they desire to live in a well-working democracy. It matters not whether these views are right or wrong, or even if these tastes are those of the authors of the present work. Such issues are entirely irrelevant. As scientists we have no basis for judging other people's tastes and as economists no basis for saying that it is wrong for a firm to do whatever business it can find. At various times, however, we will point out the consequences of allowing such services to be produced by such a central and highly monopolistic authority as the typical state.

The universe we propose to examine is assumed to consist exclusively of individuals and objects. Objects may be either tangible or intangible. Unwritten ideas, or the "mood of the times" represent examples of what we mean by intangible objects. Individuals' levels of satisfaction are assumed to be given by utility functions, which depend both on the distribution and levels of objects and on the levels of satisfaction of their fellows. As is traditional we assume that individuals choose courses of action which they expect will maximize their levels of satisfaction.

All objects are assumed to be controlled by some individual or group of individuals,[6] that is to say, they are someone's property. Free goods are ignored, but common goods are not. Let us stress at the outset that in our view "to control" is the essential positive meaning of the verb "to own." Ownership without control is an empty form, and one that tends to disappear. For purposes of simplification we ignore the possibility of inadvertent use, transfer, or change in the physical state of an object. Although a given individual may not know to whom a given object belongs, he is taken to know whether or not it is his and what the effects of his actions will be. We further assume that all consequences of actions are potentially avoidable by means of other actions, even if at some cost. If a consequence is a collective, or public, good,[7] the avoidance cost is the cost of leaving the community.

The goods (objects) exchanged by society may be either public (collective) or private. The distinction is this: for a private good, each individual gets his own amount of the good. For a public good, individuals have available to them the public's—or aggregate—level of the good. Thus, the orderliness of society (order) is a public good, while pizzas eaten are not. "Collective good" seems a better phrase than "public good" because it does not suggest that the public sector must produce public goods. In most instances goods are not entirely public or private, but rather blends of these two polar cases. These matters will be discussed at greater length in Chapter 4.

In this context, a *criminal act* is defined as any attempt by an individual (the criminal) to transfer (or alter the physical nature of) an object or individual or to benefit from its services without the permission of the individual currently controlling its use (the victim).[8]

By our definitions any criminal act necessarily involves *mens rea,* "a guilty mind." Fraud, where the permission to perform an act is obtained through deception, is also understood to be a criminal act. In general, we will not assume the existence of free perfect information.

The state provides the services "protection" and punishment, and through these it manipulates the level of order. Criminal acts may be distinguished from *punishment*. Punishment occurs when the utility level of an individual is reduced through an action initiated because that individual has previously attempted a crime. The punishment may be direct or indirect, as when loved ones are harmed. In some instances it may not even be the stated intention of the punishers to punish, as when an individual is forcibly "treated." "Hospitals" for the "criminally insane," some of whom have never committed crimes, are in this view prisons. As the psychiatrist Dr. T. Szasz observes so correctly, "The prisoner patient would have to be crazy indeed not to feel imprisoned when he is deprived of basic freedoms and when he is compelled to submit to 'treatment' against his will."[9] If "rehabilitation" is unpleasant and involuntary, it is punishment as well.

One possible refinement of this set of definitions concerns excessive punishment — that is, either punishment in excess of what is generally understood to be the appropriate response to, or consequence of, a criminal act, or punishment of an innocent. These too could be considered crimes, as could punishment that is less severe than is generally understood to be appropriate. In the first case, the new victims of a crime are the "offenders" and they, interestingly enough, are often seen as such by their society. In mid-nineteenth century Russia, people who had been punished were called "unfortunates";[10] the punishers were called "tyrants." In the second circumstance the victim is the public at large. The criminal is considered "coddled" while the reluctant punishers are called "bleeding hearts." Society is often composed of diverse groups, with different understandings of "the appropriate response." It is therefore quite possible for both views to be held in the same society at the same point in time, no doubt our present circumstance.

Contrary to Durkheim and others, we do not view punishment as mere vengeance. Durkheim argued that

> punishment has remained, at least in part, a work of vengeance . . . . The proof of this lies in the minute precautions we take to proportion punishment as exactly as possible to the severity of the crime; they would be inexplicable if we did not believe the culpable right to suffer because he has done evil and in the same degree. In effect, this gradation is not necessary if punishment is only a means of defense.[11]

This argument fails to recognize three things. First, scarce resources are required in order to be able to produce punishment. Second, various types of crimes impose different costs on society; and finally, different criminal activities have varying difficulties of apprehension. The "careful consideration" Durkheim notes may simply reflect the desire of society to allocate its resources efficiently. To the extent that more severe punishment costs the punisher more (e.g., a longer jail sentence but presumably not a larger fine) it is only rational that it be reserved for more severe crimes. Similarly, crimes with a low probability of apprehension should also be given a more severe punishment in order to confront the criminal with an appropriate "expected cost" of committing the crime. Broadly speaking, a rational society will want to have penalties and enforcement levels which cause the criminal to have the same expected cost of committing the crime as society as a whole will be forced to bear if he or she does attempt it.

To the modern economist, one way to view the role of government in society is as a controller of the levels of activities which produce "externalities," or "neighborhood effects."[12] These are effects on second parties where either the second party is benefited and the acting individual cannot require compensation for the benefit he has produced (positive externality), or the second party is harmed and cannot require compensation for the damage he has suffered (negative externality). A competitive society with no externality producing activities will invariably allocate its resources efficiently.[13] Thus, it will have no role for government. Why control a situation that is already controlling itself perfectly?[14] When externalities are present, society will not allocate its resources efficiently. Too few resources will be allocated to activities producing positive externalities and too many to those which produce negative ones. This is easy enough to show. Figure 1 depicts the case of a positive externality. In this case, marginal social benefit ($MSB$) is higher than marginal private benefit ($MPB$) by an amount which depends on the size of the externality. Marginal private and social costs, however, are the same. The curves are drawn with the conventional slopes. The social optimum occurs when marginal social benefit equals marginal social cost. When individuals are left to their own devices, they act in a manner which causes marginal private cost to equal marginal private benefit. In the present case, that results in too little of the activity being undertaken. If, however, the government subsidizes this activity by the amount "$s$" then individuals acting in their own interests will allocate society's resources efficiently.

Crimes are readily viewed as examples of activities which produce negative externalities. When the victims are fully compensated by the "thief," there is no crime—since the victims agreed (they were *fully* compensated). The case of negative externality is just the mirror image of the case of a positive one just discussed. Thus, in the absence of government intervention one expects that too much crime will occur.

According to Hobbes,[15] when people are in the "natural state" they are dominated by responses to mutual fear, by which he means "a certain foresight of future evil." These responses include not only flight but also "to distrust,

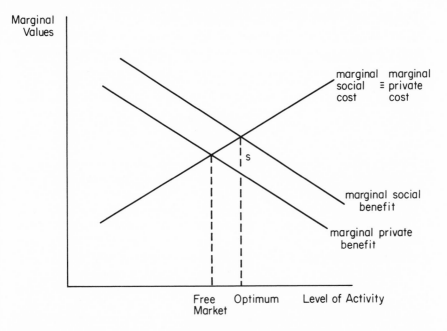

Figure 1

suspect, take heed, [and] provide so that they may not fear." One prevalent practice is to reduce one's trust in an individual who has committed crimes in the past. Tullock's[16] "discipline of continuous dealings" (or nonviolent power") is trust reduction from the potential criminal perspective. This fear of the "state of nature" is not restricted to Hobbes; the Bantu peoples of Africa believe that "In a country without chiefs, people devour one another."[17]

The government by imposing various punishments and allocating its law enforcement efforts appropriately can, at least in principle, cause *MSB = MPB*, in which case society will be efficient.[18] We may call this the "rationalist view of crime and punishment."

Donald Wittman ("Two Views of Procedure"), a modern supporter of the Durkheim view previously noted, denies that punishment is in fact meted out in this way. His counterexamples, however, only take into account the ease of apprehension and not the social cost of the crime. Robbers, for example, may perhaps be easier to catch than burglars because the victim can act as a witness. The cost to society of being a victim, however, is higher in the case of robbery because of the unpleasantness of being held at gun- or knifepoint. Litterers may be hard to catch, but society may not view the consequences of littering as very drastic. In recent years, social scientists have amassed a vast volume of evidence in support of the "rationalist" view of crime and punishment.[19] But may we note, in passing, that much of this literature seems to have missed what would appear to be one basic implication of the "rationalist view." Its notion that punishment should be set so as to have social marginal cost equal to the criminal's marginal cost can be taken to mean that, to the extent that ease of apprehension and various components of cost are measurable, actual penalties reveal society's relative preferences across groups or actions. Society, if viewed as a maximizer, reveals its tastes by its actions just as the individual does.[20] Perhaps future researchers will investigate this possibility.

We will continue to assume, then, that people are punished because society as a whole wishes to discourage the production of disorder, although actually very few (if any) of our conclusions depend on this.

Individuals desire order (the absence of disorder) both because they derive satisfaction from their property and do not wish to lose it, and because they are typically risk-averse and thus wish to avoid uncertainty about the future in general. In addition, individuals may derive satisfaction directly from the perception of order in society itself. To be more formal, we define order as:

$$G = 1 - \phi$$

where:

$G$ = Level of order

$\phi$ = Expected percentage reduction in the individual's level of
satisfaction as result of crime[21]

Admittedly, the level of order may vary from individual to individual in the society. It may vary across groups in society. Since we will be principally concerned with the social order as a whole, we will generally omit this aspect of reality.

The level of order in a society results from many factors.[22] Some of these order-generating factors may be said to determine the society's taste for criminal activity; others operate through objective constraints to determine the expected return (or schedule of returns) from such activity. In the former category are *love*, which is the weight given to the satisfaction of others in an individual's utility function; *legitimacy*, or the extent to which the current distribution of object control is considered just or right; and *guilt*, the belief that crime is "wrong" as well as other subjective sociopsychological variables.

*Relative earnings*, or the expected financial return obtainable through noncriminal activity relative to the return expected to be realized from a criminal act, is the central variable in the second category, "expected returns." The level of relative earnings is in turn determined by a number of other variables, including the distribution of income in society, the presence of legal as opposed

to criminal skills and opportunities, the level of resources being devoted to protection (which determines the probability of being successful in a criminal
endeavor), the resources devoted to punishment, and the severity of the punishment.[23] *Protection* or *defense* may be defined as "preassigned human and/or
material means whose function is to make any . . . criminal action less effective."[24] These include the use of locks, alarms, fences, guards, antiballistic missiles (ABMs), and travelers' checks, reducing one's material holdings, taking
karate lessons, practicing one's "draw," and gradations in the degree of trust one
places in other individuals.

There are various types of punishment. In some cases, the successful infliction
of the punishment depends on the use of physical coercion (or its threat). In
others, it is only necessary that the individual to be punished sees himself as a
member of the society. In this case, he is susceptible to punishment by ridicule
or ostracism, especially in close-knit communities, as well as to punishment by
means of "supernatural sanctions."[25] Among the Trobriand population of New
Guinea the chief

> has no formal mechanism for maintaining his rule — no police force or law
> courts to punish offenses . . . should anyone offend or defy him, the chief
> summons one of the sorcerers to kill the offender by black magic . . . . The
> people are genuinely afraid of magical spells and thus often doom themselves
> through an excess of fear.[26]

We will call the former *physical* and the latter *psychic* punishment.

Since the threat to the order of society may come from within or without the
borders of that society, punishment and protection are similarly directed toward
either internal or external criminals. Conquest by another society will almost
always involve the redistribution of some part of the property of the native
population among the conquerors. Similarly, pirates, hijackers, and skyjackers all
pose external threats to the level of order in a society, and the organs of external
punishment and protection are directed against them.[27]

All variables in the order-generating function vary according to time and
place. The taste variables would seem to depend primarily on the homogeneity
of the population[28] and to respond relatively little to the conscious expenditure
of additional resources. This does not mean that they do not sometimes change
very quickly, or that they might not be capable of more rapid and effective
manipulation in some future technology where thought control had reached new
levels of refinement. It is certainly possible to view large parts of educational
("schooling") and other public expenditures as being primitive attempts to induce order indirectly in this way. How effective they are is another matter.[29]

While it might be presumed in general that increasing the resources devoted to
producing order necessarily increases the level of order, this is not always so.

Sometimes a perverse result may occur for reasons which are somewhat technical and are discussed in Chapter 6. In other circumstances, however, it is easy to see why a perverse result might occur, as when increases in the level of order are attempted by means that contain contradictions. Thus, Riker (1971) suggests that redistribution of income would necessarily increase the level of order by increasing legitimacy. This might not be the case, however, unless the redistribution resulted in an entirely equal distribution (and perhaps not even then).[30] A token redistribution might serve only to convince individuals who had previously believed in the legitimacy of the distribution that they had been wrong and that the distribution is, in fact, arbitrary. Moreover, the redistribution might serve as a signal to the strongly discontented that the possessing classes have become so guilt-ridden that the subjective probability of being punished is lowered.[31] In addition, as Gordon Tullock reminds us, the redistribution of income is almost always a redistribution of *legal* income. Thus, in fact, it can be expected automatically to raise the relative return to illegal work.

Governments or states produce punishment and collective protection. Both of these services are desired because they manipulate the level of order. What types of "goods" do these services constitute? As we have observed, not all goods and services in society are of the same general type. Some are primarily "private," while others are "public," and indeed punishment and certain forms of protection have important collective (public) components. To the extent that victimization by criminals is a random event with equal probabilities of affecting everyone in society, the deterrent effect of punishment is a public good. Moreover, some forms of protection (e.g., armies and ABMs) necessarily protect everyone to the same extent. That is, they are directly public goods. As we shall see (Chapter 4), this has important implications for the structure of the industry producing those forms of protection.

Punishment exerts its deterrent effects through a number of different channels.[32] The form of punishment may rehabilitate the criminal by altering his tastes, or it may alter his opportunities for legal earnings by providing him with legally marketable skills. It may incapacitate him for further criminal activity. Execution permanently incapacitates, while jails do so on a temporary basis. In some societies pickpockets, when caught, were either publicly hanged or sent to Georgia; in others, their hands were cut off. It is often claimed that pickpockets used to practice their trade among the crowds attending the hanging of a pickpocket, and from this it must be presumed that the deterrent effect of punishment is negligible. This argument, however, misses the essential point that the hanged pickpocket was forever deterred from practicing his trade, and that individuals who had not yet acquired the skill to enter the pickpocket trade might be deterred from doing so. At least in the short run, the effect of a tax will be different on people who are already in a business and on those who are not. The recent economics literature on crime has stressed the additional argument that punishment raises the expected costs of crime to the criminal who, if rational, must then reduce his activity. At the very least, one would expect more careful planning of individual crimes, which will tend to reduce the number of crimes. In this case, *general prevention* results. Despite the current lack of popular acceptance of the deterrent effect of punishment, a growing body of econometric evidence points to its existence.[33]

It is our view that people desire to have punishment and collective protection produced, just as they desire auto repairs, haircuts, entertainment and other services, and that production of these services is governed by the usual social efficiency-seeking forces which economists typically study. We now present some evidence that the nature of punishment is indeed subject to these forces.[34]

If punishment is subject to economic or economizing forces, then one would expect the type of punishment meted out to be sensitive to certain changes in society or to certain differences between societies. For example, societies which have little or no material capital would be expected to stress corporal forms of punishment. This is consistent with observed behavior of the food-gathering societies of southeastern Australia. Since there is little property that can be used to pay compensation, punishment takes the form of the "voluntary submission of the offender to the throwing of spears or hacking with knives . . . until [the] offender is wounded, or onlookers say, 'enough'."[35] On the other hand, in societies where land and other material property were common, such as the post-Neolithic societies studied by anthropologists, those of the Germanic tribes of western Europe, in ancient Greece and Rome, and in western Europe during the Middle Ages, it was possible to expunge offenses by payment of compensation including punitive damages (fines, *wergeld,* etc.).[36] The Hebrew "eye for an eye" did not refer to the literal corporal sanction but rather to payment of a justly compensating amount.[37]

This difference in the form of punishment between societies with property and those with little or none is easy to understand if one accepts the idea that society will tend to choose its punishments in an efficient way. Compensation is preferable for the maintenance of the social order, since if compensation is arranged when the offender is caught, a large part of the effect on the victim has been only temporary. In societies without physical wealth this method is unavailable. In slave societies, slaves were always subject to corporal punishment, even when other members of society were punished by having to compensate.

When societies change, the form of punishment also changes. Thus, beginning in the later Middle Ages, we see an evolution away from the reliance on compensation. By that time the peasants of western Europe were being dispossessed of their land and property and had begun moving to the cities to become part of a vast free but propertyless working class. Compensation had once again become an ineffective punishment, because such individuals in general had little property to seize for purposes of compensation. Earlier, during the impoverished late Roman Empire and also the "silent centuries" following the collapse of the Carolingian Empire, punishments which had been traditionally applicable only to slaves were meted out to offenders from the lower class of citizens.[38]

Socially acceptable corporal punishment also has undergone a clearcut evolution since the later Middle Ages. Flogging and other forms of physical mutilation of the criminal have been replaced by incarceration and other infringements of the criminal's freedom such as "treatment," reporting to probation officers, and restrictions on movement, associations, occupation, and so forth. Usually this trend is explained by *ad hoc* suggestions that people have become more "civilized" or that they now place a higher value on human life, that is, utility functions have changed over time. These same changes, however, have several simple explanations in a traditional economic context. For one, they could simply be the result of the growth of affluence. As societies have grown richer, they have become better able to afford the higher cost of producing punishment by means of more humane (less unpleasant to the beholder) and more costly methods. Moreover, as society moves farther from mere subsistence, the severity of punishment by incarceration at or near subsistence becomes greater. In addition, technological change may also have played a role. When one removes the hand of a pickpocket or a more general thief, one not only incapacitates the criminal but also warns the general public that "this person will steal." Today the warning is accomplished by a written criminal record. The advertisement that "crime does not pay" implicit in having the maimed or branded criminal walking around can now be provided by other methods as well.

# 2 THEORIES OF THE EMERGENCE OF STATES

Traditionally, the early societies whose natures shed light on the facts of state emergence have been studied by social scientists other than economists.[1] In fact, the economic theory of markets provides a number of insights into the emergence of states.

Economists usually talk in terms of the market for any given product; other social scientists talk of society. The two concepts are related and similarly vague. A society is a group of interrelated individuals sharing some common attributes. Two of these may be, and usually are, a common language and territory. In equilibrium, a single well-defined product must always sell for only one price in any given market area. For our purposes, the essential feature of both concepts is that each sketches out a definable group of people, all in such close interrelationship with respect to some endogenous variable that it is meaningful to talk of them as a group when investigating that variable. In empirical applications, economists often talk about sub-markets; societies are similarly recognized to have component sub-societies. As this work is in some senses one in social science itself, we shall use the two concepts interchangeably. The market for the punishment and protection industries is the society. In some instances we may wish to define the market "narrowly" and in others to define it "broadly." The world is filled with societies, that is, with distinct but often interrelated markets

15

for the provision of punishment and protection, but in some senses we are increasingly justified in talking of a world market for order, and so on, in which various governments compete.

In small societies both punishment and collective protection are produced by nonspecialists such as victims of crime or their revenge-seeking family and friends, "town meetings" of citizens and/or by more specialized persons such as chiefs, leading citizens, headmen, and so forth. Sense of "duty" may motivate people to join vigilante groups. Outraged bystanders sometimes intervene to forestall or to punish crime; civilian armies rally to defend society. Observe that many of these are features of more modern, larger societies as well. It is their relative importance that has changed. In the earliest societies, no individuals devoted a large part of their working time to producing protection and collective punishment. There was no regularly or continuously functioning "full-time" institution controlling the production of collective protection and punishment and in this sense no *state*.[2]

The absence of states in small societies, in this sense, is readily explained by economic theory. *The division of labor is always limited by the extent of the market.* Since the demand for punishment and collective protection is so limited in small societies, full-time specialization does not pay. As the population of a given territory grows, however, demand increases, allowing a fuller exploitation of economies resulting from a finer division of labor[3] and fuller use of material inputs that have "large" fixed capacities ("indivisibilities"). Eventually, one supposes society reaches a size at which the demand for punishment and collective protection is large enough to support a firm specializing in their production.[4] That this may *precede* other forms of nonagricultural specialization is suggested by Fallers'[5] report:

> Throughout traditional Africa . . . full-time occupational specialization, in the sense of freedom from participation in subsistence production, is more commonly related to political tasks. Whereas full-time specialization in craft production or trade is relatively rare, the specialist in government is quite common.

The dynamic process by which such firms typically emerge is a complex mixture of force and voluntary agreement. The emergent firm, a natural monopoly at this point, is the state or government of the society.[6] Its owners are the "rulers."[7]

As society grows, the demand for punishment and protection is expected to increase for many reasons. For one, taking the rate of crime as given, the *total* amount of resources devoted to punishment must increase as the size of a society increases, if only because with more people and a constant crime rate, there will be more crimes requiring punishment and there will be more things to protect. Moreover, *ceteris paribus,* increases in the size of society also increase the relative isolation of the individual from that society; that is, the fraction of the rest of society knowing or known to any individual decreases.[8] As Linton notes, crimes against property within small groups are inherently, relatively unprofitable, for:

> Since every item of personal property is well known to most of the group's members, the thief cannot use what he steals. It is unsafe for him even to keep it in his house, since neighbors are constantly dropping in. The only things which can be taken successfully are food for immediate consumption and money. Even then the individual's character, habits, and income are so well known to the rest of the community that he can rarely "get away with it." (pp. 222–223)

Increases in society size, then, can also be expected to *raise* the *crime rate* and thus increase the per capita demand for punishment. The amount of physical punishment increases both absolutely and relatively with increases in the size of the population.

Independently of its effect on the crime rate, the increased relative isolation which comes with increased size can be expected to call forth a state, since it reduces the effectiveness of psychic punishment. If societies allocate their resources in a cost-minimizing way, this will necessarily increase the ratio of physical to psychic punishment used to produce any level of overall punishment. The reduced importance of psychic punishment should tend to increase the level of resources devoted to punishment, since physical punishment is presumably more resource intensive. Furthermore, this shift to physical punishment increases the likelihood of the emergence of a specialized firm. In the modern age this trend is reinforced by a secular decline in the perceived importance of metaphysical sanctions in general, which can be expected, *ceteris paribus,* to result in an increase in crime because of reduced feelings of guilt, and so on. We will have more to say about the consequences of this trend in Chapter 4.

Finally, it would appear that the "public" nature of protective and punishment services may encourage the emergence of a specialized firm in response to increases in society's size, at least after a certain point. The usual conclusion is that "the larger the group, the farther it will fall short of providing an optimal amount of a collective good." In other words, "free riding" is expected to increase with group size.[9] The state, with its power to tax, can be viewed as an attempt to mitigate this problem.[10]

States also specialize in the production of collective forms of external protection. Again, increases in a society's size stimulate specialization, but here threatening behavior on the part of neighboring communities may be a new, decisive stimulant.[11] Evidence on this factor is fairly abundant, both spatially and temporally.

Goody observes that "in West Africa, I have been impressed with the apparent ease with which small-scale, temporary polities of a centralized kind arose around (or in opposition to) the raiders for slaves and booty during the period prior to the coming of the Europeans."[12] The emergence of the Hebrew monarchy from the post-Mosaic theocratic anarchy in the ancient Middle East was a response to an emerging rivalry with the Philistines.[13] The emergence of a monarchic state in tribal Lithuania is sometimes attributed to attacks by the crusading Order of Livonian Brothers of the Sword.[14] The threat of conquest by industrialized western states encouraged the Meiji government of Japan (1868-1912) to complete the process of political centralization[15] begun earlier by the Tokugawa Shogunate (see Chapter 3). As a final example, we have the Prussian state created by Frederick William of Brandenburg (the "Great Elector") after the Thirty Years' War. Prussia became "not a country with an army, but an army with a country."[16]

There is also some evidence on the role of population growth in the emergence of the state in the form of data on the minimum sizes of societies where states have developed. Such evidence is of more direct value in support of the economic theory of state emergence, since the role of threats is so well known.

Despite his assertion that "there is no absolute population figure below which it is impossible to form a state," Krader, an anthropologist, observes that in fact, " . . . even relatively simple and traditional states have populations . . . numbering in at least the hundreds of thousands."[17] Sanders and Price, archeologists, suggest a minimum size of 10,000 based on comparative data from the Bronze Age (3000 B.C.E.) in Mesopotamia and sixteenth-century Mesoamerica.[18] They estimate the average size of the Sumerian state at about 17,000. Stevenson, an anthropologist who studies approximately 70 African societies, concluded that "the total population in state societies in Africa would seem to be generally larger than the total population of acephalous societies."[19] Schapera, also an anthropologist, studied four different South African "primitive" societies of diverse population sizes: Bushman (8,000), Bergdama (29,000), Hottentots (24,000), and the southern Bantu, who have four major divisions and several subdivisions ranging in size from 133,000 to 2,380,000. He observes that the Bantu "have a more elaborate system of central and regional executive officers . . . , two grades of advisory personnel at the higher levels, a well-defined hierarchy of courts and, in most tribes, separate military organizations."[20] It is also among the Bantu that official duties come closest to being the sole source of personal finance of the individual who performs them. Schwartz and Miller, in an article published in the *American Journal of Sociology*, present evidence on a group of 51 societies drawn from diverse stages of economic development and different points in time. Twenty of these societies have police, that is, a "specialized armed force used partially or wholly for norm enforcement"; of these twenty, four have no other full-time government officials, while in six the police are used only in connection with annual buffalo or reindeer hunts. The remaining ten societies which have more fully functioning governments appear to be larger on the average than those not having police.

The compactness of a given population also affects the demand for order and thus the emergence of states.[21] The reason is rather simple. The more compact a given population, the lower are transportation costs, and as a result less time will have to be expended in carrying out any transaction. In general, the lower the transaction costs, the greater the demand for any good or service, including that for collective protection and punishment. Both after all are simply demands for specific types of services. Unless the effect of a reduction in transactions costs were to raise the level of private effort to provide order more than it increased the demand for order, the demand for state services will necessarily increase.

Evidence on the effect of compaction or population density is provided by historical patterns in state formation and in the absence of states. For example, among the Eskimos, the Kimbu of Western Tanzania, and the Dakota and Sioux Indians of North America, we find both wide spatial dispersion and the absence of a central form of government despite the uniformity in culture and language among the people.[22] Nomadic pastoralists are more likely to have a state when they are compacted as a result of inhabiting an area with concentrated pasturage than when they are dispersed as a result of significant microecological variations in the quality of pastorage.[23] Historically, the drawing together of populations often has preceded the formation of a state. In ancient Sumeria, under the stimulus of irrigation (or natural disaster—i.e., massive shifts in the channels of the Euphrates River) there was a gradual drawing together of the population over the period 4000–3000 B.C.E. This was reflected not only in the growth of cities but also in the desertion of villages which became less numerous with the passage of time.[24] The first Sumerian "city-states" are dated at the end of the period, generally around the year 3000 B.C.E. Rapid urban growth in Archaic Greece starting about 800 B.C.E. was followed by the emergence of "city-states" ruled by "tyrants" in the mid-seventh century B.C.E.[25] In the Teotiahuacán Valley of Mesoamerica, the 300-year period following 300 B.C.E. saw both population growth and a shift to the alluvial plain of the valley from the surrounding slopes, perhaps as a result of trade. "Towards the end of this period, at least half of the population was concentrated into a single, huge, sprawling . . . center . . . . By the time of Christ, there was at least valley-wide political integration, comprising an area of approximately 500 km$^2$."[26] Later, the rises of the Toltec and Aztec states were preceded by significant urbanization associated with trade.[27]

This pattern, in which the concentration of population precedes the formation of "city-states," is repeated by the seventh- and eighth-century Slavic peoples of the Dnieper basin. Trade with Scandinavia, Byzantium, and the Middle East led to the concentration of population in cities. By the ninth century, "firm and durable polities, such as the Kingdoms of Kiev and Novgorod,"[28] had emerged. Later, in the middle of the twelfth century, a change in commercial relationships led to a depopulation of the Dnieper cities and a movement back to the countryside and central Russia. By the time of the Tartar invasion of 1237–40 the Dnieper states had been virtually eliminated.[29] Similarly, starting in the second decade of the fifteenth century, changed commercial relationships led to a depopulation of the Hanseatic towns on the Baltic. In 1525 the Order of Teutonic Knights in Prussia, which had functioned as a central state (by providing collective protection for the area) was dissolved.[30] Finally, Wertenbacker[31] notes that the Puritan state in early New England was, in part, undermined by a movement of population from the agricultural village to the farm.

Our next examples not only support the role of compaction through urbanization but at the same time provide "time-series" evidence supporting the causal role of population growth and on the minimum size required for state formation. Up until the late eleventh and early twelfth centuries, towns in northern and central Italy were governed on a part-time and irregular basis by prominent local men called "law-worthy" men or *boni homines.*[32] Following sharp population growth resulting mainly from migration from the countryside[33] these 200–300 towns first introduced regularly functioning chief magistrates (consuls) and then full-time government in the form of executive administrators with judicial, police, and military powers (the *podesta*). The *podesta* in turn recruited professional police, soldiers, and judges.[34] "By the first decade of the thirteenth century the *podesta* had become the rule rather than the exception."[35] Examination of the scanty and very approximate population data suggests that states emerged when populations reached 15,000–20,000.[36]

The evolution of the production of punishment and collective protection in transoceanic colonies such as those of Portugal and Spain in the sixteenth century illustrates the combined impact of a variety of demand-increasing factors. The pattern has been summarized by Lane as follows:

> So long as there was no demand except that of the first colonizers themselves, there was no economic basis for a specialized organization of government. Government and various kinds of business were all conducted by the same enterprise. When a colony was successfully established and began to grow, the market for protection increased. This expansion of the market led to increased division of labor that took the form of specialized enterprises. The force-using enterprise — government — then became one among many enterprises operating in that transoceanic colonial area (p. 409).

Finally, it is worth noting that evidence for a wide variety of societies (including China, Mesopotamia, and Mesoamerica) does *not* support the Wittfogelian hypothesis that states (and cities) typically arose in direct response to the managerial requirements of large-scale hydraulic systems.[37] The more supportive Peruvian evidence presented by Lanning[38] may be quite exceptional. Keith provides a balanced perspective in his observation that with respect to irrigation systems, concentration of population, and political centralization, each variable "reinforced and was reinforced by the others as it evolved."[39]

We trust that the evidence presented so far, while obviously far from conclusive, has at least softened the reader toward the possibility of an economic theory of the state. It certainly could not be asserted that there is no evidence for it. At this point, let us see how this view of the state relates to that of other scholars.

The view of the state expressed here is from the most general perspective somewhat atypical. The state is usually surrounded by a powerful mystique. It is not viewed as simply another of the myriad institutions contained in any society, owned of necessity by certain individuals and not by others. The state is seen in other ways; often it is viewed as the expression of some transcendental force: the "leader," the "nation," the "workers," the "general will," or "divine will." For centuries the state was rarely seen as something separate from society. Even now the terms are often confounded.

The traditional view of the state, often referred to as the "idealist theory of the state," is, as Greaves correctly observes, appealing "to those who whether because they are concerned with the enforcement of law and order or because it is to their advantage to support established institutions seek a philosophical justification of the powers that be."[40] Thus, it is always taught in state schools and represents a form of advertising.[41] What is curious is that it should be implicit in so much of social *science.*

Our view is similar to that of Max Weber. He saw the state as a "human community that (successfully) claims the monopoly of the legitimate use of physical force within a given territory."[42] This is consistent with our analysis, but we might add the quibble that the state's use of force may not always be confined to a given territory (a state for nomadic peoples) and may not always be "legitimate" in the sense of having at least the tacit support of the community. Society and the state, after all, interrelate with a lag. In the days just preceding a revolution, the state is no longer seen as simply a monopoly of legitimate force; it is seen more clearly as a preponderance of force or, sometimes, only a large force, or paper tiger. In addition, as Nozick[43] has shown, the state may possess a *de facto* monopoly of physical force without "claiming" to be its sole authorizer.

Carniero expresses a view which, while similar to ours, would seem to err in the other direction from Weber's. While Weber's analysis might be construed as overemphasizing the voluntary aspect of states, Carniero overemphasizes the conquest component. Thus, he concludes that a "close examination of history indicates that only a coercive theory can account for the rise of the state."[44] There are, however, many instances in which a clear voluntary component is present in the formation of states. While one might argue that in general the voluntary component is small, both history and legends (truly ancient history) bear out that it does exist.

According to legend the Medes, who had assembled to discuss their severe crime problem, agreed to introduce a system of monarchy with a respected citizen (Deioces) as king.[45] According to Krader,[46] Monkish chronicles report that the eastern Slavic peoples "invited the Norsemen to rule over them, pointing out that their land was rich, but unruly, and in need of government." In this way the Ukranian state at Kiev arose and was ruled by the Varangians (or Rus). Similarly, the Nilotic Alur of East Africa "extend their domain when neighboring peoples invite their chiefs to come and rule over them."[47] There is also some voluntary element present in modern democratic states where the rulers are elected. This element is reduced, however, by the general failure of electoral mechanisms to enfranchise a substantial fraction of the noninfant and sufficiently conscious population (as opposed to the "adult" population) and their universal disregard in elections of the implicit ballots of those who, in order to vote "no" to the choices offered them, do not vote at all, thus indicating a preference for still other choices.

The voluntary aspect of state rule also is illustrated by the institution of clientage in Ankole (Southwest Uganda) and by "commendations" in medieval Western Europe. In return for "gifts" of cattle from the client, the Mugabe (king) "was expected to organize retaliatory raids . . . or if [a client] lost all his cattle, either through a raid or an epidemic, to give him some to start a new herd."[48] According to Russell,[49] the poor free man usually became a serf of his own free will, "offering servile labor (to the manorial lord) in order to obtain the security, protection, and land he needed."

Given the fact that one of a ruler's tasks is to prevent genuine wars of conquest of a people,[50] the prevalence of wars to determine who shall rule may simply be a rational way for society to select the rulers. After all, wars of princes, such as the Hundred Years' War,[51] generally did not involve the nonruling parts of society. The population in this case may be thought of as desiring the war so that it may be assured of a strong defense against genuine conquest. In the Southwest African kingdom of Ankole, ". . . the succession was expected to be decided by a war to the death between the king's sons, a test which satisfied the people that their new ruler was the strongest among the eligible competitors."[52] Again, while superior weapons and tactics permit a ruler to enlarge his state[53] they simultaneously increase the demand for his services. In history, conquest and merger are often difficult to disentangle. A society caught between two rival states may, in the interests of its citizens, choose to subject itself to foreign rule by the stronger rival state.

Theocracies, of course, provide another counterexample to the pure conquest position. As Sir James Frazer[54] observed, "most primitive kings are not rulers of political communities, but persons in whom a nature god is believed to be incarnate." Similarly, Fustel de Coulanges[55] argues that in ancient Greece and Italy "it was not force . . . that created chiefs and kings in . . . ancient cities. It would not be correct to say that the first man who was king was a lucky soldier. Authority flowed from the worship of the sacred fire." From another perspective, however, these beliefs could be viewed as simply examples of the widespread acceptance in these societies of various versions of the idealist theory of the state.

There is yet another major reason why the use of force in the establishment of a state does not necessarily mean that the average person prefers to be without a state. Force theorists ignore the fact that in large groups the costs of securing more or less universal agreement to an explicit and more or less detailed "social contract" establishing a state might be quite high, if not prohibitive. In view of these contracting costs, the average person might *prefer* that a state be established by force. As Tullock observes: "Setting up a monopoly of force without requiring everybody's agreement is likely to be much faster than setting one up *with* everyone's agreement; hence, the total present discounted value of future income streams . . . will be higher."[56]

The role of conquest in the dynamic process of state emergence and expansion which is amply demonstrated in history will be discussed further in Chapter 3. On the other hand, as we shall argue later, states tend to be monopolists and therefore the consent element should not be overexaggerated.

The state often is confounded with society. Yet clearly what is good for the state may not, in fact, be good for the part of society which does not own the state, that is, the ruled as opposed to the rulers. The early socialist writers, perhaps under the influence of Hobbes and the ancient philosophical writers, were among the first in recent times to see through this basic confusion of the state with the entirety of society. Quite naturally, they then inquired into the relationship between the state and society and into the question of how that relationship might be altered for the betterment of society. It is good to recall that originally socialism was simply the name of a movement that sought to transform an existing society into one in which all individuals could achieve their "maximum potential." That the position now generally refers to the economic system "central planning" seems to reflect the general tendency of movements to become intellectually ossified and to the typical nineteenth century overemphasis on the material basis of society.[57]

At times Marx and Engels, writers in the early socialist tradition, discuss the state along lines resembling our own[58] but, as Tucker has pointed out, the Marxian analysis suffers from an unresolved tension "between [its] conception of the state as alienated social power and [its] functional definition of it as an organ of class rule."[59] This functional definition is untenable, given the frequency and historical importance of state attacks upon the "possessing classes" [e.g., Sulla, the great dictator of republican Rome, Emperor Wu of the Han (140-85 B.C.E.), seventeenth century Japanese shoguns, Indian moguls, English kings such as William II and Henry I, Joseph II of Austria, Marx's own favorite example of the two Napoleons, and more recently, Franklin Roosevelt, Hitler, Mussolini, Stalin, and Mao]. Since the possessing classes have the most to lose from crime they are certainly the best "customers" of the state. It is quite natural that they demand more punishment and collective protection than the typical member of society. They are also, however, the best customers of yacht producers and caviar vendors.[60]

It seems more natural to us to assume that the state, like any firm, is owned by someone or some group, and is run in the interests of those who own it. These are the rulers and thus, in that sense, the "ruling class." They are, however, a political class and so need not be[61] the economically dominant class, although that is not unlikely, given their preponderance of coercive force. It is the force, however, which yields the capital and not *vice versa*. Members of the dominant economic class may be their best customers, as we have already noted, and one generally pays attention to one's customers. In this and other respects our view is close to that of Mosca and Dahrendorf,[62] who focused on the political ruling class.

Lenin's Marxism exemplifies the failings of the naively applied functional half of the Marxist theory of the state; Russia, the consequences of the application of naive theory. Lenin saw the form of organization of ownership of the state as transparent. "The state is the organ of class rule"; therefore, in a heroic leap of logic, the class that rules, rules the state. The state in Lenin's view is a "shell" equally controllable by any class.[63] But of course, the state is run by its owners, in their class interests, even if this is a newly created class of commissars, who, given the reality of human nature, are unlikely to find their interests entirely the same as the general interest. To be sure, in some future utopian society men might well love each other as themselves. In postrevolutionary societies, however, revolutionary leaders are products of prerevolutionary society and are unlikely to hold all men in equal love to themselves, even if they believe they do.

When it discusses the state as alienated social power, the Marxist theory more closely approaches ours. To Marxists writing in this vein, the state results from the conflicts between the organized and the organizers, conflicts produced by the ever-deepening division of labor. The state functions as the arbiter of this struggle[64] and is the means by which civil society is kept together. Initially the state is only the mediator, but with a characteristic neo-Hegelian twist it becomes alienated and in turn becomes a power that rises above other powers. Just like ours, this version of the Marxist theory of the state is both a conquest and a consent theory. It overlooks, however, the external threat aspect of the state's function, which may have value to all classes of society. More importantly, the state results not from the conflicts produced by the division of labor, which is itself preceded by inequality of talent, and so on, but is part of the division of labor itself. As the division of labor proceeds, a separate industry to produce punishment and collective protection against internal and external threats is created. Just as hunters, merchants, farmers, and clothiers arise as separate occupations, so do rulers emerge as an occupational group. In some instances, the state emerges before other forms of specialization.

Interestingly, in *The Origin of the Family, Private Property, and the State,* Engels indirectly notes a source of the origin of the state which fits into our view. In pre-state times people lived in close affinity groups (the gens) tied by continuous close association, blood, and so forth. In such a situation, where much of the property was held communally, there was no need for people to protect property as their full-time job. One of the advantages of communal ownership is that generally there is someone around to prevent theft by means other than by force. In the case of theft by force, the individual could rely on the members of his gens to come to the defense of the group property. Similarly, crimes of violence would be avenged. The emergence of trade on a wide geographical scale, itself the product of forces such as increased population density and improved transportation, which themselves would have led to the emergence of states, also encouraged the emergence of states. This occurred not necessarily for the reason Engels saw, the increased inequality of wealth.[65] It resulted more directly from individuals spending large parts of their lives outside the physical confines of their gens. Deprived of this natural source of protection of their lives and property, they quite naturally fulfilled the desire for security through other means, that is, the creation of a state. There is some debate in the economics literature about whether or not supply creates its own demand. May we assume that no one would deny that demand generally creates its own supply?

In a neo-Marxist vein, the anthropologist M. Fried distinguishes between "secondary" states (which include all contemporary states) and the "pristine" states of a few ancient civilizations which emerged autonomously in "stratified societies"[66] to maintain stratification.[67] A stratified society "is one in which members of the same sex and equivalent age status do not have equal access to the same basic resources that sustain life."[68]

As we have just noted, however, stratification and the state are both the result of a more basic factor—namely, the expansion of population which results in an increased division of labor, particularly in societies with private inheritance. Quite clearly, the greater the stratification, the less is likely to be the feeling in the population as a whole that the current distribution of income is legitimate, and therefore, the greater will be the demand for the type of goods the state produces. This is, however, only *one* source of increased demand for state services and the emergence of states. Observe that, to the extent progress in the division of labor occurs in one society and not in others, members of that society will improve their well-being faster than those of other societies. As a consequence, the likelihood of invasion by envious neighbors also increases. For this reason also, state size and stratification are going to be positively related to the extent that the latter is a necessary consequence of the division of labor. While Fried's observation that "stratified societies lacking political institutions of state level are almost impossible to find"[69] is probably correct, it does not support his view of the state. Both stratification and the state are products of other more basic forces, the most important of which are almost certainly the steady growth in the human population[70] and the gradual perfection and spreading of markets.

It is often suggested that the difference between states and other firms is that states have the power to tax.[71] It must be remembered, however, that the power to tax is itself primarily a derivative of the preponderance of coercive force in the hands of states. Actually taxes and utility bills, both of which are for services rendered continuously and previously, differ only in that the utility company does not have its own police to enforce its demand for payment. It is the state that supplies this service, as a producer good for the other firms of society and for itself. If it were not for this police service, only moral scruples and the threat of discontinued service, analogous to exile or imprisonment in the case of states, would stand in the way of individuals refusing to pay for services received from firms other than the state. The essential distinguishing feature of the state is not that it taxes but rather its monopoly power, in particular its monopoly or preponderance of coercive force. Taxes are simply the prices that must be paid for the services of the state.

Our approach, which is to view the state as the institution controlling the levels of particular types of primarily public goods, is part of an emerging tradition. It is similar to the views of Olson,[72] Froelich, Openheimer and Young,[73] Breton, and D. Friedman, North and Thomas, and other modern public choice theorists. We are simply taking the idea a few steps forward and bringing to bear the evidence of history.

# 3 THE SIZES OF STATES

State size has at least four major dimensions. Two are the number of people served by any existing state and its geographical size. These are quantitative dimensions, analogous to the output produced by the typical firm of economic theory. Two other dimensions are the level of order $(G)$ that the state produces, which is analogous to the quality (or characteristics) of the output produced by the typical private firm,[1] and the level of resources used by the state, which corresponds to the traditional firm's revenues.[2] All, of course, are determined simultaneously; nevertheless, for analytical simplicity it is useful to consider their determination separately. In this chapter we inquire into the question of the level of political concentration, or the percentage of a given society's population which will be governed by one state. Then, in Chapter 4, we look at the resource and level of order issues, seeing if and how our conclusions in this chapter must be modified.

## 1 CONCEPTUAL FOUNDATIONS AND ILLUSTRATIONS

Let us see what the ordinary economic theory of firm sizes can predict about the long-run distributions of populations across states.[3] Suppose that in every society there are many alternative individuals capable of organizing a state. The producer with the lowest average total cost (*ATC*) in the relevant range will be the first to produce the output as the demand curve is gradually shifted by population growth. Typically, however, one does not expect that this producer will be able to expand output *ad infinitum* without raising average costs. As the existing firm increases its output, its costs eventually rise and permit the existence or entry of other firms.

When the size of the state is said to increase in the sense of gaining population, we assume that the density of that population is held constant; that is, that land increases in proportion to population.[4] With constant density, population growth means, of course, that the population is becoming more spread out spatially, which of itself will increase average costs and limit state size by increasing the costs of contract enforcement, coordination, and transportation.

Even though states are monopolies, or more accurately monopolistic competitors, for simplicity's sake, we employ an essentially competitive model in this chapter. The conclusions would not substantially differ were we to employ a more complex model. To be absolutely rigorous such a model requires assumptions which guarantee that all states produce the same level of order and that there be free emigration of population across states. While the second is plausible, at least as an approximation in the long run, the first is exceptionally unlikely. The same problem occurs with the firms of traditional concern. Typically, such firms do not all produce identical products, yet large groups of them are thought to act *as if* they did and competitive analysis is employed. A three-digit industry used in a production function study might contain products as diverse as hand guns, plumbing fixtures, and large steel girders. All use iron and steel, but as we have noted, all state outputs at root involve force. In any case, the issues raised by the negative slope of the demand curve facing the state are addressed directly in Chapter 5.

Figure 2 depicts the familiar textbook case in which two firms, each with a different cost picture, are surviving in perfect competition at a price *P*. Each maximizes profits by producing that output at which *P* is equal to marginal cost (MC). Firm 1 is more efficient than firm *n,* but the market is large enough for both to survive.

Given the level of demand for services, the central issue for determining state sizes is the shape and position of the average total cost curve of state output. Holding the level of state-produced order constant,[5] the average cost curve with respect to the size of the population served can be expected to have the traditional u-shape.[6] An initial range of decreasing average costs, resulting from indivisibilities, the finer division of labor, or perhaps from the very nature of the technology or good[7] is necessarily offset in the limit by increased transportation costs, increased coordination problems, and by the increased importance of the

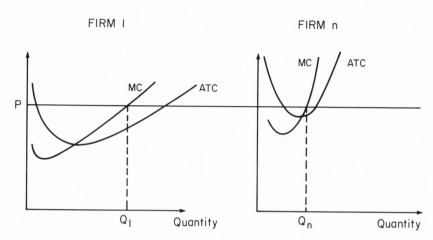

Figure 2

"shirking problem" (the need for the controller to enforce contracts, implicit or explicit, with hired labor). The "shirking problem" we believe, provides the ultimate, inescapable limit on the sizes of all firms and on state size in particular.

In general, people will "shirk" their responsibility if there are no penalties for doing so. Thus, one of the central functions of the entrepreneur, or head of a firm, is to enforce his implicit or explicit contracts with hired labor. In the absence of such enforcement, he will not only fail to obtain the effort for which he contracted but also he will no doubt lose some of his capital stock. Monitoring and enforcement are a particular type of "intermediate product" internal to the firm. Raising their levels raises output when factor inputs are held constant at *contracted for* rates. The owner's contract enforcement effort is a unique factor of production, since he does not have to enforce his contracts with himself. Being a unique factor of production, it eventually operates as a limitational factor for firm growth.

As the ruler extends his realm and is forced to increase the size of the army, police, and so forth, he necessarily acquires more contracts to enforce and therefore must spend more time seeing to it that his "employees" are acting as he wishes or more generally as they have agreed to do.[8] Even when assistant controllers are hired, *their* contractual agreements to monitor the efforts of others accurately must be enforced. As the size of the state expands, a point is reached at which the ruler either has insufficient time to increase his personal contract enforcement effort further or does not desire to do so. At that point, an upward force is increasingly exerted on costs.[9]

This upward force on costs is present even in democratic states. One must remember that, with the exception of "direct democracy," the citizen has no control over the day-to-day activities of the state (i.e., on the means, as opposed to the ends, of rule). The controllers of the state are not the public, but rather some subgroup. Even when the rulers are democratically selected in periodic elections we are still, as Sartori points out, "referring to a minority system in which the few lead and the many are led . . . . Democracy can be defined as a system where the majority designates . . . the minority that governs."[10]

To be sure, the size of this subgroup can be expanded as the size of the population grows, just as a law firm may take in new partners. This does not, however, ultimately solve the problem. A new shirking problem among the partners will inevitably emerge and worsen as the size of the controlling partnership increases.[11] Even in the limiting case of direct democracy, a shirking problem will exist because controlling the quality of the output of the state is a public good for the citizenry. The problem of shirking can be ameliorated, but it can not be eliminated.

In terms of the traditional competitive model just presented, a state can increase its size until the range of increasing average costs is reached. There will then necessarily be some pressure for the formation of new states to serve each particular society. This elementary competitive model could be enriched somewhat by the explicit introduction of a spatial dimension. The presumption is that each consumer will wish to buy from the producer with the lowest "delivered price," which results in so-called "watershed lines" between producers, at which their delivered prices are equal. In our context these would be the natural equilibrium borders between countries. As is often the case, geographical anomalies, such as mountain ranges or rivers, which raise delivered costs discretely, are often the watershed lines.[12] A similar role is played by ethnic and religious differences, since states have social as well as geographic dimensions.

The dynamics of state size adjustment can be quite complicated. Because the use of force to prevent or restrict entry is a distinct possibility, as well as for other reasons, it may take very long periods of time for rising costs to have their effect. In some historical instances, however, rulers have voluntarily introduced new states, or more commonly, allowed new states to form (e.g., by foregoing opportunities for conquest)[13] in apparent response to the increasing cost problem. Diocletian, for example, split his authority by transferring his power over the Western Roman Empire to a second "Augustus." The operation of this factor is also illustrated by Gluckman's observation that the tribal states of Southern Africa "were constantly splitting up, with segments setting themselves up as independent political communities."[14] His explanation is that increased population in the presence of vacant land results in "communications" problems. Decreases in population also appear to have their predicted effect. This is illustrated by the Black Death of the fourteenth century which killed about one-third of Europe's population. As North and Thomas point out, during this period the "required contraction in the number of political units ... came about by consolidation, merger and conquest."[15] Friedman's explanation of the same phenomenon must also be noted.

Friedman's analysis is based on the differential incentives to have large or small countries produced by differing sources of tax revenue. Taxes on trade and labor promote large countries, the former because tax revenues are maximized by having only one nation tax a single trade route or parallel trade routes. Larger countries permit higher taxes on labor since they discourage emigration. Cultural homogeneity, particularly that resulting from a common language within one t-nation,[16] has a similar effect. One could also expect that decreased population would tend to increase the size of states, because making labor relatively better paid would increase the importance of labor in total income, provided the elasticity of substitution for labor were less than one.[17]

## 2 SOME ASPECTS OF CONQUEST

Before proceeding to derive the full implications of our basic model, it may be useful to consider the issues raised by the role of conquest. This role in the dynamic process of state emergence and expansion is amply demonstrated in history. Force is a more typical method of increasing state size or forming states than the relatively costly method of explicit agreement on a "social contract"[18] or mergers or measures to encourage immigration. However, as we point out in Chapter 5, even the most extreme conquest state typically has a positive consent (or voluntary) component in its income. Of course, in the limit conquest is merely well-organized robbery or racketeering, which often increases the exploitation of the population.[19] Nevertheless, even then it is possible to view conquest itself as the taking over of a higher-cost producer's market by a lower cost producer. That force is so often the midwife of the state, should not be surprising. Because force is what states primarily produce, its use in their expansion of their market areas is quite natural.

Because conquest involves the use of force, there is a tendency for states producing more order to be able to conquer states that have lower levels of produced order and for larger states to be able to conquer smaller ones. For this reason, there may be a tendency for state sizes to be unstable, at least in the short run. However, size is not universally the decisive factor in war. There have been countless examples of military endeavors in which the outnumbered have won. Indeed, Julius Caesar rarely won when he had superior numbers and almost always won when he did not.[20] The historical importance of excellence in generalship to the determination of military success argues strongly for the "lower-cost producer" as opposed to the what might be named "big brute" view of conquest.

Costs are not determined solely by efficiency in production. The production of military might is facilitated by ready access to soldiers who are willing to fight and perhaps die, accept harsh discipline, and in modern times, possess the technical competency to use sophisticated weaponry. Societies that are relatively well-endowed with these types of individuals will be able to conquer those which are not. It might also be argued that willingness to exploit might also be a determinant of military success. Higher rates of exploitation may be associated with greater concentration of income and thus with greater savings rates. In this case, the capital that the more exploitative state had available to use for the production of conquering force might be greater. The desire to conquer, however, does not always result in conquest. On the other side, the native population of the country to be conquered might be especially resistant to becoming the subjects of high exploitation and, as we have just observed, in military affairs quantity is often less important than quality. Finally, the role of chance should not be underestimated in these and other matters.

The *ability* to remain unconquered, however, must not be identified simply with lower-cost production of order. As noted earlier in this chapter, large states may be deterred from conquering small ones because the acquisition of large and dispersed populations operates to raise their average cost of order production. Even when the large state would be the lower-cost producer, it may be deterred from conquest because the expected returns fall short of the expected costs of conquest and rule — again a familiar economic calculation. This is particularly likely when geographic barriers such as rivers and mountains are important. Roman rulers were deterred from making serious attempts to incorporate into their empire the backward Germanic tribes beyond the Rhine, while for similar reasons the Chinese emperors permitted Korea to remain separate.[21] In general, mountaineers have been more likely than flatlanders to preserve their independence. Perhaps the success of the revolt of the American colonies against the government of George III can also be placed in the category of history under the influence of geography.

History suggests that advantages in military technique are usually short-lived. Loyalties fade among widely dispersed lieutenants. The shirking effect becomes ever stronger as time passes. Large "conquest states" tend to disintegrate or to be conquered in turn. Alexander's empire did not outlive him. Genghis Khan's lasted a few generations but was then fragmented, to be partially, but again temporarily, restored by the great conqueror Timur the Lame. Similarly, the Arabian Califate was unable to maintain itself.[22] This is not to understate the importance of masses of force. The Roman Empire probably lasted quite beyond its time. The lags in the adjustment process for states are very long.

## 3 POPULATION COMPACTNESS

Independently of a population's size, its density or compactness $(C)$ itself may be expected to have an effect on state size $(S)$, both because of the direct effect of distance on the costs of producing order and because of the effect of density on the "shirking" problem itself. A reduction in "distance" will reduce the direct costs of producing order because in general transport costs will be reduced. Moreover, one also expects that the "shirking" problem will become less severe as spatial dispersion decreases which also tends to reduce costs. Thus, an increase (decrease) in population density (or compactness) can be expected not only to shift the entire average cost curve with respect to the number of people served downward (upward), but also to prolong (shorten) the range of decreasing costs. The operation of this second factor guarantees that increased density can be expected to increase state size. Figure 3 depicts the cost curve shift. It is clear that with a given $ATC$ curve of the "nearest" competitor, or more appropriately one that is shifted down by the same amount, the new equilibrium size of the firm will be increased. Mathematically one would write $\partial S/\partial C > 0$.

There is considerable evidence on the effect of density and urbanization on state size and political concentration. Changes in urbanization, of course, generally involve an increase in population density.[23] The dispersal of a given population is often accompanied by the fragmentation of states. The classic instance of this is the breakup of the Western Roman Empire. In the late fourth and fifth centuries, high urban taxes along with the looting of Roman cities by barbarians caused the population of what was still an essentially centrally ruled society[24] to be dispersed.[25] This trend toward deurbanization to avoid a threat to order was further reinforced by Islamic advances in the seventh and eighth centuries and by the Viking and Magyar raids of the mid-ninth century.[26] The specialized production of order then fell into the hands of a number of usually short-lived kingdoms,[27] a larger number of local principalities (e.g., Saxony in Germany and Aquitaine in France), and a still larger number of local magnates.[28]

Similarly, at an earlier date barbarian raids had led to the shrinkage and even abandonment of Mycenean cities in the Aegean area[29] and the replacement of a centralized state with large numbers of small rural-based "states." Changes in trade patterns produced the same form of extreme rural deconcentration of the order industry in the twelfth-century Dnieper basin and in fifteenth-century Prussia.[30]

It appears that when barbarian incursions were not accompanied by changes in the compactness of the population, they were not followed by severe political fragmentation. The period between the destruction of the Han Empire in fourth-century China and the establishment in the seventh century of the T'ang is a case in point. The cities were not destroyed, the agricultural lands of the North China

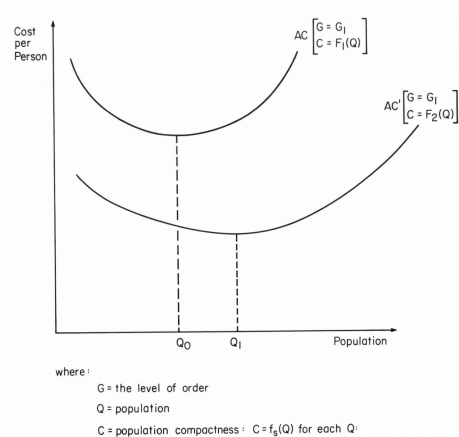

where:

G = the level of order

Q = population

C = population compactness: C = $f_s(Q)$ for each Q:
    $F_2(Q) > F_1(Q)$

Figure 3

plain remained densely populated, only three main states emerged, and full centralization returned to North China (fifth century) and to the entire area under the T'ang.[31] Similarly, barbarian invasions in Egypt during the fifth through the twelfth dynasties could not disperse the population, which out of geotechnical necessity had to be concentrated in the Nile Valley. In this case, apparently there were no cities.[32] The centralized kingdom was replaced by two relatively large states.[33] Other examples are given by Coulborn.

Urbanization not only preceded the emergence of numerous "city-states"[34] but also facilitated forcible political centralization of the entire area of Sumer (Southern Mesopotamia) under Sargon of Akkad in 2340 B.C.E. Despite invasion induced sporadic interruptions, Akkad was followed by a series of more or less centralized and highly urban empires[35] which deliberately pursued a policy of "forced sedentarization"[36] by gathering country dwellers into cities. Brundage[37] includes the continual presence of cities in the Near East as an important factor operating against the emergence there of a European type of feudalism.

Rapid urban growth in Archaic Greece, starting about 800 B.C.E.[38] and in Western Europe (starting in the eleventh and twelfth centuries B.C.E.)[39] contributed to the reconcentration of political authority. In the latter case, it is known that the urban growth resulted from a massive migratory movement out of rural areas.[40] Ultimately, much of Western Europe came to be ruled by a small number of "national monarchies" (several thousand small states had been reduced to fewer than 30 by the beginning of the twentieth century) while Greece was ruled by a small number of "city-states," which later became local states of "Hellenistic monarchies" and then of the Roman Empire.[41]

China became more and more urbanized under the stimulus of irrigation, during the seventh through third centuries B.C.E., and especially after 500 B.C.E. This was also a period of great political concentration during which some 170 small states were replaced by a remarkably stable Chinese Empire beginning with the Ch'in in 221 B.C.E. The dynamic of concentration included sacred oaths of alliance in the period of the Hegemons and conquest in the later period of Warring States. The empire was, for the most part, governed by centrally appointed salaried officials.[42]

Stimulated by foreign trade, Japan experienced rapid urban growth beginning in the late fourteenth century. This period saw the rise of commercial cities such as Nagasaki and Osaka. Again, urban growth was accompanied by sharp political concentration. First, relatively large populations were brought under the rule of "feudal lords" (the daimyō) and then, in 1603, national political concentration (a paid bureaucracy) of unprecedented scope was achieved under the Tokugawa regime.[43] In Peru, significant urban growth from 200 to 1000 C.E., was based on fishing, animal husbandry, irrigation, and agriculture and appears to have preceded the coastal empires (Huari-Tiahuanaco and Chimu). Ultimately the territories of these empires were incorporated into the relatively centralized Inca Empire, which had a population of about six million on the eve of the Spanish Conquest (1532).[44]

Something approaching a "test case" for the effect of compaction is provided by the cases of Boeotia and Attica, two Greek territories which had different degrees of urbanization yet very similar cultures, population, and territorial sizes. Attica, which was highly urbanized at Athens, had one state; Boeotia had ten states.[45] Similarly, in Peru after 800 C.E., cities on the southern coast were abandoned (apparently until the fifteenth century) and empires were replaced by small states, while at the same time empires began to emerge in the more recently urbanized central and northern coastal regions.[46]

That compaction rather than urbanization as such is the significant variable is suggested by the effect of the compaction of the East Slavs in central Russia especially after the mid-thirteenth century. This preceded the significant increase in political centralization which created the state of Muscovy by the end of the fifteenth century. Previously, in the twelfth century, the widely dispersed population had been ruled by a large number of princely states. This situation was altered by the Tartar invasion which, "by occupying the steppe regions . . . forced part of the Russian people, augmented by refugees, to occupy a smaller living space, and thus produced favorable conditions for the growth of the state by increasing the population density."[47] Along the same line, Langer considers it probable that "repeated attacks near Murom and Vladimir resulted in a population dispersement" in the direction of Moscow and Tver' in the West, "both of which emerge as major economic and political centers at the end of the thirteenth and beginning of the fourteenth centuries (C.E.).[48] In these instances, however, the effect of an external threat was also present.

The external threat aspect is not involved in the case of the rise of classic Maya civilization in the lowlands of Mexico's Yucatan peninsula about 250 C.E. Recent excavations suggest that sometime between 200–300 C.E. the highlands were rendered uninhabitable by a massive volcanic explosion, which blanketed thousands of square miles under ashes in some places yards deep.[49] Population compaction would have resulted from the migration of the survivors to the less climatically attractive lowlands, which were already inhabited.

It is not always the case that history is kind enough to provide such a simple pattern of events. Egypt provides a nice illustration of the more common difficulty of drawing definitive inferences from historical data. As we have already noted the population of Egypt necessarily concentrated itself in the 10,000-square-mile area of the Nile Valley.[50] In this circumstance, increases in population could have had two effects. The first, the demand side effect of the increased population, would have led to the proliferation of states. On the other hand, increased density of the population could have worked in the opposite direction, to increase the size of states. The problem is further complicated by the fact that in the early period of Egyptian history jungle lands were continuously cleared, producing two additional effects: an offsetting to some extent of the increase in compactness resulting from population growth which tended to reduce the size of states, and a reduction of "communications costs," a consequence of greater ease of travel that worked in the opposite direction. It might be argued, however, that the river was the cost-effective method of communication and that it did not change.[51] In fact, numerous states of various gradations in size were in time replaced by larger states and ultimately by a remarkably stable single state in 3100 B.C.E.[52] The low cost of river transportation may have facilitated this stability.

## 4  VERTICAL STRUCTURE

States typically produce more than one output, so more than one cost curve must be considered. At the most basic level are the cost curve for the preservation of order against disturbances from inside the ruled population (that of police services, etc.) and that for the preservation of order against external threats (the cost curve of military defense). It appears that in a large number of circumstances, the limitations imposed by the extent of the market have prevented rulers from reducing average costs by full-time specialization in one of the above activities;[53] nevertheless, economic pressures appear to have resulted in partial movements in that direction. It seems reasonable to presume that the range of increasing returns to scale (decreasing average total costs) is generally greater for the good protection against external threats than for the preservation of order against internal threats. There are at least two reasons why this should be. First, the pure public good aspect would appear to be more important for defense. A given army's ability to defend a certain territory is very little influenced by the size of the population *ceteris paribus.*[54] Second, it seems likely that the shirking problem may be less severe for the armed forces than for the police, because of the difference in their relationships to the "enemy." In the case of an army at war, it's foreigners—while for police, one's criminal countrymen.[55]

With this understanding we are not surprised that populous societies often divide the ruling function between a *central* state, which mainly produces preservation of order from external threats and may incorporate certain rural police functions such as the suppression of brigandage (and "High Justice"), and a larger number of *local* states which, mainly produce preservation against internal threats. This hypothesis also is consistent with Oates' ordinary least squares regressions of 1960's national data in which a statistically significant inverse correlation between the relative share of the central government in public expenditures (or public revenues) and the national population was observed.[56] Within this framework it is not surprising that as population grows, instead of seeing the emergence of complete new states, we often see a more limited form of deconcentration: the "franchising" out of some state functions to "nonsovereign" substates whose activities are subject to review by the central state.[57] This phenomenon has obvious parallels in the business world.[58]

Such a line of argument may be developed in greater detail with the assistance of Figure 4. It is assumed that the average cost of producing collective protection $(AC_1)$ turns upward later than the average cost of producing punishment $(AC_2$ not shown). The total average cost $(TAC)$ of producing a given level of order $(G_1)$ is the sum of the average costs of the two component activities. So long as the level of population is insufficient to require a ruler to undertake a

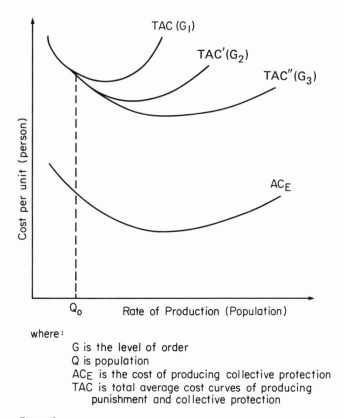

where:

      G is the level of order
      Q is population
      $AC_E$ is the cost of producing collective protection
      TAC is total average cost curves of producing
            punishment and collective protection

Figure 4

full-time contract enforcement effort, the *TAC* decreases. However, increased population transforms contract enforcement into a limitational factor and, consequently, exerts an upward pressure on costs. Ultimately, this pressure turns the *TAC* upward. Once the ruler's contract enforcement activity is limited, specialized activity in the form of a central state, producing collective protection and a local state, producing punishment, would shift *TAC* downward to *TAC'*. Later the emergence of a second local state would shift *TAC'* downward to *TAC"*.[59]

Various forms of organizational restructuring accomplish this type of deconcentration. Darius divided the Persian Empire into 20 provinces; each was ruled by a satrap, beside whom was placed a commander of the army who was responsible to the emperor. Tax collection was in the hands of collectors who paid a fixed sum to the royal treasury.[60] Eastern Europe, India, and China have seen many examples of tax farming. In Muscovy, the grand prince in Moscow appointed "lieutenants" (the *namestniki*). The latter were also full-fledged residual income recipients. They were given the responsibility for executing justice and collecting taxes in the provinces and in return paid the grand prince an annual lump sum.[61] After the 1517 conquest of Egypt, the Ottoman governor enforced the laws and defended the roads and lands from attacks of desert Bedouins under quite similar financial arrangements with the sultan in Istanbul.[62] In all of the above cases, "franchising" seems to have occurred in response to rising costs caused by increased population together with increased land (obtained, at least in part, through the conquest of new territories).

"Feudalism"[63] (e.g., Carolingian or the later "classical"), with its seignorial jurisdictions and immunities,[64] also represents a form of vertical separation (and deconcentration) of the order industry in response to rising costs. Forquin correctly warns us against the tendency to confuse feudalism, a decentralized political system, with feudalism (or better lordship) a socioeconomic organization in which great landowners exact dues and services from their tenants.[65] In this case, the payment to the overlord (or central state) for the grant of territory was not in money but in military service in the form of self-equipped and highly-trained mounted troops. The rising costs of the production of punishment, to which the many semifeudal political structures were responses, were caused not only by increases in the number of people to be ruled (as in the expansion of the Frankish kingdoms, as well as the Ottoman *timar* and Indian kingdom *jagir* systems[66]) but also by increases in the dispersion of a given population — (as in the territory of the Western Roman Empire, see Part 3). Both causes are inherent in Hintze's conclusion that "the feudal system . . . represents an attempt to create a political organization over relatively large spaces with the means of a still incompletely developed civilization."[67]

In some instances, the separation of vertical structure is less in the form of a franchise and more in the nature of a decentralized firm or self-administering "public" corporation. In the United States the city is the creature of the state, while in the British Empire one finds self-government and dominion status. Other historical examples include medieval and early modern "estates" of notables, guilds, and clergy.[68] Client kingdoms and protectorates are also examples of the phenomenon of vertical disintegration, in which the parent firm can be thought of as operating in more than one market. In the latter forms, the visible ruler is a native of the dependent society, which probably increases the population's feeling of the legitimacy of the government, and thus lowers the costs of producing order. The difficulty of operating in more than one market is often suggested as one reason why Germany, with its deep religious division between Catholics and Protestants, took so long to achieve central government.[69] Similarly, the differences in culture between northern and southern Italy may have delayed the creation of an integrated state there.

The above pattern of vertical structure often emerges in response not only to an increase in the population size and dispersion of the market served by the parent firm but also to "free-rider" problems, to changes in technology (e.g., weaponry), and to increases in the resources required to produce a given level of order, as when an external threat manifests itself.[70] There are many instances of federations or leagues of states formed in response to such threats in which the sole function of the federation is to fight off the external enemy.

The Hanseatic League of "city-states," for example, successfully waged war against a Scandinavian monarch, and the Greek response to the threat of the Persians in the fifth century B.C.E. also illustrate this phenomenon. It is important to note that when the threat disappeared so did the alliance. Athens later maintained the size of its zone of control by converting an alliance into an empire.[71] This is not the typical result. Usually the federation simply disappears after the threat is gone. The Kamakura shogunate was influential in defeating the Mongol threats in wars of 1274 and 1281, but after the defeat of the Mongols it "wobbled weakly for another half-century"[72] and then disappeared.[73] The "secession" of the American colonies from England similarly followed the removal of the French threat to the English colonists. The final disappearance of the Carolingian Empire can also be traced in part to a change in the nature of external threat which reduced economies of scale in protecting its subjects from foreigners. Saracen attempts to conquer were replaced by the raids of Vikings and Magyars, who hit, pillaged, and ran. This dissipated the effectiveness of a large national army and decentralization of the order industry to castles and strongholds proceeded to its limit.[74] Apparently, there is some tendency for federations themselves to tend to disappear when the need that prompted their establishment has done so.[75] In some instances, the former ruler of the federation assumes a ceremonial role. This approach has the advantage of facilitating a prompt reaction to any new external threat.

Local states are the most obvious but by no means the only possible example of the "franchising" out of state functions to substates. The creation of independent executive, legislative, and judicial branches of government (a dimension of Huntington's[76] "political modernization") may also be viewed as deconcentration in response to rising costs stemming from growth in the order market. The same may be true of the "military" and, more generally, Niskanen's bureaus. (Bureaus are substates which after periodic reviews receive grants or appropriations from another substate and in return supply a particular service). However, these substates are unlike the numerous punishment-producing local states because they are not responses to differences in the range of decreasing costs, but produce their service for the entire society. Such substates could be explained by the existence of similar unexhausted economics of specialization in the provision of the various subfunctions and to high costs of coordinating multiple activities.

## 5  TRANSPORTATION AND COMMUNICATION COSTS

Technological progress in transportation and communication not only reduces the direct cost of order production, such as increased population compactness, it also mitigates the shirking problem.[77] Each allows a reduction in the contract enforcement time required of the ruler in order to produce a given level of order for a given number of persons. Thus, progress in transportation and communication shifts downward the entire average cost curve and prolongs the range of decreasing costs (Figure 2). This change in average costs operates to increase state size – that is, to increase world political concentration.

Roy Wolfe, a geographer, provides several illustrations of the impact of these variables on state size.[78] We may note two. Bismarck took advantage of the railroad to centralize the many tiny principalities of north-central Europe. In North America the Maritime Provinces of Canada and the New England and Middle Atlantic states are small in comparison with provinces and states to the west. Wolfe conjectures that the observed discrepancy in sizes is due to the revolution in transportation technology (1750–1850) that took place after the founding of the original colonies.

## 6  THE FUTURE, A FIRST LOOK

A casual survey of the entire sweep of state history does not appear to reveal any clear trends in political concentration (i.e., in percentages of world society ruled by its several states). Certainly there have been large if temporary deviations from trend.[79] In a more narrowed perspective, the western world has seen an increase in political concentration starting from about 1300, the time of Dante. On the basis of the theory sketched so far, there seem to exist several powerful forces operating in recent history to increase the relative size of states. One of the most important of these is continued technological progress, which reduces communication and transportation costs and consequently reduces the effect of shirking by making it easier to gather the information necessary to combat it. This force is further strengthened by advances in management and computer sciences which operate directly on the shirking problem. The same result is produced by the continued urbanization of the populations of the world. Continued population growth, however, operates in the opposite direction – to proliferate states and reduce their relative sizes.

Other factors at work also serve to increase political concentration. A complete analysis of these requires a more general and somewhat public-good-based theory of industrial concentration, which fortunately has already been constructed elsewhere,[80] we may therefore simply summarize.

Let us view the level of concentration in any industry as resulting from an "as if" cost-minimization decision with respect to the intermediate good *decision making*. Societies can be assumed for the sake of analysis to make these decisions more or less automatically as a result of individuals acting in their own self-interest. One might call this process the institutional invisible hand. In general, we can conceive of two polar forms of decision mechanism: complete central planning and completely free markets, with all actual industry decision mechanisms arrayed somewhere along this centralization of decision-making spectrum. The more concentrated an industry, the more often are its decisions made by central planning and vice versa. A comparative statics of levels of concentration may then be generated in the familiar manner by assuming an interior solution of the cost-minimization problem (which seems to be the empirical fact). In this case, factors which raise the relative costs of either polar form will lower its relative importance in the production of decisions, which can then be readily translated into a predictable effect on levels of concentration.

The last few centuries have seen a tremendous increase in our ability to communicate and, as a result, we face a threat of the creation of a more or less uniform world culture. This can be expected to increase political concentration. The use of central planning requires that information on people's tastes be centralized. The smaller the variation in these tastes within a given population, the smaller the costs of gathering the requisite information and thus the less costly is decision making by central planners. Cultural uniformity thus promotes larger states, that is, greater concentration of political authority.[81] We appear to be closer to a single world government firm than ever before, because the underlying cost conditions have never been more appropriate for this. As we shall see, however, this is not an unmixed blessing, nor one without opposing trends.

# 4 THE QUALITIES OF STATE ACTIVITY

At this point, we turn our attention to an analysis of various determinants of the level of order and state activity in a given society. We proceed on the assumption that the size of states in both the population and territorial sense remains constant. While the theory we develop indicates how the forces with which economic theory usually concerns itself might affect the level of order and state activity, our main concern will be to understand the consequences of three exceptionally strong historical trends: increased population, the increase in the density or compactness of populations, and the decline in the metaphysical basis for order. Since the level of order in society is a public good, a comparative statics of public goods must be employed. We therefore begin with some clarification of our use of the concept "public good."

## 1  THE DEFINITION OF A PUBLIC GOOD

It is useful to assume that consumers have certain inherent desires which lie at the root of their desires for the various commodities which they buy. In making this assumption we follow a long line of recent economic thought now referred to as the "new approach to consumer behavior."[1] The desire for personal security, gratified in part by means of the public good "order," is one such desire. In general, we may suppose that there are two classes of goods capable of gratifying any desire: public and private. The desire for personal security, is gratified by many means such as personal bodyguards, private fallout shelters, personal arms, sprinkler systems, safes, and so on, as well as by such state activity as police services.[2]

The distinction between individuals' levels of personal security, which are private experiences, and the public good "order" must be remembered. Level of personal security, even if assumed to be the same for all individuals in a society, is not a public good—it is the level of gratification of individuals' desires for security and results from both the level of order and each individual's private actions.

There are various types of impurities of public goods. One occurs when the good is *crowded*. With a *pure,* as opposed to crowded, public good additional members may be added to a given population without affecting the costs of providing a given level of service. When the good is crowded, costs depend directly on the number of people in the population being served.[3] In this chapter we will proceed on the assumption that the public goods we are talking about are all *uncrowded.* In Chapter 3 we were essentially concerned with the crowding aspect of the good.

A good may also be a characteristic of some product. Cases of *"impure"* or *"mixed"* public goods may generally be transformed by this device into examples of products which are public in some of their characteristics and private in others; that is, they produce private and public joint products in the production of gratification through consumption. The hospital treatment of infectious diseases illustrates this case. Such treatment can be said to enter the arguments "probability of not catching such a disease" (the overall disease environment) and "to be cured." The former is a public good while the latter is private. In other words, the aggregate level of treatments is equal to the sum of the individual treatments while everyone (except for locational differences) experiences the same overall disease environment. In this context, one may speak of the "public intensity" of a product. Typically, states produce "public intensive" services as their products, punishment and protection being among the clearest examples of this.

## 2  THE CHOICE BETWEEN PUBLIC AND PRIVATE GOODS[4]

We will proceed on the assumption that society chooses between private and public ways of gratifying any desire (i.e., between private and public goods) in a more or less optimal manner. This is an assumption that will require some justification. First let us point out that in some senses one expects that the ultimately rational profit-seeking owners of a state would choose the optimum—unless they also exercise monopsony power in factor markets, a result discussed in some detail in Chapter 5. So, there is nothing totally wild about the assumption. On the other hand, some might argue in terms of received wisdom that by this we are suggesting that political systems fulfill the desires of society's members perfectly and that the Arrow Impossibility Theorem would make this outcome unlikely. The relevance of that theorem for actual political mechanisms, however, is open to some question, as it assumes the impossibility of individuals revealing the intensity of their preferences for various states of the world. If the intensity of preference can only partially be revealed, the theorem disappears.[5] It is our contention that in general the intensity of preferences people have are revealed, at least to some extent, in political choice processes. In modern democracies campaign contributions both financial and in terms of personal effort reflect this factor and influence elections. Kings, on the other hand, have every incentive to find out what their subjects want. All business people value information on their customers' preferences; so, too, do kings and politicians.

On the other hand, it would be absurd to argue that political systems always choose the optimum. It is too easy to construct examples in which, for instance, direct democracy could be expected to choose the worst possible alternative. Representative democracy changes the nature of individual incentives so as to produce still other problems, as we shall discuss in Chapter 6. We prefer, however, to model these problems in terms of the costs of production. In any case, a comparative statics of the optimum level of public good is part of any theory of the level, since some factors which affect the optimum will not affect the percentage deviation from it enough to invalidate a prediction based on what would happen to the optimum.

Rational choice between the public and private means of gratifying desires will often imply that both types of goods be employed in the gratification of any particular desire. This may be readily illustrated in the simple context of a two-person world by means of the familiar device of a Utility Possibility Curve (UPC).[6] If a society were to gratify any particular desire using *only* private goods, it might have the UPC labeled $A$ in Figure 5. If instead it gratified that desire using only public goods, it might have $B$. But society does not have to choose between only one or only the other.[7] Some of each type of good may be used and, in this case, the true frontier constraining social choice is the one labeled "Mixed". Assuming divisibility, this frontier is necessarily beyond frontiers $A$ or $B$ for some part of its range.

Real societies, of course, typically choose the dual mode of gratification. As we have noted, the desire for security against foreign aggression is gratified by family bomb shelters as well as by the "military." Fire protection is provided

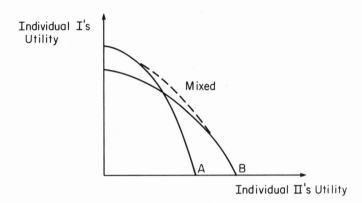

Figure 5

by sprinkler systems and fireproofing, as well as by "fire departments." Pollen-free air is provided by home electronic air purifiers, as well as by the activities of public health authorities. Similarly, protection against crime is provided by "bodyguards," bullet-proof vests, watchdogs, alarms, and locks, as well as by the "police." We may now proceed directly with some formal analysis.

Consider the usual sort of general equilibrium model. $Q$ is the private good; $G$ the public good, $L$ and $K$ the two factors of production, $L_G$ the labor used to produce $G$, and so on. Production is determined by the neoclassical production functions[8]

$$Q = F(L_Q, K_Q)$$
$$G = H(L_G, K_G) \tag{1}$$

and total resources are constrained by

$$L_Q + L_G = \overline{L}$$
$$K_Q + K_G = \overline{K} \tag{2}$$

Equations (1) and (2) together determine the production possibilities curve. This will look as it is depicted in Figure 6 unless we have the unlikely event that $F$ and $H$ exhibit identical factor intensities. In that case, it would be a straight line and relative costs would be unchanged as society changed its allocation of resources between the two goods. If the latter is the case, then we can arrive at some definitive conditions about the effects of population and density. In the former and more likely case,[9] however, we cannot. This is because the introduction of new population or the compaction of the existing population will generally change relative factor prices. If $Q$ and $G$ have different factor intensities, this will change their relative costs, thus inducing a substitution away from the

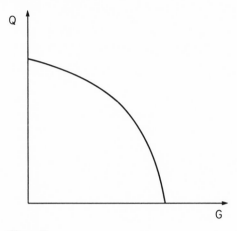

Figure 6

more expensive commodity, which will either reinforce or counteract the pure effects of changes in population or its density.

Relative costs respond to movements in relative aggregate factor quantities, society's relative resource endowments, in the familiar manner. The critical factor, as always, is relative factor intensities in production of the two types of goods. Thus if public goods tend to be relatively capital intensive, then economic growth resulting from an increase in the capital-labor ratio can be expected to increase their importance, and vice versa unless the income elasticity of demand for public goods is significantly lower than that for private. Similarly, differences in the "consumer time intensiveness"[10] of the two types of goods will result in general growth having an effect. If, for example, private goods are relatively "time intensive," which they may be, then they will *ceteris paribus* become relatively less important in the gratification of all desires as a result of a uniform improvement in technology. If public goods are land intensive, then an increase in compaction will result in a decrease in their relative levels. Whether expenditures on them increase or not, will depend on their price elasticity of demand.

When the factor intensities of the two goods are identical, then in effect, one production function is just a rescaling of the other, that is,

$$F = C \cdot H \tag{3}$$

and the relative price of the two goods is always

$$\frac{P_G}{P_Q} = C \tag{4}$$

In this case, the effects of increased population density are zero unless increased population density changes the effective technology, but in such a case we do not have a pure public good.[11] Since relative factor prices are irrelevant in our present context, let us simplify and assume that each person has $B$ units of a single resource, again measured in units of the private good $Q$. Total resources are then $Bn$.

In this context an increase in population will have a predictable effect, which we now proceed to analyze.

It is essential to assume that any increases in population do not affect the distribution of tastes in society. Increases in population ($n$) just add more people with the same tastes. Let

$$P_G = D(G, B) \tag{5}$$

be the "representative individual's demand curve for the public good. The price the individual is willing to pay per unit of the public good is a function of the level of public good and personal "income" ($B$). Society's demand for the public good is then

$$P_G = nD(G, B) \tag{6}$$

Since factor intensities are the same, however, $P_G = C(Q$ is the numerataire) and thus we have the implicit equation for the level of $G$

$$C = nD(G, B) \tag{7}$$

which under appropriate conditions may be rewritten as

$$G = h\left(\frac{C}{n}, B\right) \tag{8}$$

We are interested in the ratio

$$g = \frac{G}{Q} \tag{9}$$

Given society's overall resource constraint this is

$$g = \frac{h\left(\frac{C}{n}, B\right)}{B \cdot n - C \cdot h\left(\frac{C}{n}, B\right)} \tag{10}$$

Differentiating with respect to $n$ we obtain

$$\frac{\partial g}{\partial n} = \frac{\dfrac{C}{n^2}\, h_1\, [B \cdot n - C \cdot h] - h\left[B + \dfrac{C^2}{n^2}\, h_1\right]}{[B \cdot n - C \cdot h]^2} \tag{11}$$

where $h_1$ is the partial derivative of $h$ with respect to its first argument. Simplifying we obtain

$$\frac{\partial g}{\partial n} = \frac{-B\left[h + \dfrac{C}{n}\, h_1\right]}{[B \cdot n - C \cdot h]^2}$$

Thus

$$\frac{\partial g}{\partial n} \gtrless 0 \quad \text{if and only if}$$

$$-B\left[h + \frac{C}{n}\, h_1\right] \gtrless 0$$

or

$$-\frac{C}{n}\, h_1 \gtrless h$$

or

$$-\frac{C}{nh}\, h_1 \gtrless 1$$

The expression on the left, however, is the price elasticity of society's demand for $G$; thus, *increases in population increase (decrease) the level of pure public good at the optimum when the price elasticity of demand for those goods is greater (less) than 1 in absolute value.*

Most researchers find that the price elasticity of demand for public goods is less than 1. Thus, increasing population can be expected to lower the level of public good, at least if it is being provided at the optimum level.

## 3  THE INFLUENCE OF THE DECLINE IN THE METAPHYSICAL BASIS FOR ORDER

Order in society depends not only on what is done by government and other institutions to stop crime, promote fire safety, and so on. There is also the social environment itself. How people feel about each other and about the current distribution of material well-being will influence the number of crimes against persons and property. This will also be influenced by the extent to which certain moral precepts are followed as maxims by the public. Some people will steal more readily than others, and this will depend on how able they are to justify such actions to themselves. Economists and other social scientists should not neglect consideration of the extent to which individuals' levels of satisfaction depend on the extent to which they measure up in their own perceptions to certain ideal types (or images). Like it or not, much of our experience of happiness or sadness is internally generated. All these factors taken together produce what we have called the metaphysical basis for order. Considering the period of the last 250 years, it seems as if that basis has diminished. Senses of legitimacy, guilt, and so forth, all have declined. There are fewer people who docilely accept their place in society. Perhaps this is a result of the increased population, which should tend to increase the relative isolation of individuals from the rest of society and thus decrease the effective extent of love. On the more metaphysical plane, one of the most important forces driving in this direction is the flow of ideas which itself has led to an increase in the extent to which people choose their own roles or conceptions of themselves rather than accepting ideas handed on to them by their parents or by some other authority. People may be becoming more questioning and generally cynical.

What is the effect of the resulting secular decline in the metaphysical basis of order on the level of resources devoted to the production of order? To analyze this issue, we ignore the distinction between "order" and "personal security." This requires the assumption that relative prices of all goods other than order remain constant. In this case, we may aggregate them into the convenient fiction "all other goods." We visualize society again as choosing among alternative levels of production of other goods ($Q$) and order ($G$) offered to it by a transformation curve with the usual properties (see Figure 7).[12]

Since in every society there is some "love," some "legitimacy," and some "guilt," a positive level of order ($G_1$) would prevail even if all resources were devoted to producing $Q$. Increases in $G$ beyond $G_1$ can be accomplished only by increasing the fraction of resources allocated to the production of order.

It will make the matter more transparent if we employ community indifference curves to analyze this issue. The drawing of market demand curves for order would involve similar, if not more severe, assumptions. As always, however, there is some point in being clear about the nature of the assumptions one is employing. In this case, there are many different assumptions which will suffice.

There are two usual ways to get community indifference curves or to justify their use. Both attempt to wash out certain "income effects" either by assuming

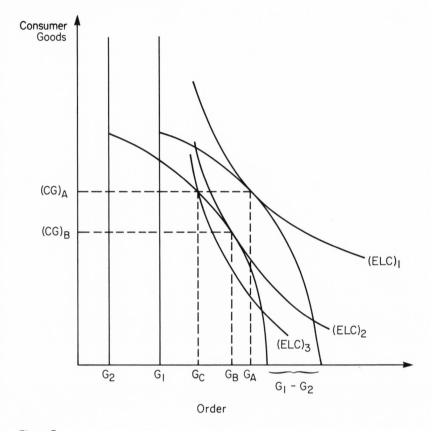

Figure 7

that the income elasticity of demands for all goods is identically one or by assuming that everyone holds all the productive resources of society in the same proportions, but perhaps not in the same amounts. Either assumption prevents the changing factor prices induced by moving along the production possibilities (P-P) curve from influencing the individual weights in the social demands for individual commodities. In the case of public choice analysis, there seems to be a growing tradition which uses a new justification. This is the so-called "median voter" model of democracy. It is argued that under majority rule all we have to do is to use the preferences of the median voter. The problem with this device, however, is that identifying the median voter on any issue may itself be endogenous to the public choice system, as when public choices are likely to affect individual levels of wealth. The "representative consumer" by any other name is still the same person.

As the second of the usual reasons seems to allow the most latitude, we employ it. In addition, we will assume in this section that everyone is somewhat risk-averse and that order itself does not enter the utility function.

Each individual in society is then assumed to receive as "wage" a given fraction ($a$) of $Q$. Social utility[13] on our assumptions is directly proportional to the consumption level ($ELC$) thus, $ELC = (1 - \phi)Q$ and we may use it as the utility function $Q$ with $\phi = \phi(G)$. The curves are rectangular hyperbolas on these assumptions.

A reduction in "love," "legitimacy," or "guilt" reduces the minimum level of order from $G_1$ to $G_2$. If these exogenous changes do not also affect the productivities of resources devoted to the production of order, the transformation curve will shift everywhere to the left by $G_1 - G_2$. One can then show that the equilibrium consensual values of both $G$ and $Q$ will decrease, which (with given resources) implies an increase in resources devoted to the production of order since everything not used for $Q$ is used in producing $G$.[14] Thus, $G$ and $Q$ must both decrease because the indifference curves become steeper going to the left along the horizontal, while the production possibilities curve, as we have just assumed, retains its slope along the horizontal.

Increases in the level of resources devoted to order will tend to increase the level of resources devoted to the state, unless the relative importance of the state in the production of order decreases at a faster rate as the level of resources devoted to order rises.[15] At the same time, however, the overall level of order will decrease.

Historically, increases in state size in terms of resource use seem occasionally to have accompanied declines in the metaphysical basis for order. Something of this nature occurred in China beginning in the nineteenth century when traditional controls and notions of right and wrong were shattered by the impact of Western nations.[16] More generally, the analysis provides a framework for interpreting "nationalist" movements in former Western colonies as attempts to increase state size in order to cope with civil strife produced by the collapse of traditional social values. Certainly the analysis is not inconsistent with recent world trends in state size.

## 4  DEMAND SIDE FACTORS

In addition to these "supply side" effects, several factors may influence the relative importance of public goods through the "demand side." A distinguishing feature of a public as opposed to a private good is that for the former no member of the defined group can to any degree exclude any other member from the use of the good by consuming or employing more of it himself. We might then say that a crucial property distinguishing one type of good from the other is that private goods are endowed with "exclusivity" while public goods are endowed with "nonexclusivity" or, alternatively, conceive of a continuous measure of exclusivity. It is possible that individuals derive satisfaction from "exclusivity" itself. Changes in tastes for "exclusivity" (e.g., resulting from changes in social cohesiveness) would then, given relative marginal costs, influence the share of public goods used in the gratification of any given desire and, by implication, would also influence state sizes.

The share of public goods might also be influenced by changes in income. It is not clear, however, whether in a world of complicated interrelationships between utility functions, "exclusivity" is a superior or an inferior good. Income can be expected to play its more traditional role, however. If desires with larger income elasticities have higher public-private "intensities," income would be observed to have a positive effect on the aggregate percentage of collective goods and vice versa. Monsen and Downs, for example, appear to suggest that the desire to express individuality through differentiated consumption patterns is relatively both income elastic and private goods intensive. In this case, material progress will to some extent exert a downward pressure on the share of public goods and, thus, presumably on the level of state activity. These are, of course, exceedingly complex issues that we hope will receive more attention in future research.

## 5  THE FUTURE AGAIN

In the previous chapter, conflicting forces were identified as exerting influences on state size. Increased population should tend to proliferate states. Increased population density, however, would tend[17] to increase state sizes, as would recent advances in communications and management science, which also serve to flatten the $ATC$ curve with respect to population. Now we have identified other factors which may shift the level of per capita resources devoted to the state and through that affect state size in the population dimension. In general, it is hypothesized that an increase in per capita resource use would cause the $ATC$ to turn upward at a lower level of population, simply because the intensity of the shirking problem and institutional size are expected to be directly related.

If we are willing to assume that the price elasticity of demand for public goods is < 1 then we expect the tendency of increased population to proliferate states to be somewhat mitigated by the tendency of increased population to decrease the level of public good (order) and thus to have the $ATC$ turn upward at higher levels of population.

Capital accumulation, on the other hand, should decrease state size, at least if Orzenchowski's results on the relative capital intensity of governments is correct. If governments are relatively capital intensive, increased capital/labor should lower their relative costs, thus increasing per capita usage. This, in turn, would cause the *ATC* in the population dimension to achieve its minimum at lower levels of population. Similarly, the increased disappearance of the metaphysical basis for order is likely to operate to proliferate states, even if that tendency is swamped by other coincident trends. As we have just seen, a decrease in the metaphysical basis of order will tend to increase the level of resources devoted to producing order. In effect, the level of produced order is increased. Again this increases per person resource expenditures and causes the per person cost curve to turn upward at lower levels of population. At the same time, a decrease in the metaphysical basis for order must cause the overall level of order, as opposed to the produced level of order, to decrease. This will worsen the shirking problem, again exerting a downward force on state size.[18]

It is not necessarily the case then that we must be moving towards even larger governments, at least in the long run. In the short run, however, because of both the gradual, indeed, almost glacial pace of the effect of increased shirking and because of the inherent frictions in the system which allow rulers to prevent fragmentation, we are likely to see larger states. The effects of improved technology are immediate – that of shirking, slow. Thus, we are likely to be confronted with larger and increasingly inefficient governments, until under the weight of truly gross inefficiency, the system collapses. This is one point of the type of theory developed here. Recognizing what is happening, we may be able to forestall the event. How, will concern us in Chapter 8.

# 5 THE MONOPOLY STATE

Although they provide services which we may not be accustomed to thinking of as "products," it appears possible to treat states as firms. The question of market structure then arises immediately. Why are the punishment and collective protection industries so highly concentrated?[1] Shoes are produced by hundreds of firms, and so are laundry and auto repair services, yet typically there are very few states producing their services for any given society. Why is it that we so rarely, and then in general so transiently, observe multiple states producing the same service in a society and what are the consequences of this "monopoly power"?

In the usual economic theory of private goods, the existence of monopoly is thought to lead to two problems: the efficiency problem and the equity problem. Because of the market power of monopoly, the monopolist recognizes that increases in the quantity of his product necessarily decrease its price. By restricting quantity supplied below the optimum, or competitive level, the monopolist is able to earn an exploitative profit. This causes society to misallocate its resources, that is, to produce less total satisfaction than it would have (the efficiency problem). At the same time, the owner of a monopoly business—presumably wealthier on the average than the customers—is made richer by the monopoly profits, thus violating our sense of equity. In the present case, however, we are dealing with a public goods monopolist. Therefore, the same conclusions may not hold. The present chapter is concerned with developing a formal monopoly theory of the state.

## 1   SOURCES OF THE MARKET POWER OF STATES

There are a number of reasons why the market power of states is typically so high. First, and perhaps most basically, it must be remembered that when the state initially emerges, the "protection-punishment" industry is a natural monopoly in that society. By virtue of its initial position of power, the first state has certain inherent advantages over potential competitors which may allow it to perpetuate its monopoly position. One such advantage is the tendency of the "customers" to identify products with their original producer. A similar tendency is found with more conventional products. Often products become so closely identified with the first firm to produce them that the brand name becomes a popular name for the item itself (e.g., Frigidaire, Coke, Jello). A second advantage derives from the initial state's ability to use its preponderance of physical force to forcibly prevent both the private production of order and competing entry by other firms. Although the use of violence to prevent entry or to eliminate rivals is not unknown as an industrial practice, in general this option is not as fully available to most firms as it is to states. This we would argue represents a real difference from the forms of forestalling competition generally available. Not a few people are lexicographically ordered against losing their lives.[2]

In addition, punishment and collective protection are goods with important public dimensions. In the context of our more general theory of industrial structure, this too can be expected to raise the level of concentration.[3] If these services were to be provided by many firms—that is, if society placed a greater reliance on market mechanisms for making decisions in this area—considerable resources would have to be expended to ensure that nonpayers did not get free rides and that resources were expended in the optimal fashion. With purely private goods these exclusionary mechanisms are less costly because of the nature of the goods. As we have shown elsewhere,[4] voluntary market mechanisms can therefore be expected to be used relatively less for public goods than for private goods because they are relatively expensive for public goods.[5] One would expect public goods industries to be more concentrated. In this regard it is interesting to note that goods which are typically privately produced, but which are "public goods intensive," in the sense of Chapter 4, also tend to be highly concentrated. The most readily apparent example is provided by news services, which over the last half-century have become highly concentrated (e.g., Associated Press, etc.).

A final reason why collective protection and punishment tend to be highly concentrated industries is also quite basic. As we observed in Chapter 3 (Section 4), the provision of protection against external threats would appear to have a prolonged range of increasing returns to scale in both quantity and quality dimensions. These are not unlimited as the breakup of large empires and other evidence attests, but they do exist. To put the matter quite simply, large armies have some advantages over smaller armies. Not only, however, are there strong increasing returns in the provision of protection against external threats but, in addition, resources allocated for this purpose will not generally be actively so employed all the time. As a result of high mobilization costs, armies typically simply stand ready to provide protection. A ruler therefore can be expected to have relatively large resources available for use, which must be kept at the ready but which cannot be used directly for their primary purpose of opposing external threats. It is only good business sense to employ these resources in the provision of protection against internal threats to order, which requires the use of similar resources. In early times, at least, the line between armed services and police was very blurred.[6] Because the ruler taxes for the services provided to all and provides these services to all free of a direct charge, competition is attenuated in the internal order industry.

Some[7] would append a further reason, namely, that decentralization in the production of physical punishment might precipitate blood feuds which are, of course, a collective bad for society as a whole. This line of argument, however, is directly contradicted by the mass of anthropological evidence summarized by Hoebel as follows:

> The fact is that there is very limited evidence for the actual occurrence of feud in primitive societies. Legal procedures or ritual devices such as regulated combat as a means of avoiding or terminating feud have been universally found to exist in such cultures.[8]

States differ typically from other firms, then, only in the amount of market power they possess in their particular business, the "coercion business." This power is not unlimited; as with every monopoly, an increased rate of exploitation will lead to a decrease in the number of customers. It will profit us to turn to the nature of the customer response in this case, if only to confront theory and evidence.

## 2   LIMITS ON EXPLOITATION

Just as all firms, so too states are confronted with demand curves for their services. Even though they possess a preponderance of force, they cannot take everything and give nothing in return.[9] They may exploit their populations, but not without limit. If they produce no collective protection, they would fall to other states by conquest. If taxes are too high, the population might elect new rulers, revolt, provide a fifth column for an invader, or emigrate. The discontent individuals feel as a result of their being exploited by a monopoly state is related to the probability of revolt, secession, emigration, successful invasion[10] or, in the case of democracy, electoral defeat. Rational rulers will only "optimally" exploit their populations.

The extent to which the state has a preponderance of force in any society necessarily varies from one case to another. Its monopoly is never complete. Often it varies according to peculiarities of the technology. There is generally more than one source of coercive power. It has been suggested, for example, that England's development of the Royal Navy instead of an army, largely an accident of geography, strongly contributed to the growth of constitutional liberty there.[11] Within tribal African states, where "weapons are simple and possessed by each warrior, each country chieftain and royal head of followers had a personal army which he could use to support him in struggles with the chief."[12] The United States Constitutional guarantee of the right of its citizens to bear arms, a right now largely abandoned, may have been motivated by the desire to impose a limit on the exploitative power of the state which the Constitution created. The other limits on the extent to which a state can or will exploit its population also vary, for numerous reasons.[13]

As we have just noted, people can leave the territory of the state.[14] Historically, a key determinant of the importance of flight as a limit on the exploitative power of the state has been the proximity of relatively empty land, or a "frontier." In the mid-twelfth century, for example, central Russia was largely vacant. People were more or less free to move from the territory of one prince (or boyar) to that of another and, interestingly, no trace of serfdom appears in central Russia until the middle of the fifteenth century.[15] This was much later than its development elsewhere in Europe, but about the same time as its appearance in Prussia, for related reasons.

Turner's "safety valve" thesis in American history is quite familiar and not inconsistent with this view. The disappearance of vacant land raises the cost of flight and consequently operates to channel discontent into revolt (Hirschman's "exit" and "voice"). Thus, in Mogul India when the rulers increased exploitation the peasants fled to areas outside Mogul jurisdiction where land was relatively plentiful.[16] The Indian peasant acquired a reputation for docility. Later when land became scarcer as a result of population growth (as a consequence of the *pax Britannica*) peasant violence apparently became more common.[17] In general, rational exploitation by a monopolist will be smaller the greater, *ceteris paribus,* is the elasticity of demand confronting him.[18] This is no doubt one of the chief advantages of a federal system such as that of the United States. Freedom of movement within a common language area places a powerful check on the exploitative ability of states (and cities),[19] a point to which we shall return later.

Because the possibility of flight places a limit on state exploitation, it will sometimes pay rulers to expend resources to curtail the ability of subjects to leave the territorial limits of their state or to expand the state to include surrounding territory.[20] Thus, in Muscovy (starting in the sixteenth century) an attempt was made to stop the peasant population of Great Russia from running away across the Urals in the direction of the Pacific.[21] Similarly, the construction of the Berlin Wall and the general restrictions on emigration from Communist (and some noncommunist) countries today facilitate exploitation of the population by these states.[22] Walls or barriers to exit never can be entirely effective, however, and, in any case they are costly, and so directly reduce the return to the rulers. Even if it were technically feasible to eliminate the possibility of emigration, the profit-maximizing ruler is unlikely to find it worthwhile to do so.

Another limit on exploitation is provided by various forms of tax resistance. Cheating, increasing the rate of consumption to avoid wealth taxes, increasing leisure at the expense of taxable output,[23] or otherwise altering the production process to facilitate tax avoidance, riots, or banditry, as well as simply shooting "revenuers," are all historical methods of limiting exploitation and reducing the return to the rulers. In the nineteenth century, the Serbs rejected agriculture for nomadic hog raising in order to avoid taxation by their Ottoman overlords. In twentieth-century Russia, the peasants' response to forced collectivization was the wholesale slaughter of stock, while eastern European peoples resisted the draft into the Czar's army by minimally maiming their children.

Exploitation is increased not only by increased taxation, but also by decreased services at a given level of taxation. During the Hundred Years' War, sporadic and brutal rebellions of French peasants, called *Jacquerie,* broke out because "their Lords burdened them with heavy impositions, yet could not protect them from bands of marauders, many of them unemployed soldiers, who roamed the countryside."[24]

Further limits on the rulers' return are provided by the possibility of reducing their psychic income.[25] Lyndon Johnson experienced this in 1967, when jeering pickets greeted him everywhere, thus eliminating the pleasure he derived from meeting his "fellow countrymen." In states where the rulers have limited direct personal access to tax revenues, this reaction may be one of the more effective citizen responses short of outright revolution.

Whatever form resistance takes, the ruler can retaliate. Tax collection forces may be increased; those refusing to give respect, taxes, and so forth, may be punished. Again, all of these require the expenditure of resources and thus reduce the ruler's income. Moreover, even where it is known that the tax resistance is doomed to eventual failure it may still occur, simply because of the built-in capacity of all animals to lose their temper.[26] An extreme example of this phenomenon is provided by *mengamok,* from which the term "running amuck" is derived. This refers to the Malay peasant whose reaction to intolerable oppression was to murder everyone he met until he was killed himself.

> Such retaliation might not reach the (district) chief personally — it was the essence of . . . *mengamok* . . . that the killer was half insane and would even kill his own family and friends . . . But a chief would not wish to provoke such a violent breach of his own law and order.[27]

Finally, *entry* of one of two types can take place in response to exploitation and this will also limit exploitation. Marginal (or complementary) entry occurs when new firms simply attempt to fill gaps in the services of the state,[28] supporting themselves either through voluntary contributions or in the more classic manner of states, that is, through force (as with Capone in Chicago). Supplanting entry (by election, revolution, secession, or invasion) involves attempts by domestic entrepreneurs, or by another state to supplant a particular state entirely.[29,30]

As in traditional economic limit price theory,[31] the simple existence of the threat of entry itself may also serve to change the level of exploitation directly. A feeling of discontent in a population, particularly when manifested by tax resistance, emigration, and so on, will provide a signal to outside entrepreneurs. Realizing this, the state may respond by acting to lower exploitation. This response is more likely to be the case where there are several known possible contenders for the crown or office or, more generally, alternative states. In this way, alternative states with acquisitive tendencies or a large supply of potential state supplanting entrepreneurs may lead to a "potential competition" so strong as to strip the state of any real power to exploit. We saw in Chapter 3 that both continued urbanization of a population and continued technological progress reducing travel and communication costs operate to reduce the shirking problem and consequently to increase political concentration. Increased political concentration, however, may not necessarily result in increased exploitation and certainly does not rule out the sharing of the accompanying efficiency benefits, if any, with the subject population, particularly if it is caused or accompanied by changes in "exogenous" variables which make flight or other forms of resistance easier. In the limit the threat of entry (a threat apparently ignored by Martin and McKenzie),[32] could force even a monopolistic ruler to pass on reduced costs of order production entirely to his subjects by way of a reduction in tax-price (or increases in the level of order). Thus Gluckman observes that in tribal African states, several accredited contenders (princes) for the main chiefship (or kingship) were to be found in the large royal family. It appears that the endemic threat of their "repetitive rebellions" provided an effective check on the rapacity of the ruler.[33]

Taking as evidence the experience of Western Europe in the fourteenth and fifteenth centuries, North and Thomas have written:

> Numerous powerful vassals of a king within any political unit were quite ready to assume control. Equally, outsiders, in the form of rival kings or dukes of other political units, were always poised, ready to take over. The constituents logically would accept the 'state' which offered them the greatest percentage of the gains from the wider administration of protection and justice. In fact the 'ideal' solution for the constituents was one in which they were delegated the 'constitutional' power to set the price (tax), whereas the opposite was true from the viewpoint of the monarch . . . . The more monopoly power an existing prince could claim – that is the less close or threatening were his rivals – the greater the percentage of rents which the state could appropriate.[34]

This raises an interesting question. If we may assume that a large supply of potential entrepreneurs for the punishment and collective protection industries provides a check, or limit, on the degree to which a given society may be exploited by its state, then what determines the level of this supply?

Historically, the social distributions of characteristics such as physical strength and ferocity appear to have played important roles in determining who shall rule. Such characteristics or, perhaps, greater experience in the use of weapons or in the discovery of new weapons (e.g., the Hittites and their use of iron) may, for example, explain why pastoral peoples were so frequently able to establish their rule over agricultural peoples.[35] This is attested to by Claiborne, who observes that:

> Some nomads were very likely able to . . . go beyond the swift swooping raid . . . and actually take over the village as permanent overlords. Their toughness and military skills would enable them to enjoy the pick of the crops – and at the same time earn their keep after a fashion, by fighting off attacks from their still-nomadic cousins.[36]

Today the production of punishment and collective protection do not appear to involve any obviously distinctive skills but may attract individuals with certain tastes; for example, sadism, the love of power, country, and so on.

Breton and Breton[37] have concluded that industrial, commercial, and "social" entrepreneurs are in reality close substitutes, with the allocation of the total stock of entrepreneurship determined by relative returns. The Bolshevik leader Bukharin (later purged by Stalin), troubled by the specter of the anarchist Bakunin's prediction of a "red bureaucracy," raised the question of whether the communist state, like other types, would inevitably become exploitative. He speculated that "in the society of the future there will be a colossal overproduction of organizers which will nullify the stability of ruling groups."[38] But is not growth in the stock of entrepreneurs more encouraged in societies relying on decentralized market systems?

States may, of course, also advertise their virtues—that is, manipulate their demand curves. Attempts by rulers to have the population view them as gods are nice examples of the use of advertising by the rulers. The Roman Emperor Diocletian deliberately introduced a form of Oriental ruler-worship in an attempt to bolster his state, a tactic which had earlier been attempted by Caligula but unsuccessfully.[39] Later emperors were often shown wearing a nimbus.[40] In sixteenth-century Western Europe monarchs advertised their "divine right."[41] Wesson[42] provides many additional examples of this phenomenon. Recent presidential elections in the United States have seen the resurrection of attempts to surround the public official or ruler with the trappings of religious sanction.[43]

In modern times, such advertising is typically one of the functions of publicly provided schooling. If the state can convince the population that its services are better than those of other states, then the rulers can capitalize on this good will by a greater degree of exploitation. Some would argue that states' general discouragement of competitive advertising is of equal importance. Generally such advertising is called "treason." Even in the United States, where there is supposed to be a constitutional guarantee of freedom of expression, people have been jailed for conspiring to *advocate* the desirability of achieving alternative systems of state ownership.[44]

Galbraith and others have asserted that the demands for private products are more contrived than those for public products. Given the amount of time that television has devoted to shows lauding the armed forces, the congress, and police, fire, and public legal services, as compared with the amount of time devoted to alcohol, cigarettes and tail fins, this is a curious assertion. It is indeed 180 degrees incorrect. If one looks only at direct advertising expenditures, one finds that the government is the tenth largest advertiser in the United States.[45]

## 3  ELEMENTARY MATHEMATICS OF THE MONOPOLY STATE

As we will now show, it is not entirely undesirable that the state should have monopoly power. States produce primarily public goods, and for public goods, monopoly is not as inefficient an organization of the market as it is for private goods. In some circumstances it is entirely efficient. This will become clear after a little formal analysis of the demand curve confronting the state. Let us employ, again, the concept of a "representative member of society" with utility function

$$U = U(G, Q) \tag{1}$$

where

$G$ = Government goods

$Q$ = All other goods

Because people might emigrate, revolt, and so on, the state must keep the difference between its offer and that of the best alternative state less than some critical level which depends on the ease of revolt, emigration, and so forth. If we let $P_G$ be the tax-price of government services, and $a$ the index which identifies the perceived best alternative state, then the state faces the revenue constraint

$$U(G, I - P_G) - U(G^a, I^a - P_G^a) = \gamma \tag{1a}$$

where $I$ and $I^a$ represent income in each situation, and $\gamma < 0$.

With a revenue constraint of this form, marginal revenue $dp_G/dG$ is

$$\frac{dP_G}{dG} = \frac{U_G}{U_Q} \tag{2}$$

the marginal rate of substitution between $G$ and $Q$, assuming $\partial I/\partial G = 0$. In this case when the monopolist (who is not also a monopsonist)[46] sets marginal revenue equal to marginal cost in order to maximize profits, he chooses a level of $G$ such that

$$\frac{U_G}{U_Q} = \frac{MC_G}{MC_Q}, \tag{3}$$

assuming that $Q$ is produced competitively so that its price is its marginal cost. Now Equation (3) is, of course, the relevant Pareto condition for the maximization of social welfare; therefore under the assumptions just made, the monopolist will produce the optimal level of public good, which is Buchanan's Theorem.

In general, however, one cannot expect that $\partial I/\partial G = 0$. If "all other goods" and government goods have different factor intensities, one expects that it will be positive and thus the monopolist will have some tendency to overproduce the level of public good.[47]

The model of citizen behavior implicit in the derivation of Equation (1a) may be employed to produce other insights into the behavior of states. For one, it is possible to use it to rigorously define the consent component of any particular state's return and then to analyze the determinants of the proportion of a state's return which is perceived as legitimate by the population. This, in turn, could lead to a more complete theory of revolution.

Let $_iU(G, Q)$ be the utility function of the $i$th individual. The amount which an individual consents to pay for the level of public good provided is not only a function of the levels of public good provided and the price charged, it also depends crucially on his perception of the alternatives available to him. Given that he will receive an amount $G_o$ of the public good, an individual would consent to pay an amount for this service which leaves him indifferent to his best alternative $(G_a, Q_a)$ and living in his consent consumption situation. His sense of being exploited is measured by the difference between what he pays and what he would consent to pay. Let $CP^i$ denote the consent component for the $i$th individual, and let $Q$ be the private good numeraire. Then $CP^i$ is defined implicitly by

$$_iU(G_o, I_i - CP^i) = {}_iU(G_a, Q_a) \qquad (4)$$

Figure 8 illustrates this calculation. Given the alternative state $(G_a, Q_a)$ and the level of "order" $G_o$ available in his current state, there is a unique level of $Q$ which together with $G_o$ leaves the citizen indifferent between the two states. When this level of $Q$ is subtracted from the citizen's current income $(I)$, we obtain $CP^i$.

Thus defined, the exploitation component has several interesting properties. For one, even when the population, or some elements of it, are feeling exploited,

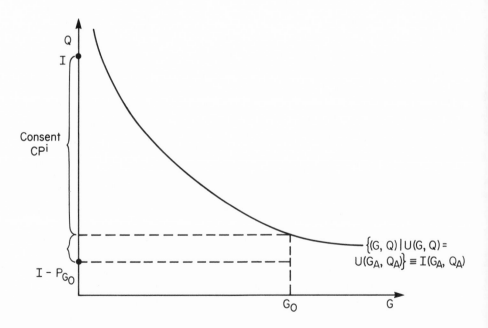

Figure 8

it may not necessarily support revolt nor may it be trying to emigrate. Revolt or emigration will require resource expenditures and the taking of risks, and these may not be justified by the expected return, the elimination of the exploitation. Thus, our view differs from those of Locke and others who read implicit consent into the absence of revolt, secession, or emigration, and is closer to those who speak of "real will" or "implicit subscription."[48,49]

Equation (4) makes one thing immediately apparent, the consent-conquest division depends crucially on the individual's perception of the alternatives to the existing state as summarized by $(G_a, Q_a)$. At one extreme, an individual in an isolated society may believe that there is no alternative to the existing state. In this case, suppressing irrelevant subscripts, $CP^i$ is defined by

$$U(G, I - CP) = U(0, I) \tag{5}$$

The ruling state is then able to extract all the consumer surplus generated by its existence and still not cause the individual to feel exploited.

At the other extreme, the individual might perceive the alternative as his optimal or ideal state. In order to simplify the exposition, assume that the entire community's preferences can be represented by (1), that is, (1) is a social welfare function. Let $F(G)$ be the cost function of the public goods industry. To some, the ideal state is one that supplies the maximum feasible level of $G$ (if that exists) and charges nothing for the service. Few people would be willing to believe such an ideal possible, so we cannot simply allow the characterization of the $G$ and $P_G$ of the ideal state to be independent of one another. The most natural alternative seems to be to assume that

$$P_{G_a} = F(G_a)$$

or that the ideal state sells its output at cost (remembering that for $G_a$, $P_{G_a}$ = total revenue). It is understood that these are opportunity costs. In this case, the ideal state occurs when

$$\frac{U_1}{U_2} = F'(G_a) \tag{6}$$

or the community indifference curve is tangent to the society's production possibilities schedule between $G$ and $B$ ($U_1 = U_G$; $U_2 = U_Q$).

It is interesting to note that the optimal state alternative approximately[50] minimizes the consent component of any existing state's receipts. To see this, set $\partial CP/\partial G_a = 0$ where the relationship between $CP$ and $G_a$ is given implicitly by

$$U(G, I - CP) = U(G_a I - F(G_a)) \tag{7}$$

Differentiating with respect to $G_a$ yields

$$U_2 \frac{\partial CP}{\partial G_a} = U_1 - U_2 F' \quad \text{or} \quad \frac{\partial CP}{\partial G_a} = F' - \frac{U_1}{U_2} \tag{8}$$

which when set to zero yields Equation (6). When his alternative is his perception of the optimal state, then the individual feels maximally exploited—i.e., $CP$ is at a minimum.

Actual perception of the alternative and hence the sense of exploitation probably lies somewhere between the two extremes of no alternative and the best alternative. Indeed, one might even suppose that this perception is related to the individual's information on other existing states. Perhaps it is their average, but more likely it is the perceived best alternative. In this case, improvement in world communication—or a successful revolutionary introduction of an improved state or one that is so perceived by other populations—can be expected to raise the probability of successful revolt in other states or at least to increase the population's sense of being exploited. Here is another reason why revolutions may be contagious, as appears to have been the case, for example, in the nineteenth century. Similarly, societies isolated by geographic conditions or by government policy can be expected to have more profitable states even if the people feel no greater discomfort. Soviet policy on emigration and outside information may simply reflect this. It should be noted, however, that some restrictions on flows of information from outside countries expounding different philosophies of government is typical of the modern age.

The alternative state the population has in mind may be a previous state or even the existing state in the (usually recent) past. Thus, sharp increases in taxes or service reductions make people feel more exploited and raise the probability of revolution.[51] In this context it is easy to understand the influence of Utopian literature.

In reality, however, society is rarely composed of homogeneous individuals. Individuals, therefore, will feel differently exploited by any state if they are charged the same amounts for its services. The state need not do this, however. Payments for its services may be made to depend on characteristics of the individual. That is, any state may practice price discrimination across its population so as to equalize rates of exploitation across its subject population. The rational ruler will do this, of course. He will more exploit those who are less able to revolt effectively or to emigrate or otherwise to react against him. Neglecting this, however, we may raise the interesting question of how senses of exploitation will vary with equal tax shares. Assuming constant tastes, the effect of income will depend on the relationship of the home state's level of $G$ to other states' level of $G$. This may be seen as follows. It is assumed that individuals have some given earnings potential which is the same in both societies. Direct calculation then yields

$$\left(1 - \frac{\partial CP}{\partial I}\right) U_2(H) = U_2(A), \tag{9}$$

where $U_2(H)$ is the marginal utility of $Q$ evaluated at the home state's level and $U_2(A)$ at the alternative state's level. This may be rewritten as

$$\frac{\partial CP}{\partial I} = \frac{U_2(H) - U_2(A)}{U_2(H)} \tag{10}$$

which is positive or negative, assuming diminishing marginal utility, depending only on whether $Q \gtreqless Q_a$.

If $P_G < P_{G_a}$, $Q > Q_a$ and $\partial CP/\partial I < 0$. Thus, assuming equal tax shares, higher income people will feel more exploited than lower income people in societies with low per capita taxes. If per capita taxes are directly related to the level of $G$, then this implies that the rich will feel more exploited, *ceteris paribus*, in societies with relatively low $G$s. Observe, however, that these results depend crucially on $\partial P_{Ga}/\partial I = 0$, that is, that the alternative state not practice price discrimination with respect to income.

The sense of exploitation may vary for reasons other than income differences across a heterogeneous population. It will then pay the state to tax discriminate against those for whom in the absence of this discrimination it would be the least exploitative, or the most subsidizing. The overtaxing of the working middle class in western democracies may reflect precisely such a phenomenon.

Finally, it is instructive to consider marginal entry. This is almost always restricted by states. Private punishment is rarely allowed. Gun control legislation restricts the private production of both internal and external protection. Private schooling is discouraged where the state produces schooling. Given this, one would expect that marginal entry reduced the consent component of the state's return, but this is not always the case.

To see this, assume that the state allows marginal entry of size $\delta$ and that this is then produced by monopolisticity competitive firms so that in long run equilibrium, total revenue equals total cost $= F(\delta)$ for these firms. Again, taking the point of view of society as a whole, the relationship defining $CP$ is

$$U\big(G + \delta, I - CP - F(\delta)\big) = U(G_a, Q_a)$$

differentiating with respect to $\delta$ one obtains

$$U_1 - U_2\left[\frac{\partial CP}{\partial \delta} + F'\right] = 0 \quad \text{or} \quad \frac{\partial CP}{\partial \delta} = \frac{U_1}{U_2} - F'$$

Thus whether or not marginal entry increases or decreases, the consent component depends on the relationship between the size of marginal cost of output and the marginal rate of substitution between $G$ and $Q$. (It is useful to remember that $F$ is measured in units of $Q$.) From this we may conclude that when the level of $G$ produced by the state is less than optimal, then allowing marginal entry will raise the consent component. If it is greater than optimal, it will lower it. In an optimal state it will have no effect. As we have seen, however, there is some tendency for the rationally run state to overproduce $G$. In this case, the tendency of states to discourage marginal entry is understandable. It is also understandable for at least one other reason. To the extent that people can see that state services can be provided by competitive firms, their perception of the optimal social order is changed. As we have seen, this too will alter the constraints on the rulers.

What individuals desire will be produced. They desire order and this calls forth specialized firms, states, which produce this order by producing collective protection against both internal and external threats and by producing punishment for violations of the existing order. Because of the inherent returns to scale in the production of these services, particularly protection against external threats to order; because of the public nature of the products; because of the extreme slowness with which adjustments in the public goods sector takes place; and because of the difference a monopoly of coercive power makes, the market for these services is inherently dominated by one firm. This firm then is able to use its monopoly power to exploit the population it serves and may be able to extend the scope of this power into other markets which are not naturally monopolistic. The question remains, is there not some way to have the service without the power, some way in which the public's desire for order can be satisfied without saddling it with an exploitative monopoly? The following chapters examine this issue.

# 6 DEMOCRACY, THE CORPORATE STATE

The monopoly power of states causes two problems: society may be led to misallocate resources by producing too much order, or at least into attempting to do so by overallocating resources to its production. Monopolies also can earn excess profits for their owners, the rulers. These are the efficiency and equity problems of the preceding chapter. The misallocation of resources is a subtle effect, one that economic theory predicts and one that can perhaps be measured using the sophisticated tools of modern econometrics, but the ordinary citizen is probably not too cognizant of it. Even if cognizant they still may find it in their own interests to leave the behavior of the rulers unchanged. The same is true of other monopolies. We are typically outraged, not by the implicit misallocation of resources they cause but by the exorbitant profits of the monopolists. Perhaps this is because for most of us envy is a stronger motivation than the desire for perfection. More likely it is simply that the profits are obvious, while the inefficiency in the form of being at the wrong point on the production possibility curve is not. Moreover, it is not at all clear that a single-owner monopoly state would misallocate resources. That issue seems to depend on the nature of the information the ruler possessed. Representative democracy, the concern of the present chapter, may be viewed as a frontal assault on the equity part of the monopoly problem. May one wonder then, why so many are surprised that equity remains one of the principal concerns of modern democracies?

At a nominal level representative democracy transfers to the enfranchised public control of the decision as to who will be the operating managers, or decision makers, of the state.[1] The value of this to the public is that it sets up the possibility that competition for public approval will result in the citizens being offered the optimal set of public goods and taxes by one or all of the candidates for any given position. In the simple context which we consider, where differences among the electorate are largely ignored so that there is an unambiguous "best" social policy, the candidate who offers the platform which is closest to the optimal policy will win. In a more complicated context it would be the one who came closest to the optimal policy of the "median voter," which, as we have noted, is an alternative way to try to validate the concept of a "representative consumer."

There are a number of reasons why in fact voters may not be offered the optimal policy package. For one, there is no guarantee that the candidates will choose to compete by offering to reduce the amount of exploitation. Competition may be entirely an illusion produced along "marketing" or other dimensions. This seems particularly likely to happen when there are only two parties of any real significance.

An industry which has only two firms of any appreciable size would be classified by most economists as a duopoly. To be sure, personal antagonism or mistrust or differences in strategic perceptions between the heads of the companies might lead to the choice of the socially optimal (price, output, quality) combination, but in general we would assume that the relatively low cost of collusion would tend to produce *de facto* monopolization; that is, the companies both would recognize their mutual interest and offer the public choices which were more narrowly in the interests of the owners of the companies. This is especially likely if it is possible for them to make side payments to each other so that the profits resulting from the exploitation of the public could be more evenly distributed than pure market choices would allow. When the nature of the demand is "all or nothing," as it is with the choice of political party, this becomes particularly important. Only one party will win. Even with only two parties, competition could be quite fierce because the loser, in the absence of side payments, would get nothing. In the United States, and one suspects other systems, side payments abound.

At a trivial level, it is often the policy of each party to appoint some members of the opposition to important and unimportant posts in the interests of national unity, to demonstrate bipartisanship, statesmanship, and so on. The division of the spoils goes deeper, however. For example, in municipal elections for judges in New York City, in the 1950s by common consent the major parties historically divided the number of judgeships. In return for this, the Republicans, who typically did not do well in Brooklyn, did not campaign very hard there, etc. Thus, each party saved resources and divided a larger set of spoils, demonstrating the common oligopolistic phenomenon of the division of the market.

The absence of effective political competition, at the local level at least, is further supported by the following evidence (Table 1) developed by Breton and Scott. Similarly, a random sample of 40 cities in the United States reveals that on the average for the period 1947–73 the majority party controlled the mayor's office 67 percent of the time.[2] Political competition does not in fact seem intense enough to eliminate the monopoly profits of modern democratic states. If we look at Congress, a similarly questionable picture of "competition" emerges. In recent years the return rate for incumbent congressmen who stand for reelection has risen to 95 percent.[3] At the same time the Campaign Reform Act of 1974, funding, as it does, the two major parties at public expense, makes entry into political competition in the form of a new party more difficult than ever before.[4] Even in the absence of collusion among parties, however, it seems unlikely that democratic control of our present type could be fully effective. It is just too indirect and occasional. There is a general presumption that some people would have to have more effective control of the decisions of a democracy than others, just as the managers of the firm typically have more control over its behavior than do the stockholders, its supposed owners; collusion among parties with respect to policies in their interests simply guarantees this.

Objectively, modern representative democracy appears highly analogous to

Table 1. Number of Years of Consecutive Political Tenure for Selected Periods and Provinces,* Canada

| (1) Province | (2) Party in Office | (3) Period | (4) No. of Consecutive Years |
|---|---|---|---|
| British Columbia | Social Credit | 1953–1972 | 19 |
| Alberta | Social Credit | 1935–1971 | 36 |
| Saskatchewan | CCF | 1944–1964 | 20 |
| Ontario | Conservative | 1943–1974 | 31 |
| Quebec | Liberal | 1897–1936 | 39 |
| Quebec | Union Nationale | 1944–1960 | 16 |
| Nova Scotia | Liberal | 1933–1956 | 23 |
| Prince Edward Island | Liberal | 1935–1959 | 24 |

*Manitoba, for example, is not in the table because the province was governed for a long time by a coalition of parties and not by a single party, so that elections were contests between Coalition and Anti-Coalition parties.

the publicly held corporation, complete with the usual problems of the "separation of ownership from control." In the industrial organization literature the distinction between ownership and control has become familiar. The essential point is that ownership is really a vector and not a scaler concept. The stockholders are commonly thought to be the owners of the firm, but it is recognized that in many instances they do not control it. When there are many stockholders, each with a negligible share of the total stock, the firm is run more or less in the interests of its "managers." The stockholders' only leverage point is that by selling their stock they can indirectly affect the managers through the value of the stock and stock options and through the influence stock prices have on the company's ability to raise funds in capital markets.

As Marris and others have pointed out, the stockholders are generally not the real owners of the firm even in law. They are simply the owners of the bundle of rights to which their ownership of the company's stock entitles them.[5] In general, these rights include a residual claim to the corporation's capital in case of bankruptcy and the collective power to remove and replace the board of directors. The latter indirectly permits them to replace and, so to control the managers. The position of a citizen of a representative democracy is essentially similar, with the perhaps important exception that he is also necessarily a customer of the firm, the state.[6] Citizens can only indirectly affect the operation of the state unless they work in its operations. The ordinary citizen of a representative democracy does not run his government. This power is held by all citizens only in "direct" democracy, and perhaps not even there. Some delegation of power to "managers" is generally involved in all public activities. Once managerial discretion exists, the stockholder–citizen in fact owns only the rights his stockholder-citizenship give him–nothing more, nothing less. In practice, citizens of various modern democracies have different amounts of legal ownership–that is, varied rights.[7] They do not have the right to rule in any but the most superficial sense. Public workers of various sorts become the new rulers de facto. In some cases, it is an elected politician who is the "ruler." The politician, however, may himself be strongly influenced by his political machine, which can be viewed as an intermediate firm headed by a manager–the political boss. Sometimes one person holds both roles. The big city political boss such as Tweed or Daley is perhaps the archetype of the political leader as new owner of the state. In general, however, politicians are typically not the only rulers because in reality much government output is only marginally controlled by the elected political leader. Even the view that the firm is run in the interests of the managers is somewhat incorrect. In general some degree of ownership, in its correct sense, is diffused throughout the firm. Everybody in the firm makes at least some decisions and has at least some degree of independence. In any but the simplest production processes, it is generally difficult to determine who akes the decisive and controlling decisions. Indeed, what the decisive and ontrolling decisions are is often difficult to determine, *ex ante* or *ex post,* a henomenon which reflects the complexity of real life. Civil service, of which ae federal judiciary is the prototype, in effect puts the ownership (control) f some parts of the state in the hands of the employees of the state just as job nure rules transfer some effective ownership of the firm to its senior em- loyees. Along the same lines, regulatory commissioners may, for their tenures i office, operate in their own, as opposed to the politicians', interests.

Modern governments produce a multitude of services and products. They are ally not so much monopolistic firms as they are loose and complicated cartels f firms producing products of various degrees of interrelatedness in demand. olice and armed forces both produce protection of property, one against ex- rnal and the other against internal threats. Fire departments also protect prop- ty against internal threats. In reality each is controlled by somewhat different oups, each group having somewhat different interests but apparently sharing a ommon understanding of their mutual interest *vis à vis* the public at large.[8]

To the extent that democracy actually did succeed in diffusing the owner- aip of the state, it would accomplish one very equitable end, redistributing the rofits accruing to the monopoly power of the state among the citizenry as a hole. This, however, only happens if the exploitative profits are in fact re- arned to the citizenry, perhaps as a tax rebate, and there appear to be difficul- es which generally prevent the citizenry's acquiring these profits in cash. One aspects then that there may be some danger that the government of a demo- atic state might be run at zero profits by producing the level of order, and so orth, associated with zero profits. If, however, as we have already demonstrated, ae profit-maximizing level of profits results in the optimal level of output or ne that is too great, then the zero profits level of output will be generally much oo great. The only case in which this would not be true is when the profit- aximizing level of profits is itself equal to zero.[9] Under such circumstances ere is no reason to want to change the structure of state ownership. When the rofit-maximizing level of profits is zero, the state in effect has only the amount f power that it is desirable for it to have. This is perhaps the best of all worlds, ad in Chapter 8 we take up how to produce this result. Representative democ- acy does not produce this result. To the extent that it forces a zero profit out- ut it produces "equity" at the expense of social "efficiency." There may be a ndency for the democratic states to become too large, for them to attempt to roduce too much order or more correctly to devote too much of their society's sources to the production of certain goods and services.[10]

The institution of world government would allow representative democracy's ndency to overallocate resources to approach the limit. When there are other overnments which do not choose their outputs in this way their existence as an alternative puts a check on the tendency of democracies to overallocate resources to producing the public good. If there is only one government, then there is no choice. This says nothing, of course, about the advisability of some sort of world confederation of states in which the free movement of population and other resources would be guaranteed. That clearly would be desirable, since by increasing the possibility of emigration it would reduce the power of all states to exploit their populations, moving us closer to the ultimate ideal. Again, we return to these matters in the final chapter; now we are concerned with democracy.

Our position thus is that representative democracy attempts but does not in fact seem to succeed in changing the ownership-control of states into one of complete equality. Public workers, including politicians, become the new owners. Such diffusion of ownership as actually occurs has two important consequences to which we now turn.

1. Since there is the absence, or at least the reduced presence of a residual income recipient in representative democracy as opposed to monarchy or oligarchy (actually there are many "recipients," with ill-defined rights) *institutional entropy* will proceed faster than it might have done. As always with states, it also will proceed farther than in other institutions because of the greater longevity of the state. Thus, the overallocation of resources to the production of order, and so on, need not actually result in having too much order relative to the socially optimal level; one could even be spending too much and getting too little.

2. Because of the generalized diffusion of the ownership of the firm among the employees of the firm, there is an increased probability that the "supply curve" of the firm will be "backward-bending", a comparative statics effect. Attempts to increase order, and so forth, through increasing demands for them may actually reduce the level of order.

We discuss each of these in turn.

(1) A more detailed exposition of the phenomenon of institutional entropy has been presented elsewhere.[11] Briefly, the notion is this. Individuals maximize their own expected utility. This may, however, include a certain amount of satisfaction, or dissatisfaction, which they derive from their perceptions of the utility of others as a result of their love, or hate, for these others. To the extent that individuals identify with the group as a whole, that is, derive satisfaction from aggregate or group average levels of satisfaction, they are considered patriotic in the context of the nation as a whole. If they do so in the ordinary context of the firm, they are sometimes said "to identify with the firm." Such individuals are very valuable to any institution. An institution composed entirely of individuals who completely "identified" with what they were doing would

never suffer from the phenomenon of institutional entropy, the gradual running down of the institution's efficiency as a result of its increasing disorganization from the point of view of fulfilling its original function.[12] In institutions with what might be called imperfect cohesion, however, there is an inherent tendency for individuals to substitute their personal well-being for the well-being of the institution as a whole. This in turn produces institutional entropy.

An example from the business world will help to clarify our position. A buyer for a department store may, to the extent that this will only affect the general well-being of "the store" and not his own particular well-being, purchase from the most sexually attractive or useful salesperson or the one with the largest expense account or the best knowledge of how to use it. The actual marketability of the merchandise being offered the department store may play only a limited role in the buyer's choices. Persons in such a position can substitute their own well-being for that of the company as a whole, and they often do. That this will be the general case follows immediately from the general private interest theory of public choice,[13] which shows that individuals will, unless they either identify with the institution or perceive themselves to be important to the outcome, or view the issue as one of overwhelming importance, always substitute their private good for the public good when given the opportunity to do so. The well-being of the firm is a public good for its employees; therefore, it is quite natural that it be sacrificed for the employee's personal well-being to the extent they can get away with it.[14]

The absence of a residual income recipient intensifies this natural force found in all firms. A residual income recipient would have the appropriate personal incentives to prevent shirking or more general substitutions of the company's well-being for the well-being of individual employees, simply because the company's interest is literally his own personal interest. Thus too, the king (ignoring income effects) has a greater incentive than does a democratic "leader" to see to it that his functionaries perform their functions as he intends them to. In modern representative democracies, incentives to prevent shirking or other forms of substitution by public workers of personal for public well-being, are more or less absent. Politicians, if they are not able to pass the buck, are held responsible only at elections; civil servants almost never. The problem, from society's point of view, is compounded by the short tenure of politicians relative to kings. This produces a tendency toward extreme myopia in their choices. Solutions must be quick, even when no quick solutions are available, because elections are always around the corner. Interestingly, the existence of political parties and the tendency of many citizens to vote for the party and not the man will tend to offset this. In any case, democracies would seem destined to be inherently inefficient producers of their public goods,[15] because no one typically has much incentive to control costs.

Perhaps it has escaped general notice, until recently, that democracies are inefficient in the management of the production of public goods. Indeed, one has the impression that in the beginning modern western democracies were perhaps more efficient than the forms they replaced. We have as an example the success of the armies of the French Assembly in the days after the revolution. The reason for this possible divergence between theory and observation is, however, readily explained in terms of the theory of institutional entropy itself. All institutions are subject to gradual disorganization—entropy—but this takes time. New institutions, perhaps after initial break-in periods, are then expected to be inherently superior simply as a result of their newness. In comparing the efficiency of alternative institutional forms empirically, the age of the institutions must be taken into account, otherwise older institutions, even though they are superior at given age, may appear to be inferior simply as a result of their greater age.

The speed at which entropy sets in will also depend on the size of the institution and the extent to which power in the institution is diffused. The first point is another reason why states typically experience more entropy than do the other firms of society. They are typically among the largest firms in society. The second point may explain the rather fantastic rate at which European Communist regimes deteriorated. If the reports of people who went to Russia in the 1920s are accepted, then things were quite different there than they are now. Perhaps Communism actually did eventually succeed in distributing power to a wider group.[16] The point is that this may not be desirable unless it can be done perfectly. More importantly, one must remember that the upper bound to the level of state inefficiency is determined by the level of exploitation which is permissible before the population revolts. Where the political ruling class is necessarily the same as the economic ruling class, which history clearly demonstrates is not necessarily always the case (consider the fate of poor Crassus),[17] the bound on state inefficiency is necessarily looser. The probability of revolt depends on the probability of success, and that depends on the resources available for the revolutionaries. Where the state controls the business sector (or *vice versa*) revolutionaries will find it harder unless, of course, they can work from within. From this perspective, it is too early to assess the success, for example, of the Chinese system. It is too early to forecast how bad things will be allowed to get in the USSR before its people actively support repossession of that state. The historical case against democracy as an efficient system is quite strong. Democracies are the most short-lived of any system of ownership of the state.[18] If one accepts the view of states developed in the preceding chapters, this follows quite naturally from their inefficiency.

Time has now passed in the story of democracy, and few would be willing to argue that its old institutions are very efficient. This is consistent with theory. Its not being generally recognized is simply a tribute to the extent to which old notions die hard. Brand loyalty in form of governments is at least as strong as that for common household products, probably considerably stronger. Indeed there is some evidence that democracy is primarily a consumer good, desired for itself, like tail fins on cars or hi-fi equipment or the arts. The evidence for this is the association between increases in income and the subsequent emergence of democracies (Chapter 7), which is not to demean it. Unlike Galbraith and others, we would never presume to stand judgment on the tastes of others,[19] lest by so doing we gave them the right to presume to judge ours.

In a modern democracy, ownership rights are not only diffused but also limited. Taxes are the property of the king and his heirs, but not the president. To be sure, it is always possible for presidents or other public officials to use public funds to acquire goods that they would otherwise have purchased themselves, and this is equally true of other public workers in modern democracies. Witness Congressional junkets and other abuses of Congressional perquisites, lavish military installations and the use of military personnel to provide for personal services, and so forth. To the extent that the use of tax revenue for personal purposes is in fact limited, however, one expects nonpecuniary returns to be of increased importance to the new rulers.

Possession of the power associated with rule provides the rulers with a unique opportunity to impose their tastes on the population as a whole. Desiring a particular religious order, they may encourage their subjects to convert. Desiring that people not engage in certain activities, they may set the law to stop them. A casual survey of history reveals the remarkable extent to which the state's power is devoted to these ends. Prohibition of the consumption of various substances or services, forced collectivization, conversion by the sword, or legal restriction on members of non-state religions have been commonplace throughout history. Even militarism and modern imperialism may be simply the desire of power-holders for more power, prestige, or simple amusement. According to Morgenthau,

> All economic explanations of imperialism . . . fail the test of historic experience . . . . What the precapitalist imperialist, the capitalist imperialist, and the "imperialistic" capitalist want is power, not economic gain . . . investigation of historic instances cited in support of the economic interpretation show that in most cases the reverse relationship actually existed between statesmen and capitalists. Imperialistic policies were generally conceived by the government who summoned the capitalists to support these policies.[20]

Because there is a more limited possibility of taking out the profits in cash under a democracy, one expects these other forms of exploitation to be more important. Military adventures may be initiated by presidents who wish to play world conqueror or savior, as may moral crusades by those who wish to go down in history as "moral."

(2) To the extent that the employees become the *de facto* owners of the

firm, the share of the "entrepreneur" in the receipts of the firm necessarily increases. This joint ownership works to increase the probability of a backward-bending supply curve of the firm in the context of the theory of the utility-maximizing firm (the comparative statics effect).

Firms attempt to maximize not only profits, but more generally the satisfactions of their controlling group. For this reason, an increase in the demand confronting the firm produces income and substitution effects with opposite signs when there exist nonpecuniary objectives whose gratification increases the money cost of producing output. Leisure is just one such objective; there are many others, as we have just discussed. For ease of exposition, however, we will continue to talk in terms of leisure.

When the demand curve confronting the firm increases, there is a tendency to substitute money for leisure by producing more output (substitution effect); but with greater "income" there is also a desire to have more leisure, and this can come only at the expense of less output (income effect). The only instance in which this has no effect on the firm's equilibrium output occurs when it is possible to perfectly substitute other factors for the inputs of the entrepreneur. Given the anti-shirking function of the entrepreneur, however, it is impossible for that elasticity to be infinite, unless everyone is fully honest.

Whether the income or substitution effect dominates depends on their relative strengths. As we have shown elsewhere,[21] in the case of monopoly the following result holds. An increase in demand (keeping the elasticity of demand constant) will lower the monopolist's desired output if and only if

$$|\epsilon_{E \cdot A}| > -\frac{(1 - \alpha_E)}{\alpha_E} \frac{1 + B}{B^2 A} P\sigma$$

where:

$\epsilon_{E \cdot A}$ = The elasticity of entrepreneurial (owner) activity with respect to the shift parameter of the demand curve $A$[22]

$\alpha_E$ = Owner's share in gross receipts

$B$ = Elasticity of demand less than 0

$P$ = Price/unit

$\sigma$ = Elasticity of substitution of entrepreneurial/activity

The strength of the income effect on the output of the firm necessarily varies directly with the share in the firm's receipts which go to the entrepreneur—that is, the residual income recipient. Thus, when the entrepreneur becomes the work force as a whole, or even only some large part of it, then, *ceteris paribus,* we increase the likelihood that increases in the demand for the firm's products will result in decreases in its output. In the present-day United States, huge public programs on occasion appear only to serve to decrease the actual output of the particular service they are intended to increase. It would be overly bold to claim that the reason for this is the presence of a backward-bending supply curve for these services, but it is certainly a possibility worthy of further examination.[23]

Of course, some might argue that the public will select the most public-spirited individuals to become its leaders, or at least that an abundance of public-spirited people will be called to government work. In this case, representative democracy would work; it is analogous to the case of a firm where all the workers "identified." The real intentions and motivations of another person are, however, often difficult to discern even after long personal contact. It seems unlikely at this point in world history that one could offer evidence that, in fact, democracies tend to choose as their leaders the most public-spirited much less the wisest of the alternatives available to them, and in a world of imperfect information that will matter as well. In addition, there are many other characteristics of public work besides "opportunity to advance the public good." Just as the opportunity to work for the advancement of the public good will attract people to public works, so will these other characteristics. It may be interesting to consider the types of people this might include.[24] This has another advantage.

By understanding the characters of public workers, we may also be better able to understand the characters of public institutions. In representative democracy, as we have already observed, there is only a limited ability to take out monopoly profits in cash. Thus, they are often taken out in kind. As a result, the characteristics of public institutions should reflect the characters of their workers to an extent not generally seen in other industries. Finally, there is the possibility that by an understanding of the selection process we might see ways to improve it.

At the outset one thing must be understood. It is not our intention to try to describe some sort of "representative public worker." There is no such person. All sorts of people do public work and are attracted to it. They come for various reasons, and different reasons are important to different individuals. What we are trying to do is to understand, on the basis of the characteristics of public work, the various types of people who will be public workers.

While we propose to discuss public workers in general, there are various possibly relevant subclassifications of these. Civil service and "other employment" is one important dichotomy. Another is between workers involved in producing the services of government and those involved in decision making as to the nature and level of these services. We do not mean to suggest that these groups possess exactly the same characteristics. The various jobs differ with respect to the relative levels of some characteristics, but not of others, and thus the individuals called to the jobs will differ. We analyze these differences and show them to have predictable consequences.[25]

If one accepts the traditional economic assumption that individuals choose their jobs in ways which maximize their own expected utility, then certain jobs will of necessity be more attractive to certain types of people. Risk averters, for example, will tend to avoid selecting occupations associated with high levels of risk, while individuals who dislike physical exertion will try to avoid occupations requiring strenuous physical effort. In general, every job can be described by a vector of its characteristics.[26] Each individual, on the other hand, has a utility function which depends on his experience of these characteristics and various other variables. The associated wage or salary is simply one of the characteristics of any particular job; others are such things as the number of hours one is required to attend to the job, nonpecuniary characteristics such as status, stress, risk, and the extent of opportunity for theft and other forms of shirking.[27] Given its levels of the various characteristics other than wage or salary relative to other available jobs, any particular job will tend to attract various types of persons in a predictable manner. Individuals with less intense dislikes (or greater likes) for characteristics of a job, other than wage or salary, will be willing to accept a lower wage and thus *ceteris paribus* will be hired first. Alternatively, if the wage is considered as given, individuals who place more emphasis on the job's other characteristics will be willing to expend more effort in acquiring it, and thus will be more likely to succeed in doing so.[28] *Ceteris paribus,* people choose jobs so as to maximize their "specific rents." This is true for public work as well as for private.

What, then, are the special characteristics of public employments in general and of the job of politician in particular? Assuming there are such characteristics, we should be able to use the foregoing analysis to predict what types of people are likely to be able to function effectively, and perhaps to see how such jobs might be restructured to attract persons more compatible with their function.

Public employments in general, and in particular those jobs involved in decision making, are characterized by a relatively large opportunity to advance the public good. A relatively high degree of job certainty results mainly from the civil service system but also from a system which always rewards loyal, long-term work for a political party or political machine. Politicians and upper-echelon appointed bureaucrats, however, have greater job uncertainty than other public employees, although recent trends may be eliminating this difference. In addition, public employment is characterized by a certain amount of power, that is, the ability to coerce others (affect them without prior consent), and large opportunities for shirking. Let us proceed to analyze the consequences of each of these characteristics in turn. Because of the very nature of any public job, there are often opportunities to advance the public good or, more generally, to alter actual public policy for the better. This opportunity is rarely large except in certain key positions but it is, almost by definition, always present to a greater degree than in private jobs. Unfortunately, the improvement in one's well-being through the increased level of the public good is generally irrelevant to an individual's choice of a course of action unless he is important to the outcome (or believes himself to be so) or he views the issue as one of overwhelming importance (that is, failure to adopt a specific policy, or achieve a specific level of public good, is viewed as an infinite disaster) or he identifies, that is, has only group levels as arguments of his utility function.[29] This follows directly from our discussion of the GPITPC (Appendix III) and from the fact that most public workers have little influence on overall outcomes. For public goods it is only the overall level that counts, since everyone obtains the public level of the good.

In the vast, diffuse bureaucracies which seem to typify public employment, few jobs can realistically be viewed as important to overall public outcomes. With respect to those few jobs with real power, such as some political, military, and appointed positions, most individuals recognize the low probability of being chosen for the position. Thus, in addition to identifiers, only those whose views of the consequences of alternate public policies are impassioned and perhaps unrealistic, or those who hold strangely optimistic views of the probability of their achieving high public office will be attracted to public work by the desire to see the public good advanced.[30] These characteristics are more likely to be present for politicians and other decision makers because of the closer connection of their work with the level of public good.

On the other hand, it cannot be denied that some people derive satisfaction from acting in what they believe to be the public interest itself—which is another type of patriot.[31] They are attracted to public work, however, not by the desire to see the public good advanced but rather by the desire to support that advancement, whether or not it is achieved.[32] They enjoy working in the public interest itself; thus public employment, particularly those positions with some real opportunities for improving the public good, seems likely to attract the patriotic, those with an unusually large, perhaps inflated sense of their own historical importance (or luck), and those who hold extreme views about the consequences of alternative policies. For these reasons, one expects public policy to be highly activist, since its character is in part determined in the interests of those who desire action for its own sake.

Patriots are extremely valuable, but only to the extent that they accurately perceive the correct policy, and only to the extent that they do not desire action for its own sake. Those with an inflated sense of their own importance and those with extreme views of consequences would seem to be dangerous people to trust with the power usually associated with important public jobs. Their attitudes and/or expectations exhibit some signs of imbalance. Most importantly, from the public's point of view, it may be impossible to distinguish between patriots and the others, especially if candidates realize that the public wants to make this distinction.

The existence of a civil service system and the lower variability, especially in the downward direction, of the revenue available to support employees which results from the market power in coercion of governments, have created (at least up to recent years) a high level of job certainty in public work. Because of this, such work is certain to attract generally risk-averse individuals. This will have consequences for adaptability of government policy because such individuals are very unlikely to wish to see change of any sort, since change necessarily brings with it an increased level of uncertainty. Reluctance to change will have especially unfortunate consequences if the social order should begin to change more rapidly; it is, of course, desirable if proposed social changes are themselves undesirable.

Politicians as well as key officials are likely to be exceptions to this general risk-aversiveness among public workers, however. By the very fact that they are politicians, we know that at one point in their lives they were willing to invest considerable resources in an endeavor of uncertain outcome. They ran for public office for the first time. The inference that they once were not entirely risk-averse is only strictly correct if politicians pay for their own campaigns and when there is genuine uncertainty about the outcome of elections. Neither is the case when there is a strong political machine. However, where there is in effect only one party, as was the case throughout the South after the Reconstruction or in northern cities in the twentieth century, then primary elections (implicit or explicit) effectively become the election, and we again have the presumption that politicians are likely not to be as risk-averse as civil servants.

The politician, in most instances, does run some risk of losing (or having to change) jobs periodically, whereas the typical bureaucrat does not, except for those upper-level bureaucrats whose positions are non-civil service; e.g., upper-echelon decision makers such as the secretary of state. This dichotomy in effective tastes for change is widened, because people who view some changes as overwhelmingly important are especially attracted to the job of politician. A difference in attitude between politicians and non-civil servants who will be required to carry out their decisions appears to be inescapable.

Public workers are thus likely to be of two divergent types. The "macro-decision makers" are more likely to prefer risks and therefore to be more willing to see things changed than will civil servants and other "micro-decision makers and production workers." This difference in tastes has predictable consequences. Changes mandated from the top may be resisted by civil servants interested in avoiding change and its consequent increase in uncertainty. As often happens, legislated reforms may never actually take place. But as we have already noted, unless the changes are desirable, this may not be bad. Finally, it must be observed that some individuals who do not like personal job uncertainty may like other uncertainty. There are, however, other reasons why public workers will resist change, to which we will turn shortly.

Ability and willingness to accept risk varies across socioeconomic groups. The rich, if only because they can afford it, seem to be more likely to take risks of a given size than the poor. The rich are therefore more likely to try for political office and, because of their superior wealth, more likely to succeed.[33] The long-run implications of this may be quite drastic. If people learn by doing, and if learning increases the more real the doing, then the children of the rich may, for lack of real practice, be relatively inept at choosing among alternatives in a world where resources are scarce, simply because scarcity is not really part of their personal experience. This is especially true for economic scarcity, which may not have been part of their experience at all when they were young and their character and capabilities were being formed. In some instances, parental training may offset this. Then too, almost all Americans may be rich enough to spoil their children at this point in time.

Acton observed that power tended to corrupt and that absolute power tended to corrupt absolutely. Actually, it is worse than that. *Ceteris paribus,* power is more valuable to people who are willing to abuse it in their own interests than to people who are not. Thus, there exists some tendency for precisely the wrong people to be attracted to positions of power. The correctness and importance of this point is rather easily seen in the context of one of the simple examples often used to "prove" that the existence of government is necessary or desirable, because of the existence of "externalities."

Consider a group of homeowners whose homes all front on the same swamp, and suppose that while the total cost of draining the swamp is less than the total benefit, it is greater than the benefit any single homeowner will enjoy from the draining. Thus, no single individual is going to drain the swamp and, to follow the usual story line, voluntary contributions will not work because some people would lie about the value to them of draining the swamp. Real "gamers" might even suggest they liked the swamp and require compensation for allowing it to be drained. But if some people would deceive, others would not; and to whom is the job of tax assessor likely to seem more valuable? *Ceteris paribus,* those who are not willing to pay their fair share must value the job more highly, since it will provide them with an excellent opportunity to avoid paying their share, while to the others this element has no value, since they wish to pay their share. Similarly, the job of police officer will appear singularly attractive to those with an interest in committing criminal acts, as well as to those who have a strong desire to enforce the law.[34] We shall shortly consider some evidence to this effect.

In addition to attracting those who would wish to abuse it, power will tend to attract those who like to exercise power for its own sake, and repel those who do not. Public officials often betray a striking tendency to prefer coercive as opposed to noncoercive solutions to problems. This follows directly from the nature of the type of individual attracted to that work.

Finally, because of the size of public institutions, because of their age, and because of the general absence in them of a residual income recipient, the opportunity for shirking there is likely to be exceptionally large. Individuals with high preferences for on-the-job leisure are likely to find public employment singularly attractive and, as a result, one expects that output per man is rather lower in the public sector than in the economy at large. Unfortunately, given the way in which we generally measure the output of a public agency, this generally is undetectable at the present time. In a number of specific instances where direct comparisons can be made, our conclusion is borne out.

Some sense of the magnitude of waste inherent in our present government is gained by comparing the costs of services when they are directly provided by government and when they are provided by low-bidding private firms. Boston uses such a system to arrange for garbage collection; Cambridge does not. Apparently[35] the per ton costs are substantially lower in Boston, even though the two cities are adjacent to each other. According to a report of the Environmental Protection Agency, private garbage collection costs only 53 percent as much as public provision of the service. The increased efficiency of the crews is credited with producing this saving. The California Task Force found that savings could be made by privately contracting a number of services rather than having them directly produced by the state. The savings ranged from $10,000 per year from contracting for legal services to $100,000 per year from contracting for bus service. Scottsdale, Arizona, has its fire protection supplied by a private contractor, at a savings of 47 percent over the costs of traditional production by governments of comparable quantity/quality.[36]

Further evidence of the differential efficiency of government is indirectly provided by a study conducted by Frech, of physician services insurance (Part B) claim processing for the Medicare Program. Both profit-seeking insurance companies and nonprofit mutual and Blue Shield firms perform this rather well-defined task. Table 2 summarizes the results of the study. In each of the three relevant dimensions of output, the profit-seeking firms are found to be significantly more efficient than the nonprofit ones. Government is, of course, analogous to a nonprofit firm.

In this context, may we simply suggest without citing any evidence that postal service could be provided more cheaply than it now is by private firms?

Table 2.  Medicare Processing Performance and Ownership

|  | Cost per Dollar Processed | Average Processing Time (Days) | Errors per $1000 Processed |
|---|---|---|---|
| Profit-seeking firms ($N = 12$) | $ 0.0715 | 18.70 | 0.1844 |
|  | (0.0178) | (10.34) | (0.0717) |
| Nonprofit firms ($N = 66$) | 0.1039 | 33.59 | 0.4426 |
|  | (0.0331) | (19.83) | (0.7576) |
| Approximate $t$-value for difference of means | 4.908 | 3.565 | 2.706 |
| Degrees of freedom | 29.9 | 31.3 | 70.9 |
| Statistical significance (one-tail test) | < .005 | .0009 | .005 |

*Note:* If variances are assumed to be different and unknown, the appropriate test statistic is an approximate $t$-value (Yamane 1967, pp. 522–24). Standard deviations are shown in parentheses.

Perhaps the same is true of education. Indeed, experimentation may reveal that most of the services we receive from government could be obtained from private firms for less.

The desire to avoid work will also tend to reinforce the tendency to avoid or resist change. It is much easier to go on doing things as they have always been done.

There is, then, no reason to believe that public work will be done only by the right sorts of people. Indeed, there is some reason to believe that public work will attract many people who, from the public's point of view, are precisely the wrong people for the job.

Representative democracy attempts to transfer ownership of the state to the citizenry at large by making them the choosers of the rulers. This would solve the equity problem of the state only if political competition forced the political ruling class to offer the optimal output at the zero profit tax level, or if there were tax rebates of the exploitative profits of the state. Neither seems to occur. What does occur is an imperfect diffusion of the ownership of the state primarily to the political leaders and other public workers. This imperfect diffusion results in a situation which appears to be worse than either monarchy or oligarchy in terms of efficiency. States, because of their longevity, their size, and the intangibility of their output, are always subject to greater entropy than are other institutions in society. Imperfect democracy intensifies this problem. The ownership of the residual income of the state is diffused throughout a wider group, and thus control becomes less effective and entropy proceeds at a faster rate. This may be the reason that democracies are historically so short-lived. Interestingly, as the possibility of taking out the exploitative profits in cash is lower than in other forms of government, most notably monarchy, the returns tend to be taken out either in the form of on-the-job leisure, and so forth, or in the form of shaping public policy to fit the tastes of the public workers as opposed to the public.

All these effects would tend to be mitigated if there were some tendency for the right people to be attracted to public work; however, theory and, to some extent, casual observation tend to suggest that this is far from being the case.

In order to tie our discussion down, it seems advisable to discuss some specific examples of the processes we have in mind. Given our orientation toward the state, it is only natural that our examples be drawn from police and military services.

We have already noted that the job of police officer will be particularly attractive to those who desire to break the law and wish to have a very useful cover for their criminal activity. New York City, one of the oldest and the largest cities in the United States provides many examples of this. According to the *N.Y. Times,* "Narcotics dealers, gamblers and businessmen make illicit payments of millions of dollars a year to the policemen of New York . . . ." The 10,000 Puerto Rican shopkeepers alone were being extorted to the tune of more than six million dollars per year. Most interestingly, of 137 cases of police misdoing reported to the authorities in one year, seven were investigated.[37] The problem is not restricted to that city, however. A study begun in 1966 showed that twenty-seven percent of the police officers observed in Chicago, Washington, and Boston slums admitted engaging in acts that could be classified as felonies or misdemeanors.[38]

Some further idea of the magnitude of police crime may be inferred from rather incidental evidence. One such piece of evidence comes from J. Edgar Hoover, late head of the Federal Bureau of Investigation, who ordered his agents to break the law in various ways a minimum of 241 times in the last 20 years of his life. To be sure, he did so because he thought he was acting in the national interest, and being a patriot he got satisfaction from that type of activity. The point remains, however, that the head of a most powerful (and model) police force was willing to break the law in order to increase his own level of satisfaction, albeit by acting for the advancement of his conception of the national interest.[39]

These are just a few examples of the ways in which some of the exploitative profits of the state are appropriated by public servants. Less order is produced by more police officers in part because the police themselves are producers of disorder and because by increasing the size of the force we provide more cover for criminals.

With the exception of Hoover, the foregoing describes instances in which the returns were appropriated in cash. In other instances, the appropriation is in kind. Those of us who have been stopped by the police for traffic violations sometimes find that we are treated with a certain amount of rudeness, arrogance, and contempt—even if the violation is only a matter of having a headlight out.[40] This is, of course, most likely to be the case if one looks odd or from outside mainstream either as a result of choice or of birth. By alienating some parts of the population in this fashion, the police acquire some part of the exploitative profits of the state in the form of psychic income. Everyone sometimes enjoys feeling superior and powerful and of course, given that the job of policeman has these possibilities, it will tend to attract those who particularly enjoy these feelings.

A third, and most important if at first less obvious, way in which the police acquire the profits of the state is through the proliferation of crimes that in actuality have little to do with order, but which are typically committed by nondangerous people—jaywalking; drinking in public, as opposed to drunk and disorderly behavior; mopery, the huge mass of traffic crimes, and so on. Potentially the job of police officer is quite dangerous, or at least it would be if all the police did was try to arrest murderers, armed robbers, and other potentially violent felons. As some current police leaders stress, however, the modern police officer's job doesn't primarily involve these activities. Other functions of the officer have become more important. It is natural that the police have an interest in the proliferation of laws; it raises the demand for their services. What we are saying is that they have an even greater interest in the proliferation of laws that are most likely to be broken by nondangerous people, and of course in extending their jobs so that they have many nondangerous reasonably straightforward things to do—e.g., filling out field interview forms on citizens stopped because they looked "suspicious."

The ability of the police themselves to appropriate the profits of the state increases with time, as a result of simple learning by doing, increases in group cohesion, and so forth. It also is a result of the operation of the adverse selection problem already alluded to. The job of policeman will tend over time to attract increasingly large percentages of power abusers. Those patriotic and public-spirited people who might have been attracted to the job by the possibilities it offered for acting on behalf of the public interest may increasingly be driven out by the guilt-by-association onus of the bad cop. While the crooked cop doesn't really mind the honest cop, unless he poses a threat of arrest, the honest cop is demeaned by association with the crooked one. One of the authors[41] conjectures the existence of a critical point after which the drift to a police force composed overwhelmingly of criminals and hooligans is inevitable save only for the intervention of an aroused and enlightened citizenry.

The armed forces represent another interesting example of the acquisition of the exploitative profits of the state by public workers in the form of personal gain or waste. Not many people appeared to be surprised by reports over the last few years of high living by military officers at public expense or of the 1976 meat inspection scandal. Although we spend staggering amounts for defense, it begins to become clear that actually we are not particularly well defended. Our recent involvement in Southeast Asia is a case in point. Actually, the American army has exhibited signs of gross inefficiency for quite a while. According to Lt. Gen. L.B. Puller's observation 50 percent of the casualties to the first force General MacArthur sent to Korea appeared to be from self-inflicted wounds. According to General Bradley, our fighting troops suffered average casualties of one-third per battle in the European theater of World War II. This is a higher rate than history records as having been suffered by many losing armies.[42] Bradley also reports with little note, an interesting observation made by General Marshall. Marshall estimated that in World War II 50 percent of our combat troops would not fire at the enemy in any given combat situation.

The military appears to be run pretty much in the interests of the academy officer class. The more troops there are the higher will be the number of high ranking positions. Officers also have an interest in the proliferation of non-, or less, dangerous positions. Perhaps this is one explanation of why the United States has the highest ratio of backup to combat troops of any army in the world — 10:1.[43]

We could of course go on, but we hope this presentation has given the reader some concrete sense of how the forces we have been discussing work out in actuality. The problem is serious. The casual evidence suggests that perhaps 50 percent of resources we now spend on government services is directly wasted. If this is even close to being correct, then the problem of the business cycle pales to insignificance before the problem of government inefficiency in representative democracy.

But this is not all. In the long run, not even the public workers benefit from the situation in the form of rents, that is, earnings in excess of their potential returns elsewhere. Competition for public jobs drives up the cost of acquiring them. The amount of schooling or the ability necessary to acquire the job is inflated beyond what will be required to perform the job by the struggle between people for these rents. Ultimately the rents tend to become capitalized. In the limit public workers earn no more than a normal return on their "investments." The tragedy is that ultimately no one gains; everyone loses. There are no villains, just victims.[44]

# 7 DEMOCRACY AS A CONSUMER GOOD[1]

The previous chapter established that democracy, rather than ameliorating the problems that citizens have with their governments, may actually make them worse. In this chapter we offer a possible explanation for the continued existence of democracies. The hypothesis examined is that democracy is desired in and of itself, that is, as a consumer good. People like to participate in government for its own sake, even if this participation results in no other benefit to them. The evidence for this view is the strong relationship between levels of income and the "democrativeness of society."[2]

## 1 EVIDENCE

The existence of a positive (but by no means perfect) relationship between income levels and "democrativeness" of political systems is supported by different types of evidence. Casual observation suggests that today's most affluent nations typically have more democratically selected rulers. Moreover, the emergence or extension of political democracy in widely different times and places is clearly linked to increases in income.

In England the political pressure of the 1820s and 1830s culminating in the enfranchisement of the new middle class by the Reform Act of 1832[3] was accompanied by a sharp rise in the real income of this social stratum.[4] Similarly, increases in the real wages of industrial and agricultural workers in the latter half of the nineteenth century[5] coincided, amid renewed political pressure and popular violence, with the enfranchisement of male workers by the statutes of 1867 and 1884.[6]

The Japanese "Taishō Democracy" movement (1912-24) enfranchised the bulk of the middle classes by 1919 and culminated in 1925 in the passage of a universal suffrage bill for men. In the early stages the demand for democratic reforms came primarily from businessmen,[7] who were enjoying unprecedented profits during the war boom of 1914-19.[8] Real industrial wages were apparently stationary during the war, but during 1920-1924 there was a precipitous rise in both real wages[9] and in demands by lower economic status urban dwellers to be allowed to participate in politics.[10]

The New Zealand Act of 1879, which significantly extended the suffrage as compared to the Reform Act of 1832[11] was immediately preceded by strong economic growth stimulated by gold rushes (1860-69) and an investment boom (1870-78).[12]

In Argentina rapidly rising incomes (during the 1880s and especially during 1904-12) and a prolonged political struggle immediately preceded the passage of the 1912 law calling for universal male suffrage by secret ballot and the democratic election of 1916.[13]

With the suffrage reforms of 1907-09 and 1918-21, Sweden became a true parliamentary democracy.[14] The 1890s period in which the suffrage movement gathered increasing force[15] was also a period of generally rising living standards that resulted from a significant upsurge in industrial development.[16]

Danish democracy, which drew its mass support from the peasantry, grew with reforms in 1834 and 1848 and finally triumphed in the 1880s. The peasants' demand for democratization of the political order (e.g., via the Farmer's Leagues in the 1840s and the United Left party of the 1870s) has been traced to a prior increase in their wealth resulting from the decision of the Reventlow Commission (1784) to give the peasants land and credit.[17]

In Athens the reforms of Solon (594 B.C.E.) which freed those enslaved for debt, wiped out the debts of farmers and removed the mortgages from their properties combined with growing general affluence from changes in agriculture and trade[18] to inaugurate the drive toward democratic rule.[19] Later, in 508 when the popular council was dissolved, the angry disfranchised masses successfully revolted and recalled Cleisthenes (the "second founder of Athenian democracy").[20]

A tenable reconstruction of the history of the extension of democratic rights in Sparta is quite similar.[21] The economic status of Spartan commoners was significantly improved after 708 B.C.E. by their seizure (or a distribution) of the conquered rich Messenian land (and "helots") on Sparta's frontier. This was shortly followed by the agitation of the commoners for political recognition. Such recognition was granted by Lycurgian reforms (700-670 B.C.E.) which provided for a regular popular assembly that elected 28 members of the Senate of Elders (the *Gerousia*) and had to grant final approval to the senate's decisions.

The early history of Rome is obscure, but apparently the land distribution of 393 B.C.E., under which all citizens secured a share of captured (Veian) land immediately north of the city, significantly improved the economic status of the "proletariat."[22] In 366 B.C.E., after an intense "patrician versus plebian" struggle, the consulship (the highest magistracy in the state) was opened to plebians.[23] A period of land distributions of newly conquered territories also preceded a "secession of the plebs" and the passage of a law in 287 B.C.E., establishing equal suffrage for men in legislation for the "plebians."[24]

After 1347-50 in Western Europe wage rates rose sharply while land values declined as a consequence of the Black Death, which reduced the population by a third or more.[25] In the following decades (the "golden age of wage labor") many cities experienced democratic agitation on the part of artisans and laborers who sought the rights of citizenship (the franchise to use modern terms) through full membership in a guild. The clearest example is provided by the revolt of the Florentine wool-workers in 1378 (the revolt of the *Ciompi*) who henceforth were to appoint three of the nine city magistrates.[26] The journeymen coppersmiths and drapers of Rouen revolted in 1382 and won a more popular constitution.[27] Other worker rebellions occurred in Lyons, Paris, and Cologne.[28] It seems quite possible that similar causes contributed to the demand for an end to villenage and the related social stigma in the English Peasants Revolt of 1381[29] and to the numerous local peasant revolts in other parts of Western Europe after the middle of the fourteenth century.[30] The Spanish historian Vicens Vives also traces "demands for personal liberty" and "great clamor for emancipation" in the Catalan countryside in 1390 to the Black Death.[31]

Similarly the great German Peasant War, the *Bauernkrieg* of 1524-25 and the numerous outbursts that immediately preceded it appear to have occurred during a period of rising prosperity among peasants and urban workers.[32] In the generation before the Reformation, the peasants generally demanded their village self-government—i.e., that they rather than the princes should choose their officials, magistrates, bailiffs, and sheriffs.[33] Later the peasants widely adopted the Twelve Articles (1525) calling for the elections of ministers by their congregations.[34]

The cases of Argentina and Japan are particularly instructive, because in both countries democratic rule was apparently aborted by the depression of the 1930s. Again, Cobban[35] has noted that the era of dictatorships beginning at the time of the Gracchi (133–123 B.C.E.) coincides rather neatly with the exhaustion of free land in Italy and the end of the great age of Roman frontier expansion.

Finally, let us review the evidence provided by a number of quantitative across-country studies. Wolf finds a positive and statistically significant simple correlation between an index of political democracy and real per capita gross national product in a group of Latin American countries.

Adelman and Morris consider a group of less developed countries and conclude that "the coefficients resulting from the factor analysis indicate that a typically western configuration of political traits is generally associated with higher average income."

Lipset classifies European and English speaking countries as "stable democracies" or as "unstable democracies" and finds that average income is higher in the former than in the latter group of countries. This student also observes that average income is higher in those Latin American countries classified as "democracies and unstable dictatorships."

In a study of 47 developing countries Simpson observes a positive correlation between a measure of political participation and national income.

Cutright constructs an index of political development (understood in a democratic sense) covering the period 1940–60 for 77 nations. He finds this index to be positively correlated with an index of economic development.

Hagen classifies the political structures of underdeveloped countries as "authoritarian," "semicompetitive," and "competitive," and observes that a composite index of economic development tends to increase as one moves from the former to the latter classification.

A.K. Smith, Jr., observes positive and often statistically significant correlation and regression coefficients between a refined version of Cutright's "index of democrativeness" and indices of urbanization, education, and communications development. His regressions are for the period 1946–65 and explain behavior in 100 nations or in various geographic subsamples of these nations.


## 2   INTERPRETATIONS AND CONCLUSIONS

Of course there are many possible interpretations of this positive relationship. A few examples are sufficient to give the flavor of the discussion.

Some students argue that poverty-stricken populations tend to become desperate and seek quick authoritarian solutions. According to Lipson:

> Where more people own at least some property, they have something to conserve and are therefore less disposed to extremist attitudes and violent actions — both of which militate against democracy. Psychologically, where the basic needs of food, clothing, and shelter are satisfied with a reasonable

amount of comfort, the resulting sense of security promotes a tendency to compromise and moderation.[36]

Lipset argues that

> Increased wealth is not only related causally to the development of democracy by changing the social conditions of the workers, but it also affects the political role of the middle class through changing the shape of the stratification structure so that it shifts from an elongated pyramid, with a large lower-class base, to a diamond with a growing middle class. A large middle class plays a mitigating role in moderating conflict since it is able to reward moderate and democratic parties and penalize extremist groups.[37]

while Hagen believes the

> expansion of industrial activity, even if it is a gradual growth of small enterprises rather than a spectacular change, creates a middle class with interests opposed to those of a traditional ruling landed group. Increased industrialization, urbanization, and geographic movement widen horizons and create new ambitions. All of these changes breed political change.[38]

Adelman and Morris do not believe that economic development and political democracy are causally related. To these students

> it appears more plausible . . . to ascribe the positive association . . . to the existence of common forces which underlie both the transformations of social institutions which typically accompany economic development and the changes in political structure characteristic of the evolution of modern political systems.[39]

The positive relationship between income and democracy has been interpreted in political and sociological terms. Surprisingly, economic interpretations have been both rare and ambiguous.

The line of explanation followed here is first that the democratic process in which consent is actively (or expressly) given (by deciding together) is itself a consumer good and second that in mass societies democratic systems are generally more expensive to operate than autocratic systems.[40]

The first possibility receives some support from White and Lippitt:

> Of all the generalizations growing out of the experimental study of groups, one of the most broadly and firmly established is that the members of a group tend to be more satisfied if they have at least some feeling of participation in its decisions . . . . If democracy is really democracy and not laissez-faire — i.e., if it emphasizes strong leadership and other factors that make for efficiency — it is usually more satisfying than autocracy. This is true at least in our own culture and probably also in most other cultures of the world.[41]

Another piece of evidence supporting the view that individuals derive satisfaction from the act of participation in political decision making is provided by the extent to which they actually do participate within democratic mass societies. If it were not for the satisfaction of participating, there are only exceptional instances in which they would. Political activity is not without cost to the individual. In mass societies, and in the absence of coercion, it is quite rational for individuals to abstain from political activity on the grounds that the nature and quality of political decisions are independent of their own political activities and that, as citizens, they will receive whatever benefits flow from political decisions even if they do not participate in making them.[42] This is the central result of the GPITPC again (see Appendix III). If they do not derive satisfaction from the feeling of participation, why else do they participate?

Measures making mass participation in state-making easier tend to be quite costly. There are the money costs of framing a constitution, establishing political parties, holding meetings and elections, protecting minority rights, gathering and assimilating various kinds of information including the "disclosure or notice of prospective actions and the announcement of the considerations underlying actions."[43] There are also the imputed costs of the participants' time, including foregone gains from specialization.[44] Carl Cohen concludes that in larger communities "the physical machinery of participation becomes exceedingly complicated and very expensive."[45] The effect of increases in population and territory ruled is illustrated by the demise of "direct" democracy in "city-states" of Early Dynastic Sumer,[46] republics of Vedic India,[47] Rome,[48] and of "town meetings" the world over.[49] Then, too, there are the indirect costs resulting from the inefficiency of democracy with respect to the levels and/or costs of public goods.[50]

It is clear that once societies have exceeded some minimum size the cost of state-making is lower under autocratic systems such as kingship for life, hereditary (next-of-kin or rotating) kingship, adoptive kingship, aristocracy, divination, fratricide, or *coup d'etat* which helps to account for their historical popularity.[51] In the future, computer technology together with recent advances in public choice theory will lower the costs of direct democracy.[52]

The remainder of the argument is readily understood by means of a simple analogy. When an individual's income is low, he or she might deem it unwise to use part of it to purchase butter or a Cadillac. In order to be better able to satisfy more urgent needs, he or she might instead purchase margarine or a Duster or perhaps do without a table spread or a car. However, at higher levels of income consumers might feel they could afford these items and purchase them. If the assumptions presented above are accepted, a similar argument can be made for active consent (or deciding together) in mass societies. At low levels of income people might prefer to do without democracy (they would not revolt or otherwise bear the cost of resisting authoritarian rule) in order to satisfy more pressing needs, but as development proceeded and incomes rose they might feel better able to afford it and increasingly engage in or support political activity designed to achieve a democratic system or to maintain democratic rights.[53,54]

Finally, it is interesting to note that the approach to consumer choice developed above is consistent with the psychological literature of the "growth actualization" school whose best-known exponents are Carl Rogers and Abraham Maslow. This view of human personality

> . . . is based on the belief that man has certain inborn, basic needs which must be satisfied if the individual is to enjoy mental health . . . it is advanced that these needs are arranged in a hierarchy of importance so that after – and only after – the first, most basic need is largely satisfied does the next need become a motivating force.[55]

Maslow stresses five basic need areas or motivators: physiological, safety or security, affection and belongingness, esteem, and self-actualization or psychic fulfillment.[56] Relatively lengthy lags of demand for democracy behind increases in income may result in the growth-actualization framework, because severe deprivation of a prior need (e.g., physiological), particularly in the early years, "even if later satisfied . . . will leave its effects on the character of the individual."[57]

The stress placed upon income should not be taken to mean that other economic and noneconomic variables are not relevant or are less important. A more complex theory might explain not only the general tendency noted above but a number of "deviant" cases such as India.

A major weakness of existing quantitative studies is that single equation estimates of the coefficient of income must be suspect when there is a reasonable likelihood that political democracy is a determinant of national income. Of course the econometricians have provided us with several simultaneous equations techniques, and in principle one of these could be employed to provide an unbiased estimate of the impact of income on the demand for political democracy. It would be more difficult to empirically disentangle the consumption argument from the view that countries differ in their distributions of various personal characteristics (i.e., in their "national characters") and that certain of these (e.g., a spirit of enterprise and industry, an inquisitive mind, or good health) are responsible for both higher incomes and heightened desires to participate in state-making.

# 8 EXPERIMENTAL REMEDIES
## *Some Preposterous Proposals*[1]

This chapter seeks to suggest ways in which a government such as that of the United States might be improved. That is the system with which I am familiar. One hopes, however, that the experiments enumerated here have applicability in other societies. We shall see. At the outset, let me stress once again that these suggestions are advanced in a very tentative fashion. It is not my intention to have them considered as some sort of platform for immediate calls to action. In truth, not enough is known, as yet, about the details and dynamics of social change. I would prefer that these experiments be treated as experiments, by being tried selectively in certain subregions of society both in terms of geography and in terms of public goods. As time passes, objective observation will teach us their actual effects. The experiments are divided into three sections.

The first set of experiments considered represents a frontal assault on the entropy problem of government institutions. As we have already argued, governments in general, and democratic governments in particular because of their size, their longevity, and the structure of their ownership under democracy, have experienced enormous amount of entropy. They have become incredibly disorganized from the point of view of providing the services they are supposed to provide in an efficient manner. Directly attacking this symptomatic area appears to offer the greatest hope for an immediate short-run improvement in our situation. These represent the least "radical," in the sense of "root" or fundamental changes in our systems of providing public services.

Our second category consists of three changes which, when taken together, would increase the intergovernmental competitiveness of the United States system, thus allowing greater scope for what are traditionally known as Teibout forces. These are already relatively strong in the United States system, although increasingly less so. The United States system consists of many alternative sub-states each providing various local public goods at different local tax prices, and its citizenry is free to move from one subjurisdiction to another at a relatively low cost. Language is technically unchanged, but local cultural differences and the existence of distance and specialized local information still create positive costs. The Tiebout hypothesis states that in the limit the resulting constraints on the behavior of the local political leaders, or "rulers", will be sufficiently great as to effectively prevent any exploitation. At the same time, the free movement of population and choice of levels of public good and tax rates by self-seeking local governors will guarantee that the correct set of levels of the public good will be produced,[2] with individuals optimally allocating themselves across the various jurisdictions. The point of modern history seems to be that we are now getting further away from that limit. Taken together, the three proposals in our second category would increase the number and quality of subjurisdictions, thus bringing us closer to satisfying the conditions of Tiebout's theorem. They accomplish this by eliminating the artificial frictions that prevent the expansion and contraction of jurisdictions within the present system. In a frictionlesss world, governments, and all the other firms' sizes as well, would be constantly shifting both vertically and horizontally in response to changes in tastes, technology, and resource endowments. We would see a proliferation of nested and continually changing federal structures. As we have already observed, the services produced by government do not all have the same degree of returns to scale. In a perfectly running, frictionless society, each of the various types of services might therefore be provided by a different subunit of an overgovernment in what would be a system of truly flexible federalism.

In actuality, the world is filled with all sorts of sources of friction. People incur transactions costs when they have to shift firms. The creation of new firms and the destruction of old ones imposes still other costs. Thus, not even in the private sector do we see a completely fluid movement from one situation to another. In the case of governments, there are also additional sources of friction: the power of government itself, the all or nothing nature of the consumption decision, and finally the higher transactions costs associated with changing governments, whether through revolution or emigration, than with changing soap suds. Perhaps the first reason is the most important. It is generally not in the interests of the present owners of any state, the powers that be, to see

fragmenting changes take place even though there are scattered historical examples in which rulers have encouraged fragmentation.[3] Moreover, because of
their market power in "coercion," states can do more to prevent entry than can
other firms. It is in the interests of the rulers to limit Teibout forces. The more
choices its citizens have, the less is the state's monopoly power. Thus, the
owners of governments will generally act to centralize authority. For all these
reasons, it is to be expected that the boundaries of government will change more
slowly than the boundaries of other firms. In some instances, since coercion is
involved they may even change in the wrong direction.

From the perspective on government just presented, it is clear that any work
on the reform of government whose objective has been a fixed ideal was mis-
directed. There is no final optimal political structure. The optimal structure is
itself subject to continual change in all its details. The real problem seems to be
that it may not be possible for the current structure to change fast enough and,
more importantly, that it does not necessarily always change in the appropriate
direction. As our discussion in Chapter 6 suggests, there are reasons to believe
that the competitiveness of the American system is decreasing. This suggests
experimenting with various means of making possible appropriate changes in the
size of governmental units or jurisdictions, allowing for fragmentation (or coalescence) when one or the other is desirable.

A third possible set of ways to improve our current situation is suggested by
the general analogy of the state with firms. Vertical disintegration is one widely
accepted antitrust technique. At present even when an industry is a natural
monopoly, because of returns to scale, because of the efficiency of a dominant
firm, or simply because enough time has not yet passed for the advantages of
being first to be dissipated, various subcomponents of the industry, or processes
associated with it, can be split off from the main company to become essentially
competitive or at the very least, more competitive. This also is the case with the
output of government. In the third section we probe the possibility that a government's performance might be improved by constitutionally narrowing the
restrictions on its limits of action, or the way in which it acts. The remaining
activities would then fall into the hands of competitive, individual efficiency-
seeking firms.

## 1  IMPROVING THE EFFICIENCY OF
GOVERNMENTS DIRECTLY

Primitive man used to decide where to hunt by casting bones to predict where
the animals would be. Animals very quickly become aware of hunting patterns,
so this was not an entirely irrational thing to do. By employing a random choice

mechanism, primitive man avoided creating any hunting patterns. Our ancestors understood that on the average in many cases a random choice was the best choice that could possible be made. In our democracy we are hunting for people of high quality for various decision-making posts, legislators for example. Might we not learn from our ancestors? At present we spend considerable sums on the electing of the typical legislator, including the costs of campaigning. According to the newspapers, many of the most powerful of these people are senile, or alcoholics, or both. Certainly their historic performance does not highly commend their intelligence or their honesty, although clearly there are exceptions. May we take it as self evident that there is room for improvement in the legislator selection process.

Why not select legislators randomly from the population at large? If you fancy an elite rule and so desire certain proportions of various characteristics we could draw a stratified random sample from those subsets of the population which meet the various qualifications. Such a choice system would be neutral with respect to such personal characteristics as the desire to use and/or abuse power, imperfect perception of probabilities, unrealistic views of the consequences of alternative public policies, and so on, and have virtually any other aggregate personality or skill properties one desired. The resources saved by foregoing campaigns could even be used to pay those selected enough to take them beyond the possibility of being bribed financially. Terms in office could be lengthened for Congress so that on-the-job training would not be wasted and the terms of office of individual members could be staggered like those of the United States Senate, so that only some fraction was replaced every election. The ending of terms in office could similarly be randomly decided. This would also reduce the probability of success through bribery. To avoid a lack of work incentives, pick few enough of them to make them feel important to the outcome.

For other jobs, such as those of police officer, it may be possible to use screening devices to test for certain adverse characteristics and to eliminate inappropriate candidates for the job. How much can be accomplished with screening devices remains to be seen, however. It is very difficult to tell about another person's true personality when the subject knows that this is being attempted and can learn about the criteria being used. Apparently, even lie-detector tests can be successfully subverted. Most importantly we must remember that in addition to the adverse selection problem, government inefficiency is caused by the more fundamental problem of insufficient incentives to perform, efficiently or at all.

As an alternative to screening perhaps we should rethink our reliance on civil service or consider how it could be altered so as both to improve the type of person attracted to public work and to alter the incentives of those employed in that way. For example, the only reason for job security to be as high as it is in the present civil service system appears to be the old desire to avoid the "spoils system." But is it really socially desirable to avoid the "spoils system?" After all, to the extent that public agencies are made up of individuals who can behave independently of the wishes of elected political leaders—which is one of the effects of our current civil service system—the leaders will not then be viewed as being responsible for the outcomes of public policy. This has the undesirable effect of removing some of their incentives to perform well, and will, therefore, *ceteris paribus,* lower the probability that their jobs will be performed properly. As it is now structured, civil service does not provide any personal, private incentives to civil servants to perform well, because advancement is generally the result not of actual performance, but of passing an exam with high marks. One wonders why so few measures of successful performance are used in the promotion decision. At the extreme, one wonders if some bureaucratic supervisory positions could not be returned to "the spoils system" so that the public—at least indirectly—could influence the bureaus.

Pursuing this line of thought raises the more interesting general possibility of relating public employee compensation to measures of their outputs, either at the level of the individual employee where that is possible, or at the level of the agency in those cases where it is impossible to identify individuals' outputs meaningfully. Such measures would, of course, have to be constructed so as to take into account the quality of service as well as its quantity, but that does not seem impossible. The hedonic price index revolution of the last 20 years has shown us that the qualities of many products can be meaningfully measured. As far as I know, the approach has yet to be applied in the public sector field, but judges' salaries, for example, could be related to the number of cases handled (adjusted for case mix and the number of decisions reversed) while public health officials could be paid according to measurements of the health of the population they serve (holding, of course, all other determinants of health constant).[4] Police departments, similarly, could have their budgets determined according to various measures of the security of the population served.

Of course, incentives in this form would do little for the efficiency problem, because if we give an incentive to the police for example, we are giving no one an incentive (since there is no one by that name). The way to proceed to make the incentive effective is to put someone in a residual income recipiency role. That person will then have the correct incentive to expend personal effort in an attempt to reduce costs. In the context of the police we might convert the police commissioner, in effect, into a contractor for police services. His own personal remuneration would be based on what was left over from the amount he was paid, after all his personnel, and so forth, were paid. The amount the commissioner was paid would in turn depend on his department's performance. Large cities could have each precinct, or subgroup of precincts, be separate contractors.

Indeed, initially it would be nice to see an experiment in which matched precincts were observed, one on such a payment system and one not.[5]

At this point it seems wise to stress that the success of these schemes depends crucially on how closely the output characteristics chosen to determine compensation really measure the true output desired, rather than inputs. The police, in their role as highway safety workers, preferably would be paid on the basis of a low accident rate and the efficiency of traffic movement, instead of the number of traffic summons issued, for example. It must be understood, moreover, that the measurement of output, by proxies, which is all that is possible with most public work, is not a once-and-for-all panacea. All proxy measures of output of necessity have some flaw; they cannot perfectly capture the full reality of what is being produced.[6] The seriousness of this problem is guaranteed in the long run, because it is generally possible for individuals through their actions to increase the inaccuracy of the proxy measures. This occurs in various ways. By focusing their efforts on those parts of the job which are most readily reflected by the proxy measure and neglecting those which are essentially ignored, individuals can cause the measure to be increasingly inaccurate. If their society is large enough, it will be in their personal interest to do so. People generally learn by doing, so they probably get better at fooling proxies as time passes and they acquire new insights, conscious or otherwise, into alternative ways in which they can advance their own interests. Thus, proxy output measures have to be revised periodically, raising the ominous questions of who is to do the revision and how are citizens to prevent the reviser and the people whose earnings are subject to the proxy measures of output from establishing trade to their own mutual advantage? This last issue will be touched on indirectly in the third section of this chapter.

To restate our position, we are suggesting that the efficiency of many government agencies could be improved by relating overall agency compensation to measures of agency output and by directing the output-related payments through an individual who has the knowledge and power to control costs.[7] There appear to be few, if any, government services which could not be at least partially converted to such a system. Education could, and so could the military, perhaps to a lesser extent. Many people do not have too much trouble accepting the former applications, at least in theory. The latter, however, is usually the case which most people bring up to object to the general principle advanced here.

In fact, the military could be compensated in a similar fashion to some extent. At the very least, a major restructuring of our defense payments system might lead to a more highly effective service. The problem of improving effectiveness in wartime is less difficult than the issue of a peacetime force, so let us begin with that. When there is an active enemy, with various targets, and so on, why couldn't we offer prizes for achieving well-defined objectives. We could simply have offered a prize for defending the South Vietnamese government, or better yet, one for the surrender of the Viet Cong, or alternatively, for the successful defense of individual combat areas. Military history contains many instances of the successful use of privateers. The British Navy which defeated the Spanish Armada was composed almost entirely of them, to cite just one example.[8] Actually the Viet Nam experience reveals the true scope for a more imaginative use of American power in the international sphere. I suspect that we could have purchased, in a straight cash deal, most of the land mass of Southeast Asia, or at least enough of it for our purposes,[9] for a fraction of what we spent in our futile military adventures there.

In peacetime the problem is more subtle, but nonetheless somewhat tractible. Weapons such as ICBMs, and some parts of our current standing forces would no doubt have to be left under continuous direct public control so that we could respond to surprises. The rest, however, might be dealt with in a more decentralized manner. Consider the Army, for example. We need a hard core cadre of professionals, ready to act in the opening phases of trouble; but it is interesting how small a fraction of our force seems really ready to go into battle in a week. Special training is almost always required before troops, supposed to be ready, are prepared for combat.[10] If this is the case, why not simply provide incentives for private citizens to acquire and to learn how to use arms: nationally funded marksmanship contests on all reasonably sized weapons; tank races and repair contests, and so on.[11] Of course, we would need to be a lot more certain that the basic principles are sound before we could entrust such a vital area to such experimentation. Nevertheless, I believe it is useful to exercise our imagination in this way. We must remember that at root the ability of the state to exploit us depends in part on our inability even to conceive of alternative ways of obtaining the same services.

## 2 INCREASING COMPETITION AMONG GOVERNMENTS

As we saw in Chapter 5, emigration to avoid exploitation is not an unknown reaction of peoples throughout history. Nor is it an ineffective force. The greater the elasticity of demand confronting any monopolist, the lower, *ceteris paribus*, is likely to be his profit. This elasticity is raised by increasing the ease of emigrating to an alternative state. The costs of emigrating may be altered by many forces. Whenever the home country's costs of exit are reduced or when the number and quality of alternative states is increased, emigration can be expected to increase. The formation of new states also directly affects the profits of existing states by reducing the demand curves they face in quality space (level of order). We would argue, therefore, that in the limit the free formation of sub-jurisdictions would imply zero profits, the monopolistically competitive equi-librium. When this is the case, it is easy to see that the correct set of levels of order would be produced and that people would be distributed across them in an optimal manner.[12]

At the same time that we increase competition across states by making it easier for them to fragment, it would be useful to restrict the federal and other government's abilities[13] to expand the scope of their activities to include public services whose cost structures do not require such large scales. Here, as else-where, there is some tendency for monopolists to be able to extend the scope of their power by tying things together; this is known in the antitrust literature as the full line forcing problem.

The production of external protection and punishment has enormous returns to scale. Ultimately, of course, these returns are limited by the presence of the shirking problem; but even so, they are limited much later than those, say, of providing fire protection, which are generally limited sooner than those of police protection, and so forth. Each service produced by the various governments within the United States has a continually shifting set of "optimal" jurisdictions. These need not be the same for each of the services, which suggests that allied substates within larger states should jointly produce those public goods with smaller optimal jurisdictions, as is somewhat the case within the federal system of the United States. Unfortunately, because of its greater power, the central state can prevent the fragmentation of its jurisdiction. Worse yet, it can often expand its scope by taking over functions that were not originally delegated to it, but rather to smaller jurisdictions, even when constrained by a constitution which requires federalism and reserves to the states certain powers. This has clearly been happening in the United States, even if it is often rationalized by other explanations. In the same way, states may expand their power *vis à vis* counties, and counties may expand their *vis à vis* municipalities. To cite just one example, school district consolidation continues despite the growing evi-dence that it increases costs and reduces educational quality.[14] Reversal of the trend toward centralization of power requires that we find a way to restrict the power of central governments, that is, to prevent them from using the superior force resulting from their monopoly of the provision of the service protection against external threats. Similarly, a way must be found to constrain states from using their legal standing, to extend into other markets more appropriately controlled by counties. Finally, there must also be a way of allowing for the flexible coalescence of the component subjurisdictions.[15]

What follows are three proposals which, taken together as amendments to the United States Constitution, would accomplish these objectives within its federal system.[16] The first two proposals would make possible actions which cannot now readily take place, while the third is a method for deciding when they can take place. No claim for originality is made; the amendments are suggested by the history of the country and by economic theory. No doubt they have been put forth by others at various times, although perhaps not in as systematic a fashion or all at once. We would like to call the three proposals taken together "a program for Republican Anarchy."

The power of the federal government can be limited. At its root the problem is simply the old one of how to limit the ability of the majority (of power, not necessarily of population) to coerce the minority, a problem that haunted Alexis de Toqueville and other students of attempts at "democratic" government. The problem has, however, a simple solution. States could be allowed to nullify the validity of any federal law for their citizens and/or within their boundaries. Thus, if the federal government should decide again to impose a draft in order to engage in some military adventure from which some members of society presumably expect to benefit, then individual states could be allowed to nullify this law within their boundaries for their citizens if they so desire. Similarly, if the federal government should decree that schools must all meet certain racial quotas (or ethnic or whatever), or that certain subjects must or must not be taught, or that certain substances must or must not be consumed, individual states might be permitted to nullify the effects of these laws within their boundaries. Not to allow such nullification is simply to allow the majority to override for its own benefit the will of some relevant minority or, in terms of the optimal jurisdiction literature for public goods, to prevent the formation of smaller jurisdictions, even though these may be optimal. This is the sense of our first proposed amendment.[17]

If within the United States as a whole, minority states may feel coerced or exploited by the national majority, then too, within a state a geographic or other minority may feel exploited by the rest of that state. This, for example, has long been the feeling of many residents of New York City.[18] The problem is found in countless circumstances, and a complete enumeration is both beyond our scope and beside the point. One of the greatest defects in the United States Constitution may be its failure to allow parts of states to secede from the state simply because the residents of such parts wanted to do so. At present, the consent of the state legislature is required. But it is a tautology that the legislature is controlled by the majority of political power, therefore, if the exploitation is severe enough, consent will not be granted. The sense of our second amendment would be to allow parts of states to secede and form new states within the union, without the direct consent of the state legislature.

But with these two proposals alone we have now created a problem. Secession of part of a state from the rest of the state, or for that matter the nullification of some federal law by a state, may impose costs on parties outside the acting jurisdiction. A state very much in the interior of a country might decide to nullify a draft law simply because the states at the exterior protect citizens of the interior automatically when they protect their own. In this age of ICBMs, which much be countered before their ultimate target can be known, some facilities of necessity protect the whole nation. Similarly, if part of a state seceded from the rest of the state, it might take with it important state facilities located there. To allow unilateral appropriation of these facilities, or to allow states to avoid payment for services rendered, would in essence allow theft—a change in the distribution of the ownership of property through someone's action without the loser's prior consent. How do we know that the gains to the seceding or nullifying group exceed the loss to everyone else? What about the important issue of compensation for change? Clearly, some outside input into the secession or nullification decisions should exist, and parties must be compensated for the adverse affects of change. After all, it is not enough to have social decision mechanisms which make "correct" decisions. Even decisions which benefit the gainers more than the losers may not be truly socially optimal unless the losers are compensated for the adverse effects of such a change. More importantly, as a practical matter it may be impossible to effect such changes unless the losers know that they will be compensated. Often the losers represent a more compact group than the gainers, and perhaps even one that is considered "expert" in such matters by the majority of the population, which may have only minute personal stakes in the issue at all. In such circumstances the potential losers are likely to be able to block improvement. If, however, they were to be compensated for the damages done them, their objections would be removed.[19]

Our third proposal provides a mechanism for making correct social decisions in a way that automatically compensates the losers. Let the people interested in a change draw up a bill of particulars, in whatever detail they deem appropriate. At this point, the federal government would hold what we have called a "compensating election."[20] Voting does not have to be a simple indication of yes or no, in particular in these days of high-speed electronic computers. Yes-or-no ballots do not allow the intensity of individual preferences to be revealed easily enough, and unless these can be revealed, paradoxes may result in nonbinary choice situations. In a compensating election, the ballot allows voters to indicate the dollar amounts they would be willing to pay to have secession or nullification occur or to prevent it. They understand that the compensation is in fact going to take place. The losing side will in fact be compensated; the winners will pay them the amounts they require for the adverse effects of the change. The side that bids the greatest amount will be required to pay the individuals on the side that loses the amount which the losers indicated it was worth to them to have the issue their way. The federal government would be paid its cost of running the election by the side that proposed the change. Any balance remaining would belong to the winning side, or could be otherwise divided.[21]

Under this proposed system any decision to secede or "nullify" would automatically compensate the losers, as would a decision not to allow secession.[22] True, some potential for gaming with the election process is present; however, this is inherent in any public choice mechanism. The pricing of public goods always has potential for gaming, as Samuelson has repeatedly and correctly stressed. The real issue is one of how to limit the potential for coercive gaming.

People like to gamble; there is evidence enough for that, and there is really nothing to prevent people from gaming on the outcome of an election. Suppose, for example, that I do not really care which side wins or loses, but I expect that the "yes" side will win by $100 million. I might then be willing to wager by voting "no" to the extent of, say, $100,000. There is the option under the compensating election scheme for people to game for the consumers' surplus to be generated by making the correct social decision. But observe that unless the "gamblers" are incorrect in their guess they will have no influence on the social outcome. If they are incorrect, they themselves pay for having caused society to make the wrong decision, and most importantly, no one who voted honestly is in any way harmed by their mistake.[23]

Let me stress again, however, my intention is to propose these as *experiments* with types of changes. While I feel that it would be desirable to begin to experiment in the directions outlined here, I do not propose that they be implemented all at once, or that any be implemented fully. Rash and hasty changes, even in the appropriate direction, have a way of not working out. Although my proposals only allow for changes to occur, actual experience with such mechanisms would seem desirable. It would be better to implement them partially and to observe the consequences. Fortunately, it is possible to do so.

The proposals depend crucially on the workability of the compensatory voting scheme. There is nothing, however, which prevents this scheme from being tried out on other issues at more local levels, for example, zoning changes within a city or a county. If some local governments would use this scheme to decide zoning changes, then the rest of us could observe the consequences. The details of compensatory voting mechanisms then could be worked out and the various risks weighed, based on actual experience.

It is absolutely crucial that this proposal be tried first on a limited experimental basis. The current distribution of wealth is very unequal. It is possible that the rich could change the rules of the game so fast under the new scheme, and still remain rich, that the population as a whole would be made much worse off and unable to afford to stop the direction of change. To be sure, some of this fear, expressed by many persons told of this proposal, may be groundless. The

rich after all have many other ways of influencing current policies and clearly
they do not always get their way, nor are their interests necessarily opposed to
everyone else's. Moreover, it must be understood that while the proposal does
give money more power, it also causes the losers in any change to be compensated. Even if the rich could influence policy under such a system, they would
have to pay their opponents, not simply the politicians, admen, and so on, for
this influence.

Similarly, experimentation with the principle of nullification could begin at
the state rather than the national level. Some states might daringly allow their
various counties to nullify within their boundaries some classes of state statutes,
or the scheme could be tried on perhaps even more restricted classes of statutes
at the federal level.[24] Laws regarding "crimes without victims" seems an appealing category to choose for testing the procedure. In some sense, selective
nullification already has been tried successfully. Some states have prohibition at
local option.

The implementation of secession might be tried in communities larger than
certain sizes. The key question is how small a unit should be allowed to secede.
If individuals can secede, and then have the power to nullify, we do have complete anarchy. It would be a constitutional or republican, to be sure, but it
would be a fairly complete anarchy nonetheless. In the beginning it would seem
wise to impose limits on the characteristics of units allowed to secede. Minimum
size is one such limitation, but in addition, population density at the fringe of
the seceding area might also be taken into account. Because these limits themselves have to be worked out, the case for caution and selective experimentation
is strengthened.


## 3 GOVERNMENTS OF MINIMAL SCOPE: THE NEW DIRECT DEMOCRACY

The final approach to improving the behavior of government being proposed is
perhaps the most radical, which is to say, the most fundamental. It is to restrict
constitutionally the manner in which governments operate so as to reduce their
scope to the minimum necessary for accomplishing their assigned task. From the
perspective of the modern economist, the function of government is to control
the levels of public goods, or externality producing activities, which is the same
thing.

To accomplish this task, governments in general do not need actually to produce public goods themselves; they can operate more indirectly. The government
can control levels of service without being involved directly in their production.
Consider sanitation services. It is one thing to decide that everyone's garbage

should be collected periodically in the interests of public health; it is quite another to leap from that to the conclusion that sanitation workers must be public employees. There is in principle no reason why such an activity could not simply be let out to the low bidding private firm, as many cities have successfully done. Only when the output is more intangible than the inputs does it make sense to try to control the level of output by directly producing the good through government,[25] and even then this requires the assumption that public control of public workers can be effective, a conclusion which at the very least appears open to some doubt. Public schooling, social insurance, fire and police protection, and so on, are perhaps all examples of goods that need not be directly produced by government. Foreign policy probably has to be produced by government; although here, too, considerable savings might occur if embassy support services (chefs, etc.) were contracted for by competitive bidding. If more public goods were handled in this way, the inherent monopoly power of the state would be minimized.[26]

It is possible, in addition, to reform the way in which we decide levels of public goods and who shall pay for them (i.e., personal tax shares). By using certain advances made in public choice theory within the last 12 years or so, it appears that we could replace our system of representative democracy with a system that automatically decided levels of public good and tax shares in a fairly optimal manner and at the same time always so compensated those opposed to a decision (those for whom it is a public bad at the margin) as to leave them no worse off.

In recent years a whole class of pricing formulas which essentially forces individuals to reveal their true preferences for the level of public good has been discovered. These are generally referred to as "incentive-compatible mechanisms" (ICM).[27] It now appears that the free-rider problem with the voluntary financing of public goods can be virtually eliminated. The compensating election scheme already discussed is one example of such a mechanism. It is particularly appropriate for yes-no issues. There are many others, however, designed for continuous choices. While it is still early in their development, laboratory experimentation has provided evidence that while gaming or attempts at free riding are not entirely eliminated by such mechanisms, they are sufficiently reduced so that groups generally choose the optimal or approximately optimal levels of public good. They do not do so otherwise.[28] Gaming reveals itself in typically small redistributions of the rents generated by the public choice towards the successful gamers.

Incentive-compatible mechanisms all work for the same basic reason. The free-rider problem itself results from the fact that if one asks people "how much," they have an incentive not to reveal their true preferences, when the amount they will have to pay depends directly on the size of their stated preferences. The same thing is true of private goods. If consumers can influence the price they pay for a private good, they typically will distort their behavior so as to pay less than when they cannot. They will act as monopsonists. By changing the institutional structure, however, so that what one pays does not depend directly on one's response, individuals can be induced to reveal their true preferences. The following example, discussed by Smith, reveals the essential device involved. Suppose we were interested in getting someone to reveal a true preference for a refrigerator. If the person believes that the revealed desired price will be the actual purchase price, (or even only that there was some positive connection between the two), then that person would have an incentive to indicate an amount less than what the refrigerator actually was worth to him or her. Suppose, however, the seller writes down on a card his reservation price and then informs the prospective buyer that if the bid is greater than the reservation price, he or she will get the refrigerator, *at the reservation price,* while if the bid is less, he or she won't get the refrigerator. In this case, individuals have an incentive to reveal their true preferences for the item, because doing so does not influence the price they will pay. This is the essence of the various incentive compatible schemes. In all of these, what each individual pays is determined by the costs of the facility and by what everyone *else* is willing to pay. Thus, no one has an incentive to lie about their preferences, unless that individual is moved to gamble on other people being willing to sacrifice some part of their shares of the consumers' surplus generated by the public good. Currently, such a scheme is being employed by the Public Broadcasting Service in a three-year experiment in which a decentralized market mechanism is used to determine the selection of programs to be broadcast over the national noncommercial television network.[29] Unfortunately, it is too early to judge definitively the success of the experiment; the same is essentially true of the lab experiments.

It appears that the mechanisms can be put into operation, that is, given a precise institutional structure for bidding and coming to a "conclusion." It seems clear that these mechanisms operate much better than does democracy when confronted with the same problems. In the laboratory, it is easy enough to construct cases where democracy will lead to the worst possible choice.[30] In general, even in such cases, the ICMs chose the socially best alternative. Nevertheless, it seems that more experience is needed before they become generally used. As suggested earlier, we need to see how such systems operate within narrowly defined categories of public decisions.

In the last 350 years, we have seen considerable advances in our understanding of the state. It was after all only relatively recently that most people stopped holding the view that it was the divine right of kings to rule society. Our progress in ideas is heartening, because at root, if we are to reform our current situation it is with ideas that we must begin. We must end our dependency on dogma, our enslavement to old ideas which do not reflect current reality. At the most basic level we must be aware of our conditioned tendencies to view the state as the earthly embodiment of some benevolent, or malevolent, transcendent force. The state is simply another human institution — it is a firm, or loose cartel. It produces goods and services which each of us appreciates in varying degrees, and that is its function, to provide goods and services.[31] But the state will typically have more market power than the other firms of society. Thus, it may exploit us by earning a monopoly profit. In democracy, we are collectively the owners of the state, in that we determine the basic rules and choose the managers, or at least can do so. As do all "owners" however, we face the problem that our employees have their own interests, and that these interests are not necessarily ours in the same degree. It is only when employees are provided with sufficient incentives to perform as we would wish, that behavior to that end is guaranteed.

# APPENDIX I
# *Entrepreneurship, Profit, and Limits on Firm Size*

## I INTRODUCTION

There is a substantial literature on the question of the existence of profit and limits on firm size under static conditions. On the one hand, there are economists such as Friedman[1] and Graaff[2] who would accept the existence of a nonmarketable factor of production called "entrepreneurship," which simultaneously is a source of profits and a limit on firm size in a static world. On the other hand, economists such as Kaldor[3] and Heady,[4] while agreeing to the existence of the factor of production entrepreneurship and its relevance as a limitational factor, would argue that this relevance exists only in a dynamic and uncertain world. Finally, economists such as Weston[5] would deny altogether the existence of a unique factor of production "entrepreneurship" and of what Friedman calls "expected non-contractual costs"[6] as a distinct distributive share and maintain that only windfall profits are legitimate.

This paper represents an attempt to contribute to this as yet unsettled, if currently neglected, controversy by making explicit the role and implications

*Source:* By Morris Silver and Richard Auster. Reprinted with permission from the *Journal of Business of the University of Chicago* (July 1969), pp. 277–81.

of entrepreneurship as a distinct factor in a static world. From another and perhaps broader point of view, the paper can be regarded as a contribution to the growing literature on divergences of interests within the firm and the costs of dealing with them.


## II  ENFORCEMENT AND PROFIT

As Friedman points out, there are two "pure" methods by which an individual can earn income from the resources he owns. First, "he can enter into a contractual agreement with some other individual whereby the latter agrees to pay a fixed sum per unit for the use of that resource—i.e., he can 'rent' the use of the resource to someone else"[7] and in this way become a contractual income recipient. Second, he can organize a firm. This involves utilizing owned and perhaps rented resources and receiving income "as the difference between the amount he receives from the sale of products and the amount he pays the resources he 'hires'—i.e., he can become a residual income recipient."[8] The individual can be assumed to make this decision on the basis of a comparison of the expected returns corresponding to these alternative courses of action. The question we now turn to is, "Why should the expected residual income differ from the expected contractual income?"[9]

Differences between expected residual and contractual earnings may in part be due to differences in incentives. It would seem to be a fact of human nature, or alternatively a response to the uninteresting and difficult kinds of work that are typically performed, that hired labor (for the present defined as wage labor) will shirk its duties unless the employer takes steps to prevent this.[10] Along the same lines, steps must also be taken to guard against embezzlement and theft by hired workers.[11] For purposes of brevity, we will call these steps "enforcement"; these should be understood to include not only watching workers in the performance of their duties but also ex post measures of performance such as counting, record keeping, plant inspection, and so on.[12] Of course, some of the latter operations would be carried out in the absence of hired labor, but, at the very least, they would be carried out more frequently when it was present.

While our argument does not require a full analysis of the question of which type of enforcement will be utilized in any given case, the following points are certainly relevant: (1) enforcement operations of the ex post type might not, given the nature of the firm's product or method of production, permit the identification of shirkers; (2) even in cases in which they did, the threat of dismissal might not be a strong enough deterrent to eliminate all losses due to the payment of "unearned" wages and maltreatment of plant and equipment.

More explicitly, the production process is conceived of as

$$Q = F(E, L_p, K_p, T_p),  \tag{1}$$

where $F$ is homogeneous of degree 1, and $E$ = enforcement; $L_p$ = production workers; $K_p$ = production capital; and $T_p$ = production land. Of course, as well as there being alternative types of enforcement (i.e., ex post and watching), there are alternative methods of producing each. For simplicity, let us lump together the two types of enforcement, in which case we write

$$E = G(O_n, L_n, K_n, T_n),  \tag{2}$$

where $G$ is homogeneous of degree 1, and $O_n$ = entrepreneur's time spent in enforcement, $L_n$ = non-production labor; $K_n$ = non-production capital; and $T_n$ = non-production land.

Now assume an individual would produce an output of $D$ dollars if he were equipped with certain production resources and told that whatever he produced belonged to him. Next, consider the alternative situation in which the individual is a hired worker – a contractual rather than a residual income recipient. Equations (1) and (2) suggest that he would not produce a product worth $D$ dollars unless his employer provided additional resources for enforcement – that is, in the absence of a need to enforce a contract with oneself, the "own" marginal product is greater than the hired marginal product. As a result, the individual's earnings would also be smaller, and this excess of residual over contractual income is *profit* – that is, a return which cannot be imputed, for the simple reason that it exists only when the individual is "self-employed."

In the above discussion it was assumed (implicitly) that the individual and his employer were equally knowledgeable about production and market conditions. It follows if nonpecuniary factors (racial discrimination, attitudes toward risk and to the giving and taking of orders, etc.) and the "costs of using the price mechanism"[13] are ignored, the individual would choose to become a residual income recipient. Of course, in the real world, differences in knowledge, tastes, and other factors are often important enough to offset "enforcement costs" and lead individuals to become contractual income recipients. Thus, nothing in our analysis implies that all individuals would have their own firms.

There are, of course, many ways in which a firm can hire labor. The above analysis seems strongest in the case of wage labor. It is weaker but, in our opinion, still relevant for other hiring systems. One alternative to wage hiring is the "piecework" system; however, this system is not appropriate for all products and methods of production – that is, in some cases the costs of installing it would be prohibitive. Moreover, even in cases in which piecework is appropriate, the interests of workers and employers would still differ. Enforcement would still be necessary to measure the quality of output and to insure that in their zeal for higher incomes workers did not abuse the firm's plant and equipment.

Another hiring approach would be to offer workers a share of the firm's receipts instead of a wage. However, this system might give rise to externality problems. Each worker might feel that his income would be the same whether he shirked or not. Such attitudes would probably necessitate that employers and/or employees undertake enforcement. Second, the returns to the employer would be maximized if labor input is carried to the point at which its opportunity cost is equal to the value of its marginal product. However, if labor receives $p$ percent of the output, laborers would carry their input only to the point where the opportunity cost of their time is equal to $p$ times the value of the marginal product of labor. Enforcement provided by the entrepreneur would be needed to guarantee that workers did not gain at his expense by restricting their labor input.[14] Finally, a share system possesses another defect that would probably cause it to be little used even if it solved the incentive problem. Workers typically know much less about production and market conditions than those who hire them, and as a result employers might find that their costs would be lower if they paid a wage and devoted resources to enforcement than if they offered a share of receipts that was greatly enlarged to compensate workers for their uncertainty bearing.

## III  ENFORCEMENT AND LIMITS ON FIRM SIZE

It is easily established that the need for enforcement places a limit on firm size. From equations (1) and (2) we have

$$Q = H(O_n, L_n, K_n, T_n, L_p, K_p, T_p), \qquad (3)$$

where $H$ is homogeneous of degree 1. At some level of output the entrepreneur would be applying all his available enforcement time.[15] Thus, further increases in output must raise the ratio of the other factors to his own time which must increase average cost and as a consequence introduce a limit on firm size. The fact that the entrepreneur could add to the enforcement time at his disposal by hiring enforcers would not prevent average costs from rising unless the employer faced a perfectly elastic market supply of nonshirking enforcers. Of course, it is precisely the scarcity of such workers and the costs of determining who is a nonshirker that are the source of our entire problem.

It might be suggested that the limit on the entrepreneur's time and the consequent rising average costs can be circumvented by erecting a pyramid of enforcers. That such arguments are incorrect can be seen by assuming the optimum ratio of enforcers to production workers to be $1/n$ and the entrepreneur is using all his available time enforcing his contracts with $n$ production workers. The entrepreneur could double output by hiring $n$ more production workers, the proper amounts of the other production factors, *two* enforcers, and spending some of his available time enforcing his contracts with the hired enforcers. However, in spite of the fact that the newly hired factors are assumed to be of equal quality and hence have the same market prices as the original set of factors (including the entrepreneur's enforcement time), total cost would more than double because of the need for the entrepreneur to spend some of his valuable time to enforce contracts with the two hired enforcers.

## IV  IMPLICATIONS OF THE ANALYSIS

The preceding arguments have established that the entrepreneur's time is a limitational factor, but it would take a major study — and even that might easily be inconclusive — to ascertain the relative importance of enforcement in explaining variations in firm size.[16] For the present, we must confine ourselves to a listing of some of the testable implications of our model with respect to concentration ratios and some casual empirical tests of these implications.

1. *Ceteris paribus* the higher an industry's cost-minimizing ratio of production labor to output, the sooner average total cost curves will turn upward, and the lower an industry's concentration ratio. Some evidence is provided by the observation that in the United States labor-to-output ratios are typically higher in manufacturing than in mineral industries, while concentration ratios are typically lower in manufacturing.

2. *Ceteris paribus* the higher the optimum ratio of enforcers to production workers in an industry, the sooner its average total cost curve will turn upward, and the lower its concentration ratio. For example, we would expect lower concentration ratios in industries (a) using more valuable factors and/or in which the degree of finish of the product(s) being handled (both intermediate and final) was high; (b) in which a firm's work force is more spatially dispersed; (c) in which production work is less interesting and/or physically dangerous or uncomfortable. Turning to some evidence: (a) retail trade is less concentrated than manufacturing; (b) agriculture and trucking are among the least concentrated industries; (c) construction work is relatively dangerous and relatively unconcentrated.[17]

# APPENDIX II
## Political Revolution and Repression: An Economic Approach

In his "The Logic of Collective Action" Olson [31] develops the broad outlines of what might be called a private interest theory of public action. It is pointed out that since the benefit to an individual from the consumption of an extra unit of a collective (or public) good is small relative to his cost of producing it, "selective incentives" are required to explain participation in production. A "selective incentive" is a non-collective benefit contingent upon the individual's participation in the production of a collective good. More recently, Tullock [42] has imaginatively formalized and applied this type of economic theory to the question of the sources of revolutionary activity. Here Tullock's analysis is used as a point of departure in grouping historical political revolutions into meaningful types and in considering who is most likely to become a revolutionary. First, however, I offer a working definition of revolution and briefly review Tullock's formal model.

## I THE PRIVATE INTEREST THEORY OF REVOLUTION

A revolutionary act is an extra-legal act (violent or nonviolent) intended by the actor to secure a change in governmental personnel, structure, or policy (see

*Source:* An earlier version of this Appendix was published by Morris Silver in *Public Choice* (Fall 1973).

[7, p. 1]). An extra-legal act (i.e., a change or transfer of a valuable resource) not ultimately to be validated by a political change is classified as "theft" or "riot". Revolution is defined as a period in which the frequency of revolutionary acts is extraordinarily high.[1] An individual who devotes a large fraction of his time, relatively speaking, to the commission of revolutionary acts is called a revolutionary.

Tullock's private interest theory of participation in revolutionary activity is conveniently summarized by his Equation (4) which I have slightly modified by including a term $V$ measuring the value of the participant's time and other resources (e.g., money spent "lobbying" in sensitive foreign capitals).

$$G_r = R_i \cdot L_v - P_i (1 - L_v) - L_w \cdot I_r + E - V$$

where:

$G_r$ = Net gain (or loss) to individual from participation, rather than remaining neutral.

$R_i$ = Private reward (e.g., income, power, status) to individual for his participation in revolution if revolution succeeds.

$L_v$ = Likelihood of revolutionary victory assuming subject is neutral.[2]

$P_i$ = Private penalty imposed on individual for participation in revolution if revolt fails.

$L_w$ = Likelihood of injury through participation in revolution.

$I_r$ = Injury suffered in action.

$E$ = Psychic income from participation.

$V$ = Value of participant's time and other resources.

An increase in $G_r$ will, according to economic theory, intensify the efforts of existing revolutionaries as well as increase the number of revolutionaries and of those who commit a revolutionary act. If the increase in revolutionary participation is great enough, the period is called a revolution. Note that since any collective good an individual expects to be produced by the revolution (e.g., "the brotherhood of man", "the dictatorship of the proletariat", the end of "imperialism") will be "consumed" by him whether he participates or remains neutral; the public good aspect drops out of the net payoff equation (i.e., it is not a determinant of participation).

The determinants of the level of psychic income from participation in revolution ($E$) include the individual's sense of duty to class, country, democratic institutions, the law, race, humanity, the rulers, God, or a revolutionary brotherhood as well as his taste for conspiracy, violence, and adventure.[3] Obviously $E$

will vary greatly from one individual to another, from one country to another, and from one time to another. In what follows, the determinants of the level and changes of $E$ (what the Marxists call "revolutionary situations") are not stressed. Such factors are undoubtedly major determinants of political stability but have received extensive treatment in the literature, including Chapter 4 of the present book. The objective conditions determining the other terms in the equation (i.e., those representing private rewards and costs) have, however, often been (implicitly) dismissed as "precipitants", "short-run," "fortuitous" and hence have received much less systematic attention than they deserve.[4]

## II  TYPES OF REVOLUTION

The private interest theory provides a basis for grouping actual revolutions according to a small but historically repetitive set of causes of significant increases in $G_r$.

### 1.  Revolutions Caused by Political Reform

Students of revolution have long been aware that revolutions frequently occur after conditions have markedly improved or while in process of improvement. Tocqueville's observations in his classic study of the French Revolution are the most frequently quoted:

> This may seem illogical – but history is full of such paradoxes. For it is not always when things are going from bad to worse that revolutions break out. On the contrary, it oftener happens that when a people which has put up with an oppressive rule over a long period without protest suddenly finds the government relaxing its pressure, it takes up arms against it. Thus the social order overthrown by a revolution is almost always better than the one immediately preceding it. . . . [41, p. 176]

While far from exhaustive, the following examples should serve to demonstrate that the violent response following the summoning of the Estates General in France is not unique.

Starting in 1780 Joseph II, the "revolutionary emperor" of Austria, undertook a series of "enlightened" reforms with respect to serfdom, religious toleration, occupational choice, and taxation. Among the responses were peasant insurrection in 1789, demands for democratic reforms including an important contribution by the democratic wing to the Belgian Revolution of 1789, and ultimately, "Jacobin" conspiracies in Vienna and Hungary in 1794 [32, V.I, pp. 341-57, 374-97; V.II, pp. 156-71]. The Prussian Revolution of 1848 was preceded by Frederick William IV's decisions in 1847 to summon a "United Diet" and to liberalize the press laws [34, pp. 107-41]. Also in 1848 the Hungarian parliament controlled by the Magyar gentry enacted the "March Laws" which

> . . . abolished preliminary censorship of the press and established jury trials for press offenses; they set up a National Guard, open to anyone with fairly modest property; . . . they [abolished] all manorial rights and jurisdictions, and all church tithes, and ended the nobles exemption from taxes" [39, pp. 105-6].

Serious peasant unrest followed in April and again in the fall [39, p. 106]. The years immediately following Russia's Peasant Emancipation of 1861 were filled with significant political ferment including demands for liberalization of the autocratic system, peasant disturbances, student disturbances in Petersburg and Moscow, the Petersburg fires, the appearance of underground revolutionary organizations, and open insurrection in Poland [8, Chap. 9-10]. The October 1905 climax of revolution in Russia was preceded by a series of significant reforms beginning in August 1904 and culminating in the Imperial Ukase of December 12 [15, pp. 47-68].[5] The reforms included: abolition of the right of peasant courts to impose corporal punishment, ending of corporal punishment in the army, ending the former policy of harassing the municipal dumas (zemstvos), ending emergency measures in "protected" areas, removing some disabilities from national and religious minorities, easing restrictions on the press, and establishing government insurance for workers. In addition, the Tsar's public announcement that open meetings of the liberal opposition would not be permitted was not enforced by the police. Finally in March 1905, Nicholas II called for the establishment of an elected consultative assembly.

In the Communist world Khrushchev's anti-Stalinist speech and reforms paved the way for the abortive revolutions in Hungary and Poland while Mao suffered through the "Hundred Flowers" debacle. The Black Revolution in the U.S. broke out only after the Supreme Court decision outlawing racially segregated schools. Most recently the student-worker rebellion in Athens was immediately preceded by an amnesty for "political prisoners", the dismantling of the military junta, and the announcement of preparations for parliamentary elections in 1974 (the first in ten years).[6,7]

The most fashionable explanation of the fact that reform often leads revolution is psychological in nature. Theorists such as Gurr argue that "discontent arising from the perception of relative deprivation is the basic, instigating condition for participants in collective violence" [13, p. 12] and speak of a "revolution of rising expectations" in which "expectations increase without an

accompanying increase in the potential for their satisfaction" [12, p. 597][8]
According to Runciman

> . . . prosperity can break the vicious cycle between poverty and conservatism
> by making people aware of the possibility of a higher standard [35, pp. 23–24].

Tocqueville remarks that:

> Patiently endured so long as it seemed beyond redress, a grievance comes to
> appear intolerable once the possibility of removing it crosses men's minds.
> For the mere fact that certain abuses have been remedied draws attention
> to the others and they now appear more galling; people may suffer less, but
> their sensibility is exacerbated [41, p. 177].

Instead of focusing attention upon the dubious possibility that reforms raise
$E$ in the equation, the private benefit approach suggests that revolutionary
activity may be induced because reforms, especially those loosely termed "revolutions from above" (and similarly reforms in response to riots [see I] or isolated acts of terror), lower the expected cost of revolution: they raise the
probability of victory $(L_v)$ while lowering the private penalty if the revolt fails
$(P_i)$, the probability of injury during participation in revolutionary activity
$(L_w)$, and the injury suffered $(I_r)$.

(1) Reforms often increase the political capabilities of the revolutionaries
(e.g., by giving them seats in Parliament, coverage in the mass media, and access
to financial contributions) which raises their $L_v$.[9]

(2) Perhaps most important in the world of imperfect knowledge, many
persons will quite rationally interpret the reforms as a sign of weakness or submission. In this event their subjective estimate of $L_v$ will rise while $P_i$, $L_w$, and
$I_r$ will decline.[10]

Taking on a new meaning within the private interest framework is Tocqueville's observation that "only consummate statecraft can enable a King to save
his throne when after a long spell of oppressive rule he sets to improving the lot
of his subjects" [41, p. 177]. A government viewed as an instrument of oppression initiating reforms which can be viewed as relaxations of oppression should
simultaneously make known the limits of the reforms and its determination to
remain in power. To this end, it must eschew "permissiveness" and, perhaps,
institute measures raising the probability of being apprehended (raise $L_w$) and/or
impose stiffer penalties (raise $P_i$ and $I_r$) for doing what is still not permitted.
History shows that failure to balance reforms with repression has not only cost
rulers their thrones but society desirable reforms.[11]

Stolypin in Russia (1905–10) appears to have been adept at juggling reform
and repression—agrarian reforms individualising land ownership were combined
with a large number of death sentences—until he himself was murdered. Lenin

(1921-22), perhaps inspired by his predecessor Stolypin, accompanied the New Economic Policy with the first mass purge of the Communist Party and the crushing of all remaining organized opposition outside the Party [23, pp. 104-5].

The above type of analysis provides a useful framework for dealing with some related sources of revolution and repression. It is not surprising that in order to forestall or limit "domino" or "demonstration" effects,[12] domestic rulers often behave in a repressive manner after serious political reforms or successful revolution in a foreign country with a similar type of regime (e.g., England after the French Revolution, 1789 [27, p. 31]). Since new revolutionary regimes are typically regarded as being weak (i.e., $L_v$ is relatively high) they typically treat all forms of dissent with a heavy hand (i.e., $P_i$ and $I_r$ are made relatively high). Thus, the usual reign of terror after a revolutionary overthrow may reflect the new rulers' determination to remain in power rather than, as Smelser suggests, their "inflexibility" or their tendency to "define the world in undifferentiated value terms" [37, pp. 323-24, 332-33].

### 2. Revolutions Caused by Defeat in War

External military defeats followed by revolutions are not unusual, as is evident from the following examples (see [17], [19]). Defeats at the hands of the French preceded English revolutions in 1204-68 and 1450-87 (the revolt of Jack Cade). The defeat of Bonaparte ushered in a period (1815-30) of revolutions in France, Belgium, Poland, Spain, Italy, Portugal. The Prussian victory in 1871 was followed by insurrection in France. Defeat preceded revolutions in Russia, Hungary, Germany, and Turkey in 1917-19.

Explanations for the observed surges in revolutionary membership,[13] activity, and enthusiasm flow easily from the private interest theory. Defeat in war lowers the expected cost of revolution by raising the probability of a victorious revolution $(L_v)$.[14] This is the case because:

1. The rulers are weakened by the defeat both materially and psychologically.
2. More importantly many persons take the defeat as evidence that they had previously overestimated the strength of the regime (it is a "paper tiger").

### 3. Revolutions Caused by Attacks on Powerful Individuals

When a government fails to adequately reward or defend, or actually attacks powerful individuals such as local government officials, owners (domestic or foreign) of large firms, large landowners, religious and military leaders, etc., it

raises the $R_i$ of these persons.[15] Often their response is called "palace revolution", "*coup d'etat*", "insurrection", "*Putsch*", or "fascist revolution" (see [20,
pp. 208-36]. A relatively clear example is provided by the 1955 revolt against
Peron in Argentina.


## 4. Revolutions Caused by Widespread Increases in Hostility toward the Regime

Some revolutions (e.g., the 1898-1900 Boxer Rebellion in China) appear to have
been preceded by increases in racial, ethnic, or class solidarity. The American
Revolution and the *Fronde* [28] illustrate the common scenario of widespread
complaints of excessive taxation followed by revolution. The Nien Rebellion
(1853-68) in China illustrates another common scenario: widespread complaints
of a decline in services followed by revolution. The Manchu state ceased to provide adequate security against banditry in the countryside which in the Nien
region ultimately brought about a situation in which revolutionaries taxed the
population and provided local defense (e.g., by setting up earth walls around the
villages) [27, pp. 214-17].[16] Clearly, such sentiments and complaints involve
increases in $E$ and, hence, in revolutionary participation.[17] The same role has
been played by the spread of new ideologies, new religions, and even *economic
affluence*.[18] However, it must be noted that increases in $E$ cause increases in
$L_v$ which induce further increases in participation. Sentiments such as "Black
Pride" make it easier for black revolutionaries to carry out their activities (the
"people" become the "sea in which the revolutionaries swim"). I am inclined to
believe that a major share of increment to revolutionary activity can be associated with the increase in $L_v$ rather than with the change in the "hearts and
minds" of the participants (i.e., the increase in their $E$).

The Warsaw Ghetto "outbreak" is a special and limiting case. We may assume
the probability of victory $(L_v)$ was believed to be close to zero but since the
inhabitants also believed that they would be killed whether or not they resisted,
$P_i$ and $L_w I_r$ are both close to zero. Resistance occurs only if $E$ is greater than
zero—it is "better" to go down fighting than passively accept destruction.


## III  WHO WILL MAKE THE REVOLUTION?

Neither the relative deprivation theory discussed above nor the social dysfunction theories we turn to next, cast very much light on the question of *who* will
become a revolutionary.

According to Pettee [33] social dysfunction leads individuals to a sense of "cramp" with revolution being intended to enlarge the range of the individual's options. To Edwards, violation of one of the "four wishes of Thomas" leads individuals to violence that is proportional to the amount of such repression.[19] Olson [30] maintains that rapid economic growth (and, presumably, rapid political or social change) is socially destabilizing because an individual's economic status becomes incompatible with his social or political status. The absence of an adequate theory to explain who will become a revolutionary is most apparent in the Marxist analysis which:

> . . . sees revolution as purely social, and as the product of the clash of interests represented in organized classes . . . in this process individuals have no part, and the Marxist offers no theory of individual behavior beyond the degree to which the individual is incorporated in the structure of the class of which he is a part . . . Marxist theory . . . ascribes key importance to the role of the few devoted people whose job is to educate the members of the supplanting class into consciousness of their duties. No explanation is offered as to which class these people will belong or how they will become aware of their mission to educate others [5, p. 154].

As Becker has pointed out in connection with criminal activity the economists' usual analysis of choice applies:

> . . . a person commits an offense if the expected utility to him exceeds the utility he could get by using his time and other resources at other activities. Some persons become "criminals," therefore, not because their motivation differs from that of other persons, but because their benefits and costs differ . . . criminal behavior becomes part of a much more general theory and does not require ad hoc concepts of differential association, anomie, and the like . . . [2, p. 176].

Neither, we may add does the theory of revolution require concepts such as "relative deprivation" and "cramp". In the private interest framework the focus is on private rewards $(R_i)$. The revolutionary is viewed as having made an occupational choice—to become a "ruler" and to this end devotes a portion of his time to politics of a certain type. Revolutionary activity itself is a form of "investment" in human resources: (1) it creates a position or, one might say, an annuity for the revolutionary;[20] (2) it provides the revolutionary with some of the organizational, communications, and military skills needed to earn the "wage" paid by society to its rulers for producing "order".

Since the expected return from a successful investment in human resources increases with the expected lifespan of the subject, it is not surprising that students of revolution have frequently noted the disproportionate participation of young persons [11, pp. 24-26].[21]

The disproportionate participation in nationalist or Marxist revolutionary movements of persons with modern higher education in economically under-developed and "third world" countries [11, pp. 23-25] may be explained not in terms of relative deprivation theory (see [37, p. 340]), but by a relatively high $R_i$ for the educated subgroup of the population. After all, it is the educated participants who get to manage the nationalized industries and serve in the expanded government bureaucracy. Further, Lasswell notes the higher revolutionary participation rates of intellectuals in nonindustrial (or traditional) as opposed to industrial (or modern) societies and, in essence, his explanation is a difference in $R_i$. Specifically he suggests [22, p. 86] that in the latter type of society

> the paths to power, wealth, respect, and other values [are] sufficiently open to intellectuals to render it unnecessary to rely upon affiliation with a revolutionary party to advance their fortunes.

A testable implication of economic theory is that, even in industrial countries, significant fluctuations in the market equilibrium real wage of "intellectual workers" (roughly college graduates, professionals, technicians, and white collar workers) lead negatively conforming fluctuations in their participation in revolutionary movements.[22]

In conclusion, one interesting indirect confirmation of the extent to which private interest calculations underlie revolutionary participation is the frequent claim that victorious revolutions become "routinized" and change little if anything of a "fundamental" nature in a society (see [37, p. 361]). Of course, from the viewpoint of the new rulers the change in the distribution of the rewards from holding power may be sufficiently "fundamental".

## REFERENCES

1. Peter Amann (ed.) *The Eighteenth Century Revolution: French or Western* (Boston: D.C. Heath and Co., 1963).
2. Gary S. Becker, "Crime and Punishment: An Economic Approach," *Journal of Political Economy,* **76,** No. 2 (March/April 1968): 169-217.
3. Daniel Bell, *The Cultural Contradictions of Capitalism* (New York: Basic Books, 1976).
4. Geoffrey Brennan, "Pareto Desirable Redistribution," *Public Choice* (Spring 1973). 43-67.
5. Peter Calvert, *A Study of Revolution* (London: Oxford University Press, 1970).
6. James C. Davies, "Towards a Theory of Revolution," *American Sociological Review,* **27** (February 1962): 5-13.
7. Harry Eckstein (ed.) *Internal War* (New York: The Free Press, 1964).

8.  Terence Emmons, *The Russian Landed Gentry and the Peasant Emancipation of 1861* (London: Cambridge University Press, 1968).

9.  Lyford P. Edwards, *The Natural History of Revolution* (Chicago: University of Chicago Press, 1927).

10. Louis Gottschalk, "Causes of Revolution," in Clifford T. Paynton and Robert Blackey (eds.) *Why Revolution?* (Cambridge, Mass.: Schenkman, 1971), pp. 99–109.

11. Thomas H. Greene, *Comparative Revolutionary Movements* (Englewood Cliffs, N.J.: Prentice-Hall, 1974).

12. Ted R. Gurr, "A Comparative Study of Civil Strife," in Hugh D. Graham and Ted R. Gurr (eds.) *The History of Violence in America: Historical and Comparative Perspectives* (New York: Praeger, 1969).

13. ——, *Why Men Rebel* (Princeton, N.J.: Princeton University Press, 1970).

14. Mark N. Hagopian, *The Phenomenon of Revolution* (New York: Dodd, Mead, and Co., 1975).

15. Sidney Harcave, *The Russian Revolution of 1905* (New York: Macmillan Co., 1964).

16. Franklin W. Houn, *Chinese Political Traditions* (Washington, D.C.: Public Affairs Press, 1965).

17. Robert Hunter, *Revolution: Why, How, When?* 4th ed. (New York: Committee for Constitutional Government, 1943).

18. Samuel P. Huntington, *Political Order in Changing Societies* (New Haven: Yale University Press, 1968).

19. Chalmers Johnson, *Revolution and the Social System* (Stanford University: The Hoover Institution on War, Revolution, and Peace, 1964).

20. John H. Kautsky, *The Political Consequences of Modernization* (New York: Wiley, 1972).

21. Harold D. Lasswell, *World Politics and Personal Insecurity* (New York: The Free Press, 1972).

22. —— and Daniel Lerner, *World Revolutionary Elites* (Cambridge, Mass.: The M.I.T. Press, 1966).

23. Maurice Latey, *Tyranny* (London: Macmillan, 1969).

24. Kenneth Scott Latourette, *The Chinese, Their History and Culture*, 4th ed. (New York: Macmillan Co., 1964).

25. Nathan Leites and Charles Wolf, Jr., *Rebellion and Authority: An Analytic Essay on Insurgent Conflicts* (Chicago: Markham, 1970).

26. Heinz Lubasz (ed.), *Revolutions in Modern European History* (New York: Macmillan Co., 1966).

27. Barrington Moore, Jr., *Social Origins of Dictatorship and Democracy* (Boston: Beacon Press, 1966).

28. Roland Mousnier, "*The Fronde*" in Robert Forster and Jack P. Greene (eds.), *Preconditions of Revolution in Early Modern Europe* (Baltimore: Johns Hopkins Press, 1970), pp. 131–59.

29. Max Nomad, *Aspects of Revolt* (New York: Bookman Associates, 1959).

ACK

126 THE STATE AS A FIRM

126      THE STATE AS A FIRM

126 — THE STATE AS A FIRM

126   THE STATE AS A FIRM

# APPENDIX III
# *The GPITPC and Institutional Entropy*

Institutions do not act—individuals act and are constrained by the institutional settings they find themselves in. Thus, we need a general private interest theory of public choice (GPITPC). §1 briefly sets down the bare outlines of such a theory and some of its most basic results. We make no claim for anything other than expositional originality with regard to that theory. It has long been implicit in much of the public choice literature and can, in part, be traced back to the earliest political economists (for example, A. Smith [8]). §2 then shows how such a theory can both explain the existence of the phenomenon of institutional entropy as well as suggest remedies for it.

## §1  THE GENERAL PRIVATE INTEREST THEORY
##     OF PUBLIC CHOICE

The political decision process is viewed as consisting of individuals who choose courses of action in what they believe to be their own interests, and a political

*Source:* An earlier version of this Appendix was published by Richard Auster in *Public Choice* (Fall 1974).

system which translates these actions into public choices, which may or may not alter the political system itself. In this view, revolution, for example, is simply a state of extraordinary activity in the political system. We now make some assumptions.

*Assumption 1.* Individuals correctly perceive their influence through the political system on public choice.

*Assumption 2.* The individual's utility function is defined over all states of the world, all of which have both public and private aspects. The individual chooses that course of action and allocates his effort in that way which maximizes his expected utility.

Uncertainty is introduced because, realistically speaking, the outcomes of the political system are themselves generally uncertain.

*Assumption 3.* The political system is weakly responsive to individual effort. That is, *ceteris paribus,* the probability that a particular public policy will emerge from the political system, is a weakly increasing monotonic function of the amount of individual effort which takes place in support of that policy. Let $\lambda_{ij}$ denote the rate at which the $i$th individual's effort increases the probability of the $j$th policy being adopted.

This is a somewhat different view of the political decision process than the usual one, e.g., Arrow [2]. There, the political system is not itself the subject of choice and change while here it is. Similarly, we do not assume that people do not or cannot reveal the intensity of their preferences. Our political decision mechanism does respond to individual effort, and these efforts are related to the intensity of the individual's preferences for one state or another. We believe this captures more fully the actuality of public choice.

Consider now any particular public policy. If it is adopted this will result in various types of expected benefits (costs) to the individual. There are those that will result from the purely public aspects of the policy. Denote these by $C_i$. An example of these is the satisfaction the individual expects to derive from his perception of the effect on collective security of a firm military stance. Then there are those private benefits (costs) which are expected to result as a consequence of the policy. Denote these by $P_{ci}$, e.g., the satisfaction the individual will derive from a greater expected probability of being promoted in an expanding army or one that is at war. In addition, should he take action in support of a policy, this acting in the public arena may itself confer private costs and benefits, the private benefits of political participation, (denote these by $p_{pi}$). The time used to participate is always a cost (as are the value of other resources expected to be used).[1] In some circumstances, however, there are additional costs (benefits) which may result depending on whether or not the policy being supported is chosen. Clearly, this is so for that particular form of participation in the public arena "revolutionary activity"; however, rewards and punishments for political activities exist in many other cases also. Quite often individuals who participate on campaign staffs find themselves, if their candidate succeeds, in high government office; wealthy financial backers become ambassadors. Political participation, in cash or in kind, for this last class of motives has essentially the economic structure of a bet. The key variable in the individual's decision is his subjective evaluation of the probability that one side or other will win.[2]

In general, individuals will distribute their time and other resources to and among various policies so as to set the marginal benefit of a course of action equal to its marginal cost. Which policies then will individuals choose to support most strongly? These are the policies which the political system will "choose."

Before proceeding to the central result of GPITPC, which provides a partial answer to this question, it will make things somewhat more rigorous if we introduce the concept of a *negligible increment to satisfaction*. An increment to satisfaction is "negligible" if it is either less than what might be called the individual's threshold of perception or if it is his prior expectation that it is less than the costs (subjective or objective) of calculating its precise rate.[3] Let us then suppose (for simplicity) that there exists, for all individuals, a number $\delta$ such that if the increment to satisfaction obtaining from a course of action is less than $\delta$, it is a negligible increment to satisfaction. Clearly negligible increments to satisfaction are irrelevant to the individual's decision calculus.


## Theorem

Given a particular individual and two policies $(B_0, B_1)$ with expected levels of public-public good benefits (costs) $C_0$, $C_1$, and expected levels of private-public good benefits (costs) $P_{po}$, $P_{p1}$, and expected levels of private-private benefits (costs) $P_{co}$, $P_{c1}$ to some individual, then, unless

1. the individual is important to the outcome[4] ($\lambda_{ij}$ "large") or
2. $(C_1 - C_0)$ is infinite, or
3. $(P_c - P_{co})$ is infinite (and maintaining Assumptions 1-3), he will choose to support $B_0$ over $B_1$ whenever

$$P_{po} > P_{p1} \tag{i}$$

irrespective of $(C_1 - C_0)$, and $(P_{co} - P_{c1})$

Proof

Because they are the consequences of a public good, the individual obtains whichever $(C_i, P_{ci})$ is implied by the political system's choice irrespective of whether or not he has supported the policy. His expected rate of return to acting in favor of $B_1$ (and against $B_0$) involves $(C_i, P_{ci})$ therefore only to the extent that the individual's acting influences the probability of one policy or another being chosen. In the case under consideration, the choice is between $B_0$ and $B_1$. Acting in favor of $B_1$ raises its probability of being chosen and lowers the probability that $B_0$ will be chosen. Therefore, the individual's rate of return to acting in favor of $B_1$ (and against $B_0$) involves $(C_i, P_{ci})$ in the form

$$\lambda_{i1}C_1 - \lambda_{io}C_o + \lambda_i P_{c1} - \lambda_{io}P_{co} \tag{ii}$$

Assuming equal effectiveness on the individual's part, that is, a single well-defined "importance to the outcome" $= \lambda_i = \lambda_{i1} = \lambda_{io}$, Equation (ii) becomes

$$\lambda_i(C_1 - C_0) + \lambda_i(P_{c1} - P_{c0}) = \lambda_i DC \tag{iii}$$

and as long as

$$\lambda_i < \delta/|DC|$$

the differences $(C_1 - C_0)$ and $(P_{c1} - P_{co})$ are irrelevant for the individual's choice.                                                          q.e.d.[5]

This is similar to what Tullock [9] has shown in the context of revolutionary activity.[6] It is, as he notes, nothing but the "free-rider problem" [6] viewed from a slightly different perspective. Given our assumptions, expected utility will always be higher when the $P_{pi}$ are higher, because whether or not one supports the policy one desires one must obtain the public-public and private-public benefits from it if it is adopted, i.e., one is a free rider. If the individual believed that his actions could influence the outcome, then any finite difference $|DC|$ would affect his allocation of effort. As long as he believes he is not important to the outcome, however, there is no private incentive to *acting* unless $|DC|$ is infinite, in which case what is really a "negligible influence" and not a precisely zero influence) is counter-balanced by the "overwhelming importance" of the issue. This perhaps explains public-spirited actions in times of war.

Corollary I

*Ceteris paribus* individuals support, or support most strongly, those policies which they expect to have the greatest level of $P_p$. Thus, when given the opportunity, individuals will generally sacrifice the public for their private good.

Corollary II

Individual's public actions can only be manipulated by altering their expectations of the $P_{pi}$ unless they can be (or are) convinced that

1. $|DC|$ is infinite; or that
2. they are important to the outcome

Of course, one way to make $|DC|$ infinite is to convince people that $B_0$ is infinitely bad. This may account for the tendency to exaggerate the defects of opposing views which so characterizes the political arena.

It is interesting to recall that Rousseau [5] argued that individuals should vote the "general will," as opposed to their private interests. In this way he felt democracy could work. *Ceteris paribus* an individual's influence over the outcome declines directly with the number of other individuals in the unit of democracy; therefore, if Rousseau is accepted, a presumption against democracy's being an effective political system for large units exists. From the perspective of GPITPC, increased "democratization," especially if coupled with increased centralization, is seen as something other than a panacea.

Finally, we may observe that GPITPC provides a simple explanation for the existence of positions with some public power in all institutions and societies. By creating a position of power one makes someone (the office holder) important to the outcome, and unless someone is in fact important to the outcome (that is, has power) GPITPC tells us that public actions for which there is little or no private reward at all would not take place at all.


## §2  INSTITUTIONAL ENTROPY

Perhaps the most pervasive phenomenon of the contemporary U.S. (world?) institutional scene is the apparent inability of old-large institutions to function effectively; the Armed Forces and the Post Office are but two particularly conspicuous examples as are the hospitals, the universities . . . . The GPITPC provides us with a simple way of understanding some of the causes and remedies for the phenomenon of institutional entropy, as well as explaining why one expects it to be strongest in "nonprofit" institutions.

On the surface the phenomenon is surprising. Learning should make older institutions better, not worse. As essential feature of learning, however, is the discovery of past mistakes and their correction. GPITPC points to the existence of a tendency to keep on with mistakes. Observe only that the *general* improvement in the institution's efficiency which would result as a consequence of the discovery and elimination of a mistake is a public good, that is automatically for everyone in the institution and thus essentially irrelevant to the actual choice the institution's political system will make.

This tendency for its efficiency to be irrelevant for its member individuals' choices of courses of action is likely to be most severe in those circumstances where the inefficiency of the institution as a whole does not reflect back on any one individual, but is diffused throughout the institution or worse yet, throughout society as a whole. Thus, it is precisely the "nonprofit" sector which one expects to be the most conspicuous area of waste and inefficiency in society, and note that our opening list is from that sector. While an entrepreneur, that is the residual income recipient of the firm, may have a sufficient private incentive to try and see to it that his supervisors do not accept kickbacks for punching employees out long after they have in fact left the plant, who has such an incentive in the Post Office?[7] The popular notion that the nonprofit form is superior from the point of view of society as a whole finds no support in GPITPC.

From this perspective one can readily understand the importance, in the absence of sufficient institutional social cohesion, of a single entrepreneur. Only when the political system is, in effect, also the residual income recipient, is there sufficient incentive to discover and correct mistakes. Because of the diffusion of the receipt of residual income which one finds in the modern corporation (between stockholders and managers and among the managerial group). they must experience this entropy as well.

Two other forces, also readily understood in terms of GPITPC, tend to strengthen this natural running down of institutions' efficiencies. For those benefiting from the continued existence of the mistake, its elimination is often a catastrophic private bad. That is, the issue is more likely to be of "overwhelming importance" to those who benefit from the mistake than to members of the institution in general. For these people, their private interest will dictate opposition to the policy "eliminate the mistake." But then, unless someone with comparable influence over the outcome of the political system has, or can develop, a comparable private interest in the elimination of the mistake, the policy "eliminate the mistake" will not be chosen (or will have a lower probability of being chosen) simply because less effort will be exerted in its behalf. Again, mistakes will tend to accumulate, and the institution's level of efficiency will progressively deteriorate. In addition, because they are directly involved, the "general public" is likely to consider those who benefit from the mistake as "experts" on the matter, and they may thus in fact be important to the outcome of the political system on the issue.

GPITPC suggests that there are at least two methods of reducing the forces responsible for institutional entropy:

1. Create a countering private interest in eliminating the mistake.
2. Eliminate the private interest in keeping the mistake.

Muckrakers, and political entrepreneurs, provide the society at large with some amount of approach (1).[8] They are limited, however, in their effectiveness by the fact that they act on what people believe to be good for all. That is, in some circumstances they do not affect the individual's perception of $P_{pi}$. When they are able to do so, however, they become effective. In any case, one suspects that other institutions would do well to facilitate the emergence of muckrakers.[9] But observe, facilitating such an emergence provides a public good which also operates against the interests of those who form the muck—that is, benefit from it. Thus, GPITPC does not lead one to expect to find many institutions with massive facilitation. People who "rock the boat" are often fired.

Approach (2) is familiar to economists under the title "compensation principles." One relatively easy way to eliminate the private interests opposing the elimination of a mistake would be to buy them off. If it is a "mistake" from the point of view of the institution as a whole, then this compensation can be made and still leave everyone else better off. Consider, for example, the case of taxicabs in New York City. These are licensed, and the market price of the license relative to its costs of production betrays the existence of some measure of monopoly profit. It is generally agreed that things would be better for all, taken as a whole, if additional licenses were issued so as to drive their price down and eliminate the shortage of cabs which the high price reflects. This is opposed, of course, by the current holders of the licenses, many of whom have only one license and would thus be impoverished by the change, and who are in any case simply earning a normal return on their investment having bought the license at, or near the current price.[10] If they were bought off, however, their resistance would disappear. Thus, GPITPC is not without its own public policy recommendations. *Beneficient social change can be facilitated by the general establishment of more or less automatic compensation mechanisms for the adverse private affects of such change.* This would appear to be recognized, if only implicitly, by many institutions. The phenomenon of "kicking him upstairs" no doubt reflects something like this.

## AFTERWORD

One cannot deny that questions of "what should public choices be" are interesting, if only for aesthetic reasons. GPITPC does not suggest that there is much hope, however, that the simple articulation of *optimal* public choices (which affects only the perception of the $C_i$), will have, in and of itself, any appreciable effect on *actual* choices. The singular lack of success that the economics profession has had in its greater than 200-year advocacy of free trade — as a long run world optimal policy — is but one striking illustration of the futility of this course of action. Acting on what individuals believe is good for all is not enough. Having and *using* a fully developed GPITPC will allow us to have a greater influence on actual public choices, and at that point the work on optimal policies would attain something other than a simply aesthetic relevance.

## REFERENCES

1. G.A. Ackerlof, "The Market for 'Lemons': Qualitative Uncertainty and the Market Mechanism" *QJE* (August 1970): 488–500.
2. K.J. Arrow, *Social Choice and Individual Values,* 2d ed. (New York: Wiley, 1963).
3. N.E. Devletoglou, "Thresholds and Transactions Costs," *QJE,* 85 (February 1971): 163–70.
4. J. Richelson, "A Note on Collective Goods and the Theory of Political Entrepreneurship," *Public Choice* (Fall 1970).
5. J.J. Rousseau, *Social Contract.*
6. P.A. Samuelson, "The Pure Theory of Public Expenditure," *R.E. Stat.,* 36, No. 4 (November 1954): 387–389.
7. M. Silver and R.D. Auster, "Entrepreneurship, Profits, and Limits on Firm Size," *Journal of Business of the University of Chicago,* 42, No. 3 (July 1969): 277–81. (Reprinted as Appendix I.)
8. A. Smith, *Wealth of Nations* (Modern Library, Random House, 1937).
9. G. Tullock, "The Paradox of Revolution," *Public Choice* (Fall 1971): 89–99.

# LIST OF REFERENCES
# (in Chapters 1-8)

REFERENCES

1. P.H. Aranson and P.C. Ordeshook, "A Prolegomenon to a Theory of the Failure of Representative Democracy," in Auster and Sears (eds.), *American . . .* , pp. 23–46.
2. Robert M. Adams, *The Evolution of Urban Society: Early Mesopotamia and Prehispanic Mexico* (Chicago: Aldine, 1966).
3. Irma Adelman and Cynthia Taft Morris, "Factor Analysis of the Interrelationship between Social and Political Variables and Per Capita GNP," *Quarterly Journal of Economics* (November 1965): 555–78.
4. Johannes Andenaes, *Punishment and Deterrence* (Ann Arbor, Michigan: University of Michigan Press, 1974).
5. Stanislav Andreski, *The Uses of Comparative Sociology* (Berkeley, California: University of California Press, 1965).
6. ——, *Military Organization and Society* (2d. ed.,: Berkeley, California: University of California Press, 1968).
7. Kenneth J. Arrow, *Social Choice and Individual Values* (2d. ed., New York: Wiley, 1963).
8. ——, *The Limits of Organization* (New York: W.W. Norton, 1974).
9. R.D. Auster, "The GPITPC and Institutional Entropy," *Public Choice,* **19** (Fall 1974): 76–83.

10. ——, "Some Economic Determinants of the Characteristics of Public Workers" in Robert D. Leiter and Gerald Sirkin (eds.), *Economics . . . ,* pp. 185–98.

11. R. D. Auster and B. Sears (eds.), *American Re-evolution: Papers and Proceedings* (Tucson, Arizona: Department of Economics, University of Arizona, May 1977).

12. ——, "Renting the Streets" in R. D. Auster and Sears (eds.), op. cit.

13. ——, "The Level of Public Goods Under Anarchy," 1977, mimeo.

14. ——, "Private Markets in Public Goods (or Qualities), "*Quarterly Journal of Economics* (August 1977): 419–30.

15. ——, and Morris Silver, "Collective Goods and Collective Decision Mechanisms," *Public Choice,* **13** (Spring 1973): 1–17.

16. Z. Bairey, "The End of Theocratic Anarchy in Ancient Palestine," Department of Economics, University of Arizona, mimeo.

17. R. Bataglio, J. Kagel, J. Winkler, R. Fisher, R. Basmann and L. Krasner, "A Test of Consumer Demand Theory Using Observations of Individual Consumer Purchases," *Western Economic Journal,* (Dec. 1973): 411–28.

18. Gary S. Becker, "A Theory of the Allocation of Time," *Economic Journal,* **75** (September 1965): 493–517.

19. ——, "Crime and Punishment: An Economic Approach," *Journal of Political Economy,* **76**, No. 2 (March/April 1968): 169–217.

20. H. S. Bennett, *Life on the English Manor* (Cambridge, England: Cambridge University Press, 1956).

21. Theodore C. Bergstrom and Robert P. Goodman, "Private Demands for Public Goods," *American Economic Review,* **LXIII**, No. 3 (June 1973): 280–96.

22. M. Bloch, *Feudal Society* (London: Routledge and Kegan Paul, 1965).

23. Alfred Blumstein, Jacqueline Cohen, and Daniel Nagin (eds.), *Deterrence and Incapacitation; Estimating the Effects of Criminal Sanctions on Crime Rates* (Washington, D.C.: National Academy of Sciences, 1978).

24. Joseph B. Board, Jr., *The Government and Politics of Sweden* (Boston: Houghton Mifflin Co., 1970).

25. Derk Bodde, "Feudalism in China," in Coulborn (ed.), *Feudalism . . . ,* pp. 49–92.

26. Thomas E. Borcherding and Robert T. Deacon, "The Demand for the Services of Non-Federal Governments: An Econometric Approach to Collective Choice," *American Economic Review,* **LXII**, No. 5 (December 1972): 891–901.

27. Omar Bradley, *A Soldier's Story* (New York: Holt, 1951).

28. Albert Breton and Raymond Breton, "An Economic Theory of Social Movements," *American Economic Review,* **59**, No. 2 (May 1969): 198–205.

29. Albert Breton, *The Economic Theory of Representative Government* (Chicago: Aldine Publishing Co., 1974).

30. ——, and T. Scott, "The Economic Theory of Representative Government: A Reply" *Public Choice,* **XX** (Winter 1974): 129–143.
31. Gene A. Brucker, Florentine Politics and Society: 1343–1378 (Princeton, New Jersey: Princeton University Press, 1962).
32. Burr C. Brundage, "Feudalism in Ancient Mesopotamia and Iran," in Coulborn (ed.), *Feudalism . . .* , pp. 93–119.
33. P.A. Brunt, *Social Conflicts in the Roman Republic* (New York: W.W. Norton and Co., 1971).
34. Martin Buber, *Paths in Utopia* (Boston: Beacon Press, 1949).
35. James M. Buchanan, "Before Public Choice," in Tullock (ed.), *Explorations . . .* , pp. 27–37.
36. ——, *The Limits of Liberty: Between Anarchy and Leviathan,* (Chicago: University of Chicago Press, 1975).
37. Nikolai Bukharin, *Historical Materialism* (New York: International Publishers, 1925).
38. Robbins Burling, *The Passage of Political Power* (New York: Academic Press, 1974).
39. C. Delisle Burns, *The First Europe* (New York: Allen and Unwin, 1948).
40. Gilbert A. Cahill, *The Great Reform Bill of 1832* (Lexington, Mass.: D.C. Heath and Co., 1969).
41. Robert L. Carniero, "A Theory of the Origin of the State," in Jennings and Hoebel, (eds.), *Readings . . .* , pp. 424–32.
42. F.L. Carsten, *The Origins of Prussia* (London: Oxford University Press, 1954).
43. Richard E. Caves and William F. Murphy II, "Franchising: Firms, Markets, and Intangible Assets," *Southern Economic Journal,* **42,** No. 4 (April 1976),: 572–86.
44. Neil W. Chamberlain, *Beyond Malthus: Population and Power* (New York: Basic Books, 1970).
45. Edward P. Cheyney, *The Dawn of a New Era: 1250–1453* (New York: Harper and Row, 1936).
46. V. Gordon Childe, *Social Evolution* (Cleveland: World Pub. Co., 1951).
47. Carlo M. Cippolla, *Before the Industrial Revolution* (New York: W.W. Norton and Co., 1976).
48. Robert Claiborne, *Climate, Man, and History* (New York: W.W. Norton and Co., 1970).
49. M.V. Clarke, *The Medieval City State* (Cambridge, England: Speculum Historiale, 1926).
50. Alfred Cobban, *Dictatorship* (New York: Charles Scribner's Sons, 1939).
51. Michael D. Coe, *Mexico* (New York: Praeger Publishing Co., 1962).
52. Carl Cohen, *Democracy* (Athens, Georgia: University of Georgia Press, 1971).
53. Yehudi A. Cohen (ed.), *Man in Adaptation: The Biosocial Background* (Chicago: Aldine, 1968).

54. ——, (ed.), *Man In Adaptation: The Cultural Present* (2d. ed., Chicago: Aldine 1974).

55. Donald Collier, "Development of Civilization on the Coast of Peru," in Steward (ed.), *Irrigation . . .* , pp. 19–27.

56. Elizabeth Colson, *Tradition and Contract: The Problem of Order* (Chicago: Aldine, 1974).

57. J.B. Condliffe, *New Zealand in the Making* (2d. ed., London: Allen and Unwin, Ltd., 1959).

58. Rushton Coulborn (ed.), *Feudalism in History* (Hamden, Conn.: Archon Books, 1965).

59. ——, "A Comparative Study of Feudalism," in Coulborn (ed.), *Feudalism . . .* , pp. 185–395.

60. L.M. Court, "Entrepreneurial and Consumer Demand Theories for Commodity Spectra," *Econometrica,* **8,** No. 1 (April 1941): 135–62; No. 2 (July/October 1941): 241–97.

61. Phillips Cutright, "National Political Development," *American Sociological Review* (April 1963): 253–64.

62. Robert A. Dahl, *A Preface to Democratic Theory* (Chicago: University of Chicago Press, 1956).

63. Joseph Dahmus, *The Middle Ages* (Garden City, New York: Doubleday and Co., 1968).

64. Rolf Dahrendorf, *Class and Class Conflict in Industrial Society* (Stanford, Calif: Stanford University Press, 1957).

65. Otto A. Davis and Andrew B. Whinston, "On the Distinction Between Public and Private Goods," *American Economic Review,* **57** (May 1967): 360–73.

66. Phyllis Deane, *The First Industrial Revolution* (Cambridge, England: Cambridge University Press, 1965).

67. Harold Demsetz, "The Exchange and Enforcement of Property Rights, *Journal of Law and Economics,* **7** (October 1964): 11–26.

68. Isaac Deutscher, "Roots of Bureaucracy," in *Marxism in Our Time* (Berkeley, Calif. Ramparts Press, 1971).

69. A.S. Diamond, *Primitive Law* (London: Longmans, Green and Col, 1935).

70. ——, *The Evolution of Law and Order* (London: Watts and Co., 1951).

71. Stanley Diamond, "The Rule of Law Versus the Order of Custom" in Robert Paul Wolff (ed.), *The Rule of Law* (New York: Simon and Schuster, 1971).

72. David C. Douglas, "Introduction," in Edouard Perroy, *The Hundred Year's War* (Bloomington, Ind.: Indiana University Press, 1959).

73. Anthony Downs, *Inside Bureaucracy* (Boston: Little, Brown, and Co., 1966).

74. Richard S. Dunn, *The Age of Religious Wars* (New York: W.W. Norton and Co., 1970).

75. Emile Durkheim, *The Division of Labor in Society* (Glencoe, Ill.: The Free Press, 1933).

76. Wolfram Eberhard, *A History of China* (Berkeley, Calif.: University of California Press, 1969).

77. William F. Edgerton, "The Question of Feudal Institutions in Ancient Egypt," in Coulborn (ed.), *Feudalism . . .*, pp. 120–32.

78. Victor Ehrenberg, *The Greek State* (2d. ed., London: Methuen and Co., 1969).

79. Isaac Ehrlich, "Participation in Illegitimate Activities: An Economic Analysis," Ph.D. Dissertation, Columbia University, 1970.

80. ——, "Capital Punishment and Deterrence," *Journal of Political Economy* (August 1977): 741–88.

81. T. Olawale Elias, *The Nature of African Customary Law* (Manchester, England: Manchester University Press, 1956).

82. Bryan Ellickson, "A Generalization of the Pure Theory of Public Goods," *American Economic Review* (June 1973): 417–32.

83. Mark Elvin, *The Pattern of the Chinese Past* (Stanford, Calif.: Stanford University Press, 1973).

84. Friedrich Engels, *The Origin of the Family, Private Property, and the State* (Moscow: Foreign Languages Publishing House, 1948).

85. Richard Faber, *The Vision and the Need* (London: Faber and Faber, 1966).

86. Lloyd A. Fallers, "Social Stratification and Economic Processes," in Melville J. Herskovits and Mitchell Harwitz (eds.), *Economic Transition in Africa* (Northwestern University Press, 1964).

87. Wallace K. Ferguson, *Europe in Transition: 1300–1520* (Boston: Houghton Mifflin Co., 1962).

88. Guy Forquin, *Lordship and Feudalism in the Middle Ages* (New York: Pica Press, 1976).

89. W.G. Forrest, *A History of Sparta* (London: Hutchison University Library, 1968).

90. Tenney Frank, *An Economic History of Rome* (2d. ed., Baltimore: Johns Hopkins Press, 1927).

91. Henri Frankfort, *Kingship and the Gods* (Chicago: University of Chicago Press, 1948).

92. Gunther Franz, "Origins in the Ancient Law and the Divine Law, Defended," in Kyle C. Sessions (ed.), *Reformation and Authority* (Lexington, Mass.: D.C. Heath and Co., 1968), pp. 1–8.

93. John Fraser, "Comment," *Public Choice* (Fall 1972): 115–18.

94. T.E. Frech, "The Property Rights Theory of the Firm: Empirical Results from a Natural Experiment" *Journal of Political Economy*, **84**, 1 (February 1976): 143–152.

95. Bruno S. Frey, "Why Do High Income People Participate More in Politics?" *Public Choice* (Fall 1971),: 101–5.

96. ——, "Reply," *Public Choice* (Fall 1972): 119–22.

97. Morton H. Fried, *The Evolution of Political Society* (New York: Random House, 1967).

98. David Friedman, "A Theory of the Size and Shape of Nations," *Journal of Political Economy* (Feb. 1977): 59–77.
99. Carl J. Friedrich, *Constitutional Government and Democracy* (Waltham, Mass.: Blaisdell Publishing Co., 1968).
100. Norman Frolich, Joe A. Oppenheimer, and Oran R. Young, *Political Leadership and Collective Goods* (Princeton, New Jersey: Princeton University Press, 1971).
101. Numa Dénis Fustel de Coulanges, *The Ancient City* (Garden City, New York: Doubleday and Co., 1936).
102. John Kenneth Galbraith, *The Affluent Society* (College ed., Cambridge, Mass.: The Riverside Press, 1960).
103. ——, *The New Industrial State* (Boston: Houghton Mifflin Co., 1967).
104. F.L. Ganshof, *Frankish Institutions Under Charlemagne,* (Providence, Rhode Island: Brown University Press, 1968).
105. Nicholas Georgescu-Roegen, "Concepts, Numbers, and Qualities," in *Analytical Economics* (Cambridge, Mass.: Harvard University Press, 1966), pp. 17–46.
106. G. Germani, "The Transition to a Mass Democracy in Argentina," in S.N. Eisenstadt (ed.) *Readings in Social Evolution and Development* (London: Pergamon Press, 1970), pp. 313–36.
107. Jacques Gernet, *Ancient China* (Berkeley, Calif.: University of California Press, 1968).
108. R. Ghirschman, *Iran* (Baltimore: Penguin Books, 1954).
109. McGuire Gibson, "Population Shift and the Rise of Mesopotamian Civilization," in Colin Renfrew (ed.), *The Explanation of Cultural Change* (London: Duckworth, 1973), pp. 447–63.
110. Ronald M. Glassman, *Political History of Latin America* (New York: Funk and Wagnalls, 1969).
111. Max Gluckman, *Politics, Law, and Ritual in Tribal Society* (Chicago: Aldine Publishing Co., 1965).
112. B.G. Gokhale, *Ancient India* (4th ed., Bombay: Asia Publishing Co., 1959).
113. Jack Goody, *Technology, Tradition, and the State in Africa* (London: Oxford University Press, 1971).
114. R. Graves, *I Claudius* (New York: Smith and Haas, 1935).
115. H.R.G. Greaves, *The Foundations of Political Theory* (2d. ed., London: London School of Economics and Political Science, 1966).
116. Alexander J. Groth and Robert L. Curry, Jr., "Individual System Preference: A Model of Rational Choice," *Public Choice,* **XXIII** (Fall 1975): 11–23.
117. J.M. Gullick, *Indigenous Political Systems of Western Malaya* (London University of London Press, 1958).
118. Everett E. Hagen, "A Framework for Analyzing Economic and Political Change," in *Development of the Emerging Countries: An Agenda for Research* (Washington, D.C.: The Brookings Institution, 1962), pp. 1–38.
119. John W. Hall, "The Castle Town and Japan's Modern Urbanization," in John W. Hall and Marius B. Jansen (eds.), *Studies in the Institutional*

*History of Early Modern Japan* (Princeton, N.J.: Princeton University Press, 1968), pp. 169–88.

120. Mason Hammond, *The City in the Ancient World* (Cambridge, Mass.: Harvard University Press, 1972).

121. B. H. L. Hart, *Strategy,* rev. ed. (New York: Praeger, 1954).

122. Denys Hay, *The Medieval Centuries* (New York: Harper and Row, 1964).

123. ——, *Europe in the Fourteenth and Fifteenth Centuries* (New York: Holt, Rinehart, and Winston, Inc., 1966).

124. John G. Head and Carl S. Shoup, "Public Goods, Private Goods, and Ambiguous Goods," *Economic Journal,* **79** (September 1969): 567–72.

125. Frederick A. Hermens, *The Representative Republic* (Notre Dame, Indiana: University of Notre Dame Press, 1958).

126. Otto Hintze, "The Formation of States and Constitutional Development: A Study in History and Politics," in Felix Gilbert (ed.) *The Historical Essays of Otto Hintze* (New York: Oxford University Press, 1975).

127. Albert O. Hirschman, *Exit, Voice, Loyalty* (Cambridge, Mass.: Harvard University Press, 1970).

128. Thomas Hobbes, *De Cive* (New York: Appleton-Century-Crofts, 1949).

129. Gerald A. J. Hodgett, *A Social and Economic History of Medieval Europe* (London: Methuen and Co., 1972).

130. E. Adamson Hoebel, *The Law of Primitive Man* (Cambridge, Mass.: Harvard University Press, 1961).

131. ——, *Anthropology: The Study of Man* (4th ed., New York: McGraw-Hill, 1972).

132. Frank Hole, "Investigating the Origins of Mesopotamian Civilization," in Cohen (ed.), *The Biosocial . . . ,* pp. 354–62.

133. Franklin W. Houn, *Chinese Political Traditions* (Washington, D.C.: Public Affairs Press, 1965).

134. Samuel P. Huntington, *The Soldier and the State* (New York: Random House 1964).

135. ——, *Political Order in Changing Societies* (New Haven, Conn.: Yale University Press, 1968).

136. G. L. Huxley, *Early Sparta* (Cambridge, Mass.: Harvard University Press, 1962).

137. J. K. Hyde, *Society and Politics in Medieval Italy: The Evolution of the Civil Life, 1000–1350* (New York: St. Martin's Press, 1973).

138. Thorkild Jacobsen, "The Function of the State," in H. Frankfort et al., *The Intellectual Adventures of Ancient Man* (Chicago: University of Chicago Press, 1946), pp. 62–92.

139. Charles and Barbara Jelavich, *The Balkans* (Englewood Cliffs, N.J.: Prentice-Hall, 1961).

140. Jesse D. Jennings and E. Adamson Hoebel, *Readings in Anthropology* (3d. ed., New York: McGraw-Hill, 1970).

141. Bob Jessop, *Social Order, Reform, and Revolution* (New York: Herder and Herder, 1972).

142. Gregory Alan Johnson, *Local Exchange and Early State Development in*

*Southwestern Iran,* University of Michigan, Museum of Anthropology, Paper No. 51 (Ann Arbor, 1973).

143.  A.H.M. Jones (ed.) *A History of Rome Through the Fifth Century, Vol. II: The Empire* (New York: Walker and Co., 1970).

144.  Bertrand de Jouvenel, *Sovereignty* (Chicago: University of Chicago Press, 1957).

145.  Solomon Katz, *The Decline of Rome* (Ithaca, New York: Cornell University Press, 1955).

146.  Robert G. Keith, *Conquest and Agrarian Change: The Emergence of the Hacienda System on the Peruvian Coast* (Cambridge, Mass.: Harvard University Press, 1976).

147.  Suzanne Keller, *Beyond the Ruling Class* (New York: Random House, 1963).

148.  Hans Kelsen, *The Pure Theory of Law* (Berkeley and Los Angeles: University of California Press, 1967).

149.  V.O. Key, Jr., *Public Opinion and American Democracy* (New York: Alfred A. Knopf, 1964).

150.  H.D.F. Kitto, *The Greeks* (Chicago: Aldine, 1964).

151.  Jeanne N. Knutson, *The Human Basis of the Polity* (Chicago: Aldine, 1972).

152.  H.G. Koenigsberger, "The Reformation and Social Revolution," in Joel Hurstfield (ed.), *The Reformation Crisis* (New York: Barnes and Noble, Inc., 1966), pp. 83–94.

153.  Lawrence Krader, *Formation of the State* (New York: Prentice-Hall, 1968).

154.  Leonard Krieger, *Kings and Philosophers, 1689–1789* (New York: Norton and Co. Inc., 1970).

155.  Kelvin J. Lancaster, "A New Approach to Consumer Theory," *Journal of Political Economy,* **74** (April 1966): 132–57.

156.  Frederic C. Lane, *Venice and History* (Baltimore: Johns Hopkins Press, 1966).

157.  Lawrence N. Langer, "The Medieval Russian Town," in Michael F. Hamm (ed.), *The City of Russian History* (Lexington, Kentucky: University Press of Kentucky, 1976).

158.  Edward P. Lanning, *Peru Before The Incas* (Englewood Cliffs, N.J.: Prentice-Hall, 1967).

159.  Richard LaPiere, *The Freudian Ethic* (New York: Duell, Sloan, and Pierce, 1959).

160.  Kenneth Scott Latourette, *The Chinese, Their History and Culture* (4th ed., New York: Macmillan Co., 1964).

161.  Robert Leiter and Gerald Sirkin (eds.), *Economics of Public Choice* (New York: Cyrco Press, 1975).

162.  Gerhard E. Lenski, *Power and Privilege* (New York: McGraw-Hill, 1966).

163.  Paul M.A. Linebarger, *Government in Republican China* (New York: McGraw-Hill, 1938).

164.  Ralph Linton, *The Study of Man* (New York: Appleton-Century-Crofts, 1964).

165. Seymour M. Lipset, "Some Social Requisites of Democracy: Economic Development and Political Legitimacy," *American Political Science Review* (March 1959): 65–105.
166. Leslie Lipson, *The Politics of Equality* (Chicago: University of Chicago Press, 1948).
167. ——, *The Democratic Civilization* (New York: Oxford University Press, 1964).
168. James M. Litvack and Wallace E. Oates, "Group Size and the Output of Public Goods: Theory and an Application to State-Local Finance in the United States," *Public Finance,* **25** (1970): 42–58.
169. Dennis Lloyd, *The Idea of Law* (Baltimore: Pelican, 1964).
170. William C. Lockwood, *The Economic Development of Japan* (Princeton, New Jersey: Princeton University Press, 1954).
171. Robert S. Lopez, *The Birth of Europe* (New York: M. Evans and Co., 1966).
172. Robert H. Lowie, *Primitive Society* (New York: Harper and Brothers, 1920).
173. ——, *The Origin of the State* (New York: Russell and Russell Inc., 1962).
174. Emil Lucki, *History of the Renaissance 1350-1550: Book V – Politics and Political Theory* (Salt Lake City, Utah: Utah University Press, 1964).
175. Bryce Lyon, *A Constitutional and Legal History of Medieval England* (New York: Harper and Brothers, 1960).
176. R.M. MacIver, *The Modern State* (London: Oxford University Press, 1964).
177. William McCord, *The Springtime of Freedom* (New York: Oxford University Press, 1965).
178. Martin McGuire, "Group Segregation and Optimal Jurisdictions," *Journal of Political Economy,* **82,** No. 1 (January/February 1974): 112–32.
179. Lucy Mair, *Primitive Government* (Baltimore: Penguin Books, 1964).
180. Bronislaw Maiinowski, "An Anthropological Analysis of War", *American Journal of Sociology,* **46** (1941): 521–53.
181. "Marine! The Life of Lt. Gen. Lewis B. (Chesty) Puller, USMC (ret.)," Davis, Burke (Boston: Little, Brown, 1962).
182. R. Marris, *The Economic Theory of Managerial Capitalism* (New York: Free Press of Glencoe, 1964).
183. Dolores T. Martin and Richard B. McKenzie, "Bureaucratic Profits, Migration Costs, and the Consolidation of Local Government," *Public Choice,* **XXIII** (Fall 1975): 95–100.
184. Alden Mason, *The Ancient Civilization of Peru* (Baltimore: Penguin, 1969).
185. H.B. Mayo, *An Introduction to Democratic Theory* (New York: Oxford University Press, 1960).
186. Charles K. Meek, "Ibo Law," in Jennings and Hoebel (eds.), *Readings . . . ,* pp. 247–58.
187. Charles E. Merriam, *Political Power* (New York: Collier, 1964).
188. John Stuart Mill, *Principles of Political Economy,* Books I-II (Toronto: University of Toronto Press, 1965).

189. Kenneth E. Miller, *Government and Politics in Denmark* (Boston: Houghton Mifflin Co., 1968).
190. Jora R. Minasian, "Television Pricing and the Theory of Public Goods," *Journal of Law and Economics,* 7 (October 1964): 78–80.
191. D.S. Mirsky, *Russia: A Social History* (London: The Cresset Press, 1931).
192. E.J. Mishan, "The Relationship Between Joint Products, Collective Goods, and External Effects," *Journal of Political Economy,* 77 (May/June 1969): 326–48.
193. Joseph Monsen and Anthony Downs, "Public Goods and Private Status" *The Public Interest,* No. 23 (Spring 1971): 64–76.
194. Barrington Moore, Jr., *Social Origins of Dictatorship and Democracy* (Boston: Beacon Press, 1966).
195. Hans J. Morgenthau, *Politics Among Nations* (3d. ed., New York: Alfred A. Knopf, 1963).
196. Gaetano Mosca, *The Ruling Class* (New York: McGraw-Hill, 1939).
197. Richard Muir, *Modern Political Geography* (New York: Wiley, 1975).
198. R.F. Muth, "Household Production and Consumer Demand Functions," *Econometrica,* 34, No. 3 (July 1966): 699–708.
199. Y.K. Ng, "The Possibility of a Paretian Liberal: Impossibility Theorems and Cardinal Utility," *Journal of Political Economy,* 79 (November/December 1971): 1397–1402.
200. William A. Niskanen, Jr., *Bureaucracy and Representative Government* (Chicago: Aldine-Atherton, 1971).
201. Douglas C. North and Robert Paul Thomas, *The Rise of the Western World* (Cambridge, England: Cambridge University Press, 1973).
202. Robert Nozick, *Anarchy, State, and Utopia* (New York: Basic Books, Inc., 1974).
203. Wallace E. Oates, *Fiscal Federalism* (New York: Harcourt, Brace, Jovanovich, 1972).
204. Mancur Olson, Jr., *The Logic of Collective Action: Public Goods and the Theory of Groups* (Cambridge, Mass.: Harvard University Press, 1965).
205. —— and Richard Zeckhauser, "An Economic Theory of Alliance," *Review of Economics and Statistics,* 48, No. 3 (August 1966): 266–79.
206. W.P. Orzechowski, "Labor Intensity, Productivity, and the Growth of the Federal Sector", *Public Choice* (Fall 1974): 123–26.
207. Herbert L. Packer, *The Limits of Criminal Sanction* (Stanford, Calif.: Stanford University Press, 1968).
208. Angel Palerm and Eric R. Wolf, "Ecological Potential and Cultural Development," in Pan American Union, *Studies in Human Ecology,* Social Science Monograph III (Washington, D.C., 1960), pp. 1–37.
209. J.H. Parry, *The Sale of Public Office in the Spanish Indies Under the Hapsburgs* (Berkeley, California: University of California Press, 1953).
210. P.H. Partridge, *Consent and Consensus* (New York: Praeger Publishers, 1971).

211. Mark Pauly, "Cores and Clubs," *Public Choice,* **6** (Fall 1970): 53–65.

212. Henri Pirenne, "From Medieval Cities," in Alfred F. Havighurst (ed.), *The Pirenne Thesis* (Boston: D.C. Heath and Co., 1958), pp. 11–27.

213. John Plamenatz, Man and Society: *Political and Social Theory, Bentham through Marx,* **II** (New York: McGraw-Hill, 1963).

214. A. F. Pollard, *The Evolution of Parliament* (2d. rev. ed., New York: Russell and Russell Inc., 1964).

215. Roger Portal, *The Slavs* (New York: Harper and Brothers, 1969).

216. David M. Potter, *People of Plenty: Economic Abundance and the American Character* (Chicago: University of Chicago Press, 1954).

217. Fredric L. Pryor, *Public Expenditures in Communist and Capitalist Nations* Homewood, Illinois: Irwin, 1968).

218. Carroll Quigley, *The Evolution of Civilizations* (New York: Macmillan Co., 1961).

219. A. R. Radcliffe-Brown, "Preface" in M. Fortes and E. E. Evans-Pritchard (eds.), *African Political System* (London: Oxford University Press, 1940), pp. xi–xxiii.

220. Paul Radin, *The World of Primitive Man* (New York: Henry Schuman, 1953).

221. Robert Redfield, "Primitive Law," in Paul Bohannan (ed.), *Law and Warfare: Studies in the Anthropology of Conflict* (Garden City, New York: The Natural History Press, 1967).

222. Edwin O. Reischauer, "Japanese Feudalism," in Coulborn (ed.), *Feudalism . . .* , pp. 26–48.

223. ——, *Japan: Past and Present* (New York: Alfred A. Knopf Inc., 1964).

224. William H. Riker, *Federalism* (Boston: Little, Brown and Co., 1964).

225. ——, "Public Safety as a Public Good," in Eugene V. Rostow (ed.), *Is Law Dead?* (New York: Simon and Schuster, 1971), pp. 370–85.

226. Carroll L. Riley, *The Origins of Civilization* (Carbondae and Edwardsville, Illinois: Southern Illinois University Press, 1969).

227. William A. Robson, *Civilization and the Growth of Law* (New York: The Macmillan Co., 1935).

228. Hans Rosenberg, *Bureaucracy, Aristocracy, and Autocracy: The Prussian Experience, 1660–1815* (Cambridge, Mass.: Harvard University Press, 1958).

229. W. W. Rostow, *Politics and the Stages of Growth* (Cambridge, Mass.: Cambridge University Press, 1971).

230. Georg Rusche and Otto Kirchheimer, *Punishment and Social Structure* (New York: Columbia University Press, 1939).

231. Jeffrey Burton Russell, *Medieval Civilization* (New York: John Wiley and Sons, 1968).

232. Keith P. Russell, "Comment," *Public Choice* (Fall 1972): 113–14.

233. Philip C. Salzman, "Political Organization Among Nomadic People," in Cohen (ed.), *The Cultural . . .* , pp. 268–284.

234. Kurt Samuelson, *From Great Power to Welfare State* (London: Allen and Unwin Ltd., 1968).
235. Paul A. Samuelson, "The Pure Theory of Public Expenditure," *Review of Economics and Statistics,* 36, No. 4 (November 1954): 387–89.
236. William T. Sanders, "Cultural Ecology in Nuclear Mesoamerica," in Cohen (ed.), *The Biosocial . . . ,* pp. 336–43.
237. ——, "Population, Agricultural History, and Societal Evolution in Mesoamerica," in Brian Spooner (ed.), *Population Growth: Anthropological Implications* (Cambridge, Mass.: M.I.T. Press, 1972), pp. 101–53.
238. —— and Barbara J. Price, *Mesoamerica* (New York: Random House, 1968).
239. A. Sandmo, "Optimality Rules for the Provision of Collective Factors of Production," *Journal of Public Economics,* 1, No. 1 (April 1972): 149–57.
240. ——, "Public Goods and the Technology of Consumption," *Review of Economics Studies* (October 1973): 517–28.
241. Giovanni Sartori, *Democratic Theory* (Detroit: Wayne State University Press, 1962).
242. I. Schapera, *Government and Politics in Tribal Societies* (New York: Schocken Books, 1967).
243. Joseph A. Schumpeter, *Capitalism, Socialism, and Democracy* (3d. ed., New York: Harper Row, 1950).
244. Richard D. Schwartz and James C. Miller, "Legal Evolution and Societal Complexity," Cohen (ed.), *The Cultural . . . ,* pp. 560–67.
245. James R. Scobie, *Argentina: A City and A Nation* (2d. ed., New York: Oxford University Press, 1971).
246. William Seagle, *The Quest for Law* (New York: Alfred A. Knopf, 1941).
247. J. Thorsten Sellin, *Slavery and the Penal System* (New York: Elsevier, 1976).
248. Elman R. Service, *Profiles in Ethnology* (rev. ed., New York: Harper and Row, 1971).
249. Stanford J. Shaw, "Introduction," in *Ottoman Egypt in the Age of the French Revolution* (Cambridge, Mass.: Harvard University Press, 1964).
250. Aylward Shorter, *Chiefship in Western Tanzania* (Oxford, England: Clarendon Press, 1972).
251. Morris Silver and R. D. Auster, "Entrepreneurship, Profit and Limits on Firm Size," *Journal of Business University of Chicago,* 42, No. 3 (July 1969): 277–81. (Appendix I.)
252. Morris Silver, "A Demand Analysis of Voting Costs and Voting Participation," *Social Science Research,* 2, No. 2 (August 1973): 111–24.
253. ——, "Political Revolution and Repression: An Economic Approach," *Public Choice,* 17 (Spring 1974): 63–72.
254. ——, "Towards a Consumption Theory of Political Democracy," in Leiter and Sirkin (eds.), *Economics . . . ,* pp. 140–53.
255. ——, "Punishment, Deterrence, and Police Effectiveness: A Survey of the

Recent Econometric Literature," in Ernest van den Haag and Robert Martinson (eds.), *Crime Deterrence and Offender Career* (Report prepared for the Office of Economic Opportunity under Grant Number 20071G-73), 1975 (Xerox).

256. ——, "Economic Theory of the Constitutional Separation of Powers," *Public Choice* (Spring 1977): 95–107.

257. R. Simpson, "The Congruence of Political, Social and Economic Aspects of Development," *International Development Review* (June 1964): 21–25.

258. Gideon Sjoberg, *The Preindustrial City* (Glencoe, Illinois: The Free Press, 1960).

259. Adam Smith, *The Wealth of Nations* (New York: Modern Library, 1937).

260. Arthur K. Smith, Jr., "Socio-Economic Development and Political Democracy: A Causal Analysis," *Midwest Journal of Political Science,* **13,** No. 1 (February 1969): 95–125.

261. F.B. Smith, *The Making of the Second Reform Bill* (Cambridge, England: Cambridge University Press, 1966).

262. Vernon Smith, "Incentive Compatible Mechanisms for the Provision of Public Goods," in R.D. Auster and B. Sears (eds.), *American . . . ,* pp. 97–106.

263. ——, "The Principle of Unanimity and Voluntary Consent in Social Choice," *Journal of Political Economy,* **85,** No. 6 (1977): 1125–39.

264. ——, "Incentive Compatible Experimental Processes for the Provision of Public Goods, *Research in Experimental Economics,* (Greenwich Conn.: JAI Press, 1979 forthcoming.

265. ——, "Experimental Economics: Induced Value Theory," *American Economic Review.*

266. Julian H. Steward (ed.), *Irrigation Civilizations: A Comparative Study* (Washington, D.C.: Pan American Union, 1955).

267. ——, "Some Implications of the Symposium," in Steward *Irrigation Civilizations . . . ,* pp. 58–78.

268. Michael Spence, "Product Selection, Fixed Costs and Monopolistic Competition" *Review of Economic Studies* (June 1976): 217–36.

269. George J. Stigler, "The Division of Labor is Limited by the Extent of the Market," *Journal of Political Economy,* **59** (June 1951): 185–93.

270. Robert F. Stevenson, *Population and Political Systems in Tropical Africa* (New York: Columbia University Press, 1968).

271. Joseph R. Strayer, *Western Europe in the Middle Ages* (New York: Appleton-Century-Crofts, 1955).

272. ——, "Feudalism in Western Europe," in Coulborn, (ed.), *Feudalism . . . ,* pp. 15–25.

273. ——, *On the Medieval Origins of the Modern State* (Princeton, New Jersey: Princeton University Press, 1970).

274. C.F. Strong, *A History of Modern Political Constitutions* (New York: C.P. Putnam's Sons, 1963).

275. Thomas S. Szasz, *Law, Liberty, and Psychiatry* (New York: Collier Books, 1963).
276. Mark Szeftel, "Aspects of Feudalism in Russian History," in Coulborn (ed.), *Feudalism . . .* , pp. 167–82.
277. Irene Taviss, *The Computer Impact* (Englewood Cliffs, New Jersey: Prentice-Hall, 1970).
278. Romila Thapar, *A History of India* (Baltimore: Penguin, 1966).
279. James W. Thompson, *Economic and Social History of Europe in the Later Middle Ages (1300–1500)* (New York: The Century Co., 1913).
280. Charles M. Tiebout, "A Pure Theory of Local Expenditures," *Journal of Political Economy* (October 1956): 416–24.
281. Charles Tilly, "Reflections on the History of European State-Making," in Tilly (ed.), *The Formation of National States in Western Europe* (Princeton, N.J.: Princeton University Press, 1975), pp. 3–83.
282. N.S. Timasheff, *An Introduction to the Sociology of Law* (Cambridge, Mass.: Harvard University Press, 1939).
283. Arnold Toynbee, *Hellenism* (New York: Oxford University Press, 1959).
284. ——, *Cities on the Move* (New York: Oxford University Press, 1970).
285. George M. Trevelyan, *British History in the Nineteenth Century and After* (New York: David McKay Co., Inc., 1937).
286. Robert C. Tucker, *The Marxian Revolutionary Idea* (New York: W.W. Norton and Co., 1969).
287. Henry Tulkens and Alex Jacquemin, "The Cost of Delinquency: A Problem of Optimal Allocation of Private and Public Expenditures," Center for Operations Research and Econometrics Discussion Paper No. 7133, Universite Catholique de Louvain, August 1971 (mimeographed).
288. Gordon Tullock, *Toward A Mathematics of Politics* (Ann Arbor: University of Michigan Press, 1967).
289. ——, (ed.), *Explorations in the Theory of Anarchy* (Blacksburg, Virginia: Public Choice Society, 1972).
290. ——, "The Edge of the Jungle," in Tullock, (ed.), *Explorations . . .* , pp. 65–75.
291. ——, *The Social Dilemma: The Economics of War and Revolution* (Blacksburg, Virginia: University Publications, 1974).
292. ——, "The Transitional Gains Trap," *Bell Journal of Economics* 6, No. 25 (Autumn 1975): 671–78.
293. Frederick J. Turner, *The Frontier in American History* (New York: Henry Holt, 1948).
294. George Vernadsky, *The Mongols and Russia* (New Haven: Yale University Press, 1953).
295. Sir Paul Vinogradoff, *Outlines of Historical Jurisprudence* (London: Oxford University Press, 1922).
296. Jaime Vicens Vives, *Approaches to the History of Spain* (Berkeley, California: University of California Press, 1967).

297. Daniel Waley, *The Italian City-Republics* (New York: McGraw-Hill, 1969).
298. Richard L. Walker, *The Multi-State System of Ancient China* (Hamden, Conn.: Shoestring Press, 1953).
299. Imanuel Wallerstein, *The Modern World-System* (New York: Academic Press, 1974).
300. Max Weber, *Essays in Sociology* (New York: Oxford University Press, 1946).
301. J. Wenders, "Collusion and Entry," *Journal of Political Economy,* **79** (Nov/Dec. 1971): 1258–77.
302. T.J. Wertenbaker, *The Puritan Oligarchy* (New York: Charles Scribner's Sons, 1947).
303. Robert G. Wesson, *The Imperial Order* (Berkeley, California: University of California Press, 1967).
304. K.C. Wheare, *Federal Government* (4th ed., New York: Oxford University Press, 1964).
305. Paul Wheatley, *The Pivot of the Four Quarters* (Edinburgh: Edinburgh University Press, 1971).
306. Ralph K. White and Ronald Lippitt, *Autocracy and Democracy: An Experimental Inquiry* (New York: Harper and Brothers, 1960).
307. John A. Wilson, *The Burden of Egypt* (Chicago: University of Chicago Press, 1951).
308. Karl A. Wittfogel, *Oriental Despotism* (New Haven, Conn.: Yale University Press, 1957).
309. Donald Wittman, "Two Views of Procedure," *Journal of Legal Studies,* **3** (January 1974): 249–56.
310. ——, "Punishment as Retribution," Theory and Decision, **4**, Nos. 3/4 (February/April 1974): 209–39.
311. Charles Wolf, Jr., "The Political Effects of Economic Programs: Some Indications from Latin America," *Economic Development and Cultural Change* (October 1965): 1–20.
312. Alan Wolfe, "New Directions in the Marxist Theory of Politics, *Politics and Society* (Winter 1974): 131–59.
313. Roy I. Wolfe, *Transportation and Politics* (Princeton, N.J.: D. Van Nostrand Co. 1963).
314. Anthony Wood, *Nineteenth Century Britain:* (London: Longmans, 1960).
315. Michael Young and Peter Willmott, *The Symmetrical Family* (New York: Pantheon Books, 1973).
316. Alfred Zimmern, *The Greek Commonwealth* (New York: Random House, 1956).

# NOTES

## INTRODUCTION AND CHAPTER I

1. In the usual probabalistic sense of modern science.

2. See Auster, "Private Markets in Public Goods (or Qualities)"; all qualities are public goods, albeit often crowded.

3. Aggregate consumption adjusts between 80–90% in 15–20 years. Individual consumption items such as housing services may take as long as 15–20 years. Autos might take 4–5 years (according to L. Taylor in private conversation).

4. Bataglio et al. point out that with seven observations an absolute percentage error of as much as 3.5% will prevent the determination of the slope of a demand curve as being different from –1 even when price is measured perfectly.

5. An institution is a formal organization, that is, an organization of human activity by means of rules, as opposed to completely free interaction which is another form of organization.

6. In a slave society, some people may partially control others. This does not mean that these people are objects; they are simply more constrained than others. Every living thing faces constraints. For some purposes, however, it might be useful to consider these individuals as quasi-objects.

7. See also Buchanan (1975), pp. 67–71, and Tullock (1974), p. 10, for a recent exposition of a similar position.

8. This emphasis on *current* control is consistent with J. S. Mill's view of the evolution of private property:

Enough is known of rude ages both from history and from analogous states of society in our own time, to show that tribunals (which always precede laws) were originally established, not to determine rights, but to repress violence and terminate quarrels. With this object chiefly in view, they naturally enough gave legal effect to first occupancy, by threatening as the aggressor the person who first commenced violence, by turning, or attempting to turn, another out of possession (p. 201).

9. Page 120.

10. Timasheff, p. 100.

11. Page 8. Durkheim's idea is expanded and applied by Donald Wittman in his "Punishment as Retribution."

12. There are at least two other approaches: control the level of public goods, or produce the optimal set of "property rights." All three views are, of course, interrelated.

13. A result sometimes referred to as "the Central Theorem of Classical Welfare Economics."

14. It is sometimes argued that the government might be viewed as functioning in such a situation so as to ensure competitiveness. The presence of market power in the hands of any individual, however, necessarily implies the existence of an externality producing activity – namely, "output restriction." Under competition the individual bears the full costs of reducing output, but when market power is present, this is no longer true.

15. Page 24.

16. Tullock (1972), p. 73.

17. Schapera, p. 105.

18. See the seminal discussions of Becker and Ehrlich.

19. For example, Erlich (1977).

20. Social attitudes toward crimes are, moreover, not given. They may evolve to reflect different eases of apprehension. For example,

... in the Trobriand (as in many other places in Melanesia) it is vital to the self-respect of a native that he should be reported a good gardener and well supplied with food, and the shame and ridicule attaching to a theft of vegetables (very difficult to detect) would make life insupportable [A. S. Diamond (1951), p. 50].

21. Alternatively, $\phi$ might be more objectively defined as the expected percentage reduction in the individual's "wage" as a result of criminal acts.

22. Tulkens and Jacquemin.

23. Ehrlich.

24. Tulkens and Jacquemin, p. 5.

25. For a further discussion of the latter type of punishment, see A. R. Radcliffe-Brown and Timasheff, p. 108.

26. Service, p. 240.

27. Along the same lines the Frankish kings were mainly concerned with the professional thief (*criminosus*) "who could not be dealt with under the system of kindred responsibility because he was as a rule without family ties and by flight could easily evade the justice of the clan" (Seagle, p. 75).

28. This in turn is based on common ancestry, culture, religion, economic status, etc. See Malinowski, pp. 257–58.

29. Crisis situations have interesting effects. When a crisis occurs or a "great national leader" arises, the sense of oneness of the people increases and this in turn increases the level of order, which increases the people's satisfaction. To a certain extent their common perception of this improvement may further their sense of oneness and induce further rounds of

improvement, unfolding a type of "multiplier" process. It is interesting to speculate on the stability of this process; however, this work will not consider dynamics explicitly.

30. Efforts in modern times to actually redistribute income have not been very success-ful, which leads one to wonder if there are not some natural limits on our ability to redis-tribute. In the U.S. the total costs of welfare programs in 1968 amounted to $18,000 per family of four in the bottom 20% of the income distribution—hardly what they were re-ceiving. See the discussion between G. Tullock and L. Thurow, *American Re-evolution, Papers and Proceedings,* Auster and Sears eds.

31. See also Appendix II.

32. Andenaes, Packer, pp. 48–53.

33. Andenaes, Blumstein, Cohen, and Nagin, Ehrlich (1977), Silver (1975).

34. The following discussion was to a large degree inspired by the seminal researchers of LaPiere, Chapter 7, and Rusche and Kirchheimer, Chapters 2 and 3.

35. A. S. Diamond (1951).

36. Certain crimes, such as incest, which were considered high spiritual offenses, were, however, excepted. See Bloch, p. 129; A. S. Diamond (1935), pp. 283, 304, 320–21; S. Dia-mond, p. 133; Hoebel (1961), p. 121; Radin, p. 258; Rusche and Kirchheimer, Chapters 2 and 3; Sellin, pp. 14–18, 25–29; and Vinogradoff, pp. 177, 190–91.

37. It seems as if the Talmud does not even say "an eye *for* an eye"; it says "an eye *instead* of an eye." Why "instead"? As the oral tradition, without whose aid the under-standing of Torah is impossible, makes clear "instead" means something of equal individual importance to an "eye." We are indebted to Rabbi B. C. Schloime Twerski, Talmudic Re-search Institute, Denver, for discussion of this point. See also Tractate *Baba Kama,* 83, side 2. Simply requiring compensation is still not enough to achieve the social optimum, however, unless criminals are always caught.

38. Sellin, pp. 29, 39–41. Some may wonder about recent exposes of modern torture. These, however, appear notable because they are exceptions.


## CHAPTER 2

1. F. Engels is one exception. Marx's great collaborator used anthropological data to construct or test a theory of the state. The relationship between ours and Engels' theories is explored in this Chapter. Interestingly many of the pre-20th century economists em-ployed our type of data.

2. This definition follows in the footsteps of several anthropologists: Childe, p. 158, refers to full-time "ruler," Fried, p. 235, speaks of "specialized institutions" responsible for "differential access to basic resources . . . and defense," Wittfogel, p. 239, says the state involves "government by professionals," and Johnson, p. 2, speaks of a "specialized de-cision making organization." Our view is similar to that expressed by Hans Kelsen:

> To be a state, the legal order must have the character of an organization in the manner and specific sense of this word, that is, it must establish organs who, in the manner of division of labor, create and apply the norms that constitute the legal orders, it must display a certain degree of centralization. The state is a relatively centralized legal order (p. 286).

See also Elvin.

3. Ultimately these are economies of scale which result from the various forces usually cited [e.g., by Smith (Book 1, Chapter 2, Chapter 3, p. 17) and others].

4. See North and Thomas, p. 7. For a lucid general discussion of the factors responsible for the proliferation of "strategic elites" and survey of the sociological literature regarding the "division of labor," see Keller, Chapter 3.

5. Page 119.

6. Sometimes a society passes first through an intermediate (non-state) stage in which employees (e.g., jailers and policemen) have become full-time specialists but not their employers (superiors).

7. All firms (organizations) are owned (controlled). In our view Lenski's "proprietary theory of the agrarian state" (pp. 210–17, 318–19) is best understood as an attempt to deal with the questions of the magnitude and form of exploitative "earnings" by ruling states. A general analysis of these questions is presented in Chapter 5.

8. Thus, Young and Willmott, p. 287, take note of the "paradox of modern society," that "as people have become more and more dependent upon each other, as the ever expanding division of labor has brought more millions within its net, they have not necessarily felt any the more united to those whom they were bound by ties of self-interest. They may feel less."

9. Olson (1965), p. 35. This conclusion does not hold if individuals are allowed to take some account of the effects of their actions on others and learn by experience. If they can, then anarchy can provide more or less than the optimum level of public good and size can cause the level provided to increase or decrease (Auster mimeo 1977).

10. See North and Thomas, pp. 6–7.

11. A number of sacred texts postulate the existence of a golden age which preceded the emergence of the state. According to the epic of the Aryanization of India (ca. 1000–700 B.C.E.), "with the passage of time conditions changed and men turned wicked; there were thefts, strife, and insecurity . . . the gods were alarmed, and when men prayed to them to be saved, Brahmadeva created a code of law and enforced it through his son Virajas. Thus was the state born, and thus was born the first king . . . " (Gokhale, p. 102). The Buddhist version differs in that it attributes the origin of the state not to divine intervention but to the fact that "weary of the oppressive conditions, the people elected a king . . . . " (Gokhale, p. 102). The view that the state was preceded by a golden age is not inconsistent with our stress upon the demand-increasing effects of increased society size.

12. Page 18.

13. Bairey.

14. Lucki, pp. 27–28.

15. Moore, pp. 245–250.

16. Rosenberg, pp. 33–40.

17. Pages 42–43.

18. Pages 74–75.

19. Page 11.

20. Page 64.

21. This factor is noted by Durkheim (Book II, Chapter 2).

22. Hoebel (1961), pp. 67–68; Shorter, pp. 39–40, 67, 97; and A. S. Diamond (1951), p. 28.

23. See Salzman.

24. Hole, p. 358; Gibson, p. 454.

25. Hammond, pp. 163–164.

26. Sanders and Price, pp. 140–41.

27. Sanders and Price, pp. 33–34; Coe, pp. 151–53; Sanders (1968), pp. 340–41; Sanders (1972; Steward, p. 64; Adams, pp. 74–76; Palerm and Wolf, pp. 3–5.

28. Krader, pp. 68–69.

29. Krader, pp. 68–69; Pirenne, pp. 25–27; Portal, pp. 37–38; Szeftel, pp. 168 and 180.

30. Carsten, pp. 102 and 113.

31. Page 341.

32. Waley, p. 56.

33. Waley, p. 14.

34. Hyde, p. 102.

35. Waley, p. 68.

36. Waley, pp. 35, 37, 68.

37. Wheatley, pp. 256–98.

38. Pages 80–82.

39. Page 12.

40. Page 24.

41. The myth of the original ancestor and social contract theories of the state all tend to support the legitimacy of the existing distribution of power. Some African societies have attempted order production by a belief in common ancestry or a legendary founding of their settlement by a great hero (Elias, pp. 14–15). People tend to feel at least partially bound by their past commitments and similarly to feel bound by the past commitments of their ancestors. When society devotes resources to propagating these myths or beliefs it produces order indirectly.

42. Page 78,

43. Pages 117–118.

44. Page 426.

45. Herodotus, as reported by Lipson, pp. 66–67.

46. Page 74.

47. Goody, p. 18.

48. Mair, pp. 166–67.

49. Pages 217–18. See also Bennett.

50. See Nozick, p. 17. Indirect evidence supporting this line of reasoning is provided by the frequency with which states defeated in war must confront internal hostility and revolution. Of course, other explanations of this linkage should not be ignored (see Appendix II).

51. See Douglas.

52. Mair, p. 210.

53. See Andreski (1968), pp. 81–83.

54. Reported in Mair, pp. 229–30.

55. Page 178.

56. (1974), p. 25.

57. See Buber for an excellent analysis of the early socialist literature and where it went wrong.

58. See Wittfogel, Chapter 9.

59. Page 59; see also Keller, pp. 47–54.

60. To be sure, struggles often arise because the "rich" typically desire more punishment than the "poor" just as the "strong" desire less than the "weak." The reader should consult Buchanan (1972) for an illuminating analysis of this type of struggle.

61. A. Wolfe.

62. Pages 301–7.

63. Priest-run societies where the priests themselves are interested in ascetism might provide an interesting counterexample to the notion that the economic rulers run the state.

64. See Deutcher.

65. And inconsistent with the factor price equalization theorem of international trade.

66. Pages 231–32.
67. Page 235.
68. Page 186.
69. Page 185.
70. Plamenatz, pp. 351–56.
71. For example, Arrow (1963).
72. (1968), p. 15.
73. Pages 53–56, 75–76.

## CHAPTER 3

1. See Auster (1977).
2. This last is determined by the other two only for a given efficiency in production – which may not be the case.
3. This seems the most direct way of approaching the issue of optimal jurisdiction size. See also McGuire or the most general, but still somewhat incomplete analysis in Auster-Silver (1973).
4. In the presence of large vacant lands the population, as it increases, could actually be expected to spread itself out so as to maintain a roughly constant density because of diminishing returns to land and labor in the production of both material and psychic well-being.
5. In general, the higher this level of order the higher the minimum ATC.
6. The reader will now recognize that we are talking about a crowded, as opposed to a pure, public good (Ellickson, McGuire, Pauly). In terms of that literature, we are discussing the emergence of new jurisdictions. Our approach differs from that of most previous researchers in that our focus is on the institutions which have to produce the level of order.
7. See Chapter 2.
8. Pryor (pp. 102–3) finds, for 18 countries in 1858 and 29 countries in 1958 that total military personnel and population are significantly positively correlated.
9. The shirking problem although recognized by the earlier economists (Cantillon, Smith, Mill, Marx, and Marshall, for example; it can also be found in the Bible) fell into disuse until revived by the authors in a still often-neglected piece included here as Appendix I. See Rosenberg, Chapter 5, for a fascinating discussion of the attempts of Prussian Kings Frederick William I and Frederick II to deal with the shirking problem.
10. Page 116. Here the people who perform the role of political leadership are a class in much the same way that doctors and lawyers are. See also Mosca, Chapter 2.
11. See Chapter 6.
12. R. Wolfe, Chapter 2; R. Muir, Part 7.
13. See part (2).
14. Page 37.
15. Page 80.
16. The largest political unit in which tax policy is effectively coordinated (p. 61).
17. That the issue depends on the E.S. is not noted by Friedman. He avoids simultaneous equations bias quite cleverly, however, by using annexation data, thus circumventing the issue of the endogenous nature of taxes.
18. The Mayflower Compact is an exception.
19. Tullock (1974), pp. 17–19. The situation of the American Indians being a case in point.

20. Hart, pp. 53–58.

21. Wesson, p. 44.

22. Andreski (1968), p. 86.

23. Sjoberg (pp. 69–77) discusses the issue of the impact of the state on the growth and diffusion of cities. A related topic. MacIver (p. 53), on the other hand, believes that "the city is the first condition of empire" but he attributes this to "concentration of wealth."

24. Ostrogorsky, pp. 34–35; Jones, preface.

25. Burns, pp. 100–101; Katz, pp. 97–98.

26. Pirenne, especially pp. 26–27; Strayer (1955), p. 60; Hodgett.

27. A.S. Diamond (1951), p. 129; Hay, p. 25.

28. Hay (1964), p. 35, Lloyd, p. 242.

29. Hammond, pp. 152–53.

30. See Chapter 2.

31. Coulborn, pp. 261–62; Bodde, p. 50; Latourette, pp. 116–19; Eberhard, pp. 99–102, 107–65.

32. Hammond, p. 150.

33. Edgerton, 125–26; Coulborn, 261–62.

34. Previously noted in Chapter 2.

35. Or at least by a small number of large states such as Isin and Larsa, Hatti, Mittani, etc. The urban focus of these empires moved northward in Mesopotamia probably as a result of gradual salting-up of the south (Hammond, p. 67; Claiborne, pp. 283–85). Adams (p. 68) has strongly attacked the view that large-scale irrigation management played a major role in centralization.

36. Hammond, p. 55.

37. Pages 118–19.

38. Hammond, pp. 163–64.

39. Lopez, pp. 258–59.

40. Cipolla, p. 141. Urban fertility and mortality were approximately the same.

41. Hammond, pp. 208–10; Tilly, p. 76.

42. Eberhard, pp. 51–56, 62, and 68; Gernet, Chapters 3–4; Bodde, pp. 50 and 69; Walker, Chapter 2.

43. Reischauer, p. 44; Hall, pp. 279–80.

44. Keith, pp. 9–13; Lanning, pp. 115–22, 127–41, 151–71; Service, p. 353; Carniero, p. 430; Collier; Máson, pp. 100–107.

45. Ehrenberg, pp. 27–31.

46. Lanning, p. 140–41.

47. Portal, p. 54; see also Vernadsky, pp. 341 and 350.

48. Page 15. Langer also cautions against the assumption that all areas experienced a heavy loss of life and were turned into virtually depopulated deserts. Many areas were plundered, but the "brunt of the invasion fell on Riazan, Vladimir, and Southern Russia."

49. *New York Times,* January 10, 1977.

50. Riley, p. 36, Wilson, p. 14.

51. Toynbee, p. 47.

52. Riley, p. 36; Wilson, p. 43, Frankfort, pp. 17–20; Edgerton, pp. 121–126. While construction of the irrigation system (mainly accomplished by clearing the jungle lands) appears to have gone on for a long time before national unification (Wilson, p. 31) its effect towards promoting national unity was no doubt also positive.

53. There may be other explanations as well. These are implicitly discussed in Chapter 5, where the monopoly power of states is considered.

54. This neglects the issue of food and siege.

55. Military technology may also be more amenable to large scale since heavy equipment is more important there.

56. Pages 195–209.

57. See Chamberlain's seminal discussion (pp. 129–32, 136–37).

58. See Stigler; Caves and Murphy, p. 574. It might be argued that if population grows and becomes less culturally homogeneous (e.g., as a result of conquest) substates will proliferate in response to *diversity in demand* for state services rather than in response to cost considerations. However, this does not necessarily follow: Firms can and often do produce different "qualities" for different markets.

59. We ignore the possibility of higher information costs resulting from the disintegration of technically compatible operations.

60. Ghirshman, p. 144. For Latin America see Glassman, pp. 84–86, 92–102.

61. Portal, pp. 66–68 and 112–13; Mirsky, pp. 147–49.

62. Shaw, pp. 3–7. Note also the widespread Indian practice of leaving an established ruler in charge of a conquered territory with the understanding that a fixed percentage of his states' revenue (*chauth*) would be turned over in return for external protection by the conquerors (Burling, pp. 69–70).

63. Feudal societies have existed not only in Western Europe (see Bloch; Forquin, Ganshof, pp. 50–53; Lyons, pp. 129–34; Strayer, 1965), but also in Japan under the Tokugawa shoguns (Coulborn, pp. 279–80; Reischauer) and perhaps in China (Bodde); see also Andreski's excellent discussion (1965, pp. 152–62). The sale of positions in the bureaucracy by 17th and 18th century French monarchs has been viewed as a step in the direction of replacing feudalism by a centralized state (Moore, pp. 57–63). See also Wallenstein's discussion of "prebendalization" in China (pp. 57–59). Parry explains this method of recruiting civil servants by noting: "Taxation could not easily be increased, for grants of direct taxation were still regarded in most countries as extraordinary measures to meet particular emergencies, and indirect taxation tended to become fixed by custom (p. 2)."

64. Immunities are explicit or *de facto* promises that (within defined limits) the overlord will not intervene into relations between a lord and his vassals or serfs [Andreski (1965), pp. 155–56].

65. Pages 12–13.

66. Forquin, p. 19, Jelavich and Jelavich, p. 20; Burling, pp. 55–56, 82–83.

67. Page 169.

68. Krieger, p. 4.

69. Dunn, pp. 48–55 and 69–79.

70. See Olson and Zeckhauser.

71. Clarke, pp. 179–180; Faber, 19–20; Toynbee (1959), pp. 105–110.

72. Coulborn, p. 21.

73. Reischauer, pp. 31–33.

74. Coulborn, p. 206; Strayer (1965), pp. 21–22.

75. Federations for no purpose (e.g., imitation) just seem to fall apart. See also Wheare.

76. (1968), p. 94. See also Dahl, p. 136; Huntington (1964), pp. 32–33; Pollard, p. 255, Riker (1964); Strong, p. 235.

77. Andreski (1968), pp. 79–80.

78. Pages 47–49.

79. Andreski (1968, pp. 75–78) suggests that oscillations in the military balance between offense and defense have been important in causing oscillations in political concentration.

80. Auster-Silver (1973).

81. But Andreski (1968, pp. 88–90) notes that improvement in communications may sometimes foster nationalism which operates as a "frictional factor." In addition, recent research (R.D. Auster, 1978) suggests that completely homogeneous populations have no free-rider problem. Unfortunately approximately homogeneous populations may have a large one.


## CHAPTER 4

1. Court, Muth, Lancaster, Becker . . . .

2. Sandmo makes rigorous the notion of the "use" of a public good, also by employing the approach we use here. In some instances, how much of the good an individual gets may vary, even when the good is a public good. In feudal times, the closer one was to the fort, the more protected he was against attack. See also Davis and Whinston, Demsetz, Minasion, Mishan. . . .

3. Ellickson.

4. The material in this section is partly based on Auster-Silver (1973).

5. See Ng or Tullock (1967). The new incentive compatible mechanisms, which are discussed in Chapter 8, are ultimate counterexamples.

6. The curves are drawn on the usual convexity assumptions about tastes and the technology. One cannot infer that Figure 5 is generally the case; however, given the world we live in, it seems likely to be.

7. As would seem to have been suggested by Head and Shoup, who use a diagram similar to ours, but implicitly assume an "all private" or "all public" social choice. Their notion of a good resembles our notion of a desire and in this sense we assume that many goods are in their third category of "ambiguous goods."

8. Homogeneous of degree one with $[F_{L \cdot K}]$ and $[H_{L \cdot K}]$ negative semidefinite of rank 1.

9. More likely at least on the basis of Orzechowski's work.

10. See Becker (1965).

11. Earlier it was argued that the same level of services would be more easily provided by public goods with higher density. A sort of reverse crowding was postulated. Missiles perhaps provide an example of such a good (Auster-Silver). Similarly, Borcherding and Deacon, using a different methodology, observe positive correlations between a measure of urbanization and per capita state expenditures on fire, police, and sanitation in regressions including total population as an independent variable. Bergstrom and Goodman, however, find that (for all states taken together) population density is positively correlated with total municipal expenditures on police but negatively correlated with total general expenditure. The regression coefficients of density for the 10 individual states included in the study fluctuate in sign and statistical significance. See also Litvack and Oates.

12. We also assume away the problem that an increase in the level of order will necessarily decrease the shirking problem and therefore increase the extent of returns of scale, possibly causing society to have a different shape for its production possibilities curve.

13. See Chapter 1. At this point we employ the objective definition of order — i.e., the expected percentage reduction in the individual's "wage" as a consequence of crime. The two are equivalent for risk-neutral individuals and the argument in the text is valid so long as the person is not a risk-seeker.

14. If, for example, a reduction in guilt lowers the relative marginal productivity of resources devoted to order production (e.g., because informants are less likely to come for-

ward to the police ) the intercept of the transformation curve on the $G$-axis decreases by more than $G_1 - G_2$ – the curve shifts to the left and becomes steeper. Under this circumstance an increase in the equilibrium value of $Q$ (decline in resources to order production) is conceivable. This would depend in part on elasticities of demand.

15. The level of order will decrease, thereby increasing shirking. This tends to decrease the importance of returns to scale and, therefore, the importance of the state in the production of order. It could in and of itself lead to secession (see Chapter 5).

16. Linebarger, pp. 19–21.

17. Through its effect on the shirking-monitoring problem and through that on the shape of the ATC curve.

18. The paragraph which follows represents the views of Auster as opposed to Silver.

## CHAPTER 5

1. The state is generally recognized as being possessed of monopoly power. Among the Ashanti of the Gold Coast only the king may kill and the penalty for suicide is decapitation, the same as for any homicide (Schapera, pp. 236–37). The punishment is actually carried out. Among the ancient Mesopotamians, a single god, Enlil, represents the state as sheriff and commander of the armed forces. The king was viewed as the human whose function was to exercise Enlil's monopoly (Jacobsen). It appears that even the word "monopoly" itself is derived from the "king's Monopoly" or his exclusive right to produce certain things.

2. That is, would give up everything else rather than lose them.

3. See the discussion at the end of chapter 3.

4. Auster-Silver (1973).

5. Of course, this may only be a perception of a cost difference rather than a real difference. Taxes require tax collectors and tax assessors, and this creates other problems which we will turn to in Chapter 6.

6. In the U.S. the police were exempt from the draft.

7. For example, Diamond (1951), p. 24.

8. (1972), pp. 516–17. The supporting anthropological evidence can be found in Hoebel (1961), pp. 120–21, 139, 158; Lowie, p. 400, 450; Mair, pp. 17–41, 59–60; Meek, p. 250; Colson, pp. 34–44; and Redfield. For similar evidence on Greece and Rome, see Robson, pp. 91–92.

9. An organization that forcibly takes without producing service is not a state at all but a gang of armed robbers or racketeers. History, however, is full of borderline cases in which it is difficult to tell which "princes" were robbers and which were cops (see Lane, p. 414; Claiborne, pp. 266–67). Moreover, as Lane (p. 414) has noted: "A plunderer would become in effect the chief of police as soon as he regularized his 'take,' adapted it to the capacity to pay, defended his preserve against other plunderers, and maintained his territorial monopoly long enough for custom to make it legitimate."

10. A classic example is provided by the crumbling during the 18th century of the predatory Mogul state in India in the face of small and divided European forces (Moore, p. 324).

11. Friedrich, pp. 60–61; North and Thomas, p. 97 ff.

12. Gluckman, p. 136.

13. See Frolich, Oppenheimer, and Young, pp. 62–65.

14. See Breton, pp. 93–96.

15. Szeftel, pp. 169–171.

16. Moore, pp. 238, 332.

17. Moore, pp. 355, 378-85; Jessup, pp. 108-9.

18. Niskanen expresses a similar view (pp. 130-31). Similarly, the U.S. founding fathers' concern with States' Rights may have come from their desire to limit the power of all levels of government (see also Chapter 3).

19. This is essentially the Tiebout hypothesis. It is discussed in more detail in subsequent chapters.

20. See Martin and McKenzie.

21. Szeftel, pp. 176-77.

22. Admittedly, this may only be exploitation of one part of the population for the benefit of another, which may always be the case.

23. Breton, pp. 87-90.

24. Dahmus, p. 351.

25. Merriam, p. 161.

26. Tullick (1972), p. 66.

27. Gullick, p. 118.

28. Breton, pp. 90-93.

29. Tullock (1971) has imaginatively applied what might be called the private interest theory of public choice to the question of the sources of revolutionary activity. Silver uses Tullock's analysis as a point of departure in grouping historical revolutions into meaningful types and in considering who is most likely to become a revolutionary (see Appendix II).

30. Our emphasis here on exploitation by the state should not be misunderstood. Some part of the return to any state is perceived as the legitimate payment for services rendered. The production of order in society must be paid for.

31. See Wenders.

32. Page 98.

33. Pages 137-38.

34. Page 98.

35. In addition to the Hittites, prominent examples include the Hyskos in Egypt, the Kassites in Mesopotamia, and the Mongols in China and elsewhere. See also Krader, pp. 49-52, and Lowie (1962), pp. 20-21.

36. Pages 266-67. See also de Jouvenal, p. 28.

37. Page 202.

38. Page 310. A cardinal principle of Confucianism, "the man on the throne should be worthy and any worthy man is eligible for the throne," encourages ambitious men to believe they can do a better job than the current rulers (Houn, p. 43). No wonder the present communist rulers of China are reported to consider Confucianism subversive.

39. See Graves, "I Claudius."

40. Burns, pp. 113-21.

41. Krieger's (pp. 6-8, 11) perceptive comments are worth quoting: "The idea of divine right, in its application to kingship, went back to the Middle Ages; in this sense it signified the sacred origination of the royal office . . . . The divine right of kings, however, was a more modern product, developing during the 16th and 17th centuries to extend the sanctity of the king's 'body politic' into his natural body. This extension was a response both to the psychological need for a visible symbol . . . and to the political need for a distinctive blessing upon kings vis-à-vis the more indiscriminate anointment of any office holder in the hierarchy of public authorities . . . . For kings, their position at the apex of the divinely constructed social ladder called for obedience even when the benefits of their government were not in evidence."

42. Pages 80-86.

43. In a recent talk in Tucson, Gene McCarthy complained that he'd been outmaneuvered here. Carter claimed to talk to Jesus, while Ford said he had a regular relationship with God, leaving Gene only the Holy Spirit.

44. This position is Auster's, as opposed to Silver's.

45. For an extended discussion of the interface between government and the media the reader might consult the Sunday discussion in *American Re-evolution* (Auster, Sears eds.).

46. These matters are discussed in greater detail in R.D. Auster (August 1977).

47. Of course, one should not ignore the possibility that the government, through its activities of requiring forms, plans, prior approval, etc., so hampers production in the private sector that $\partial I/\partial G$ is negative. If the rational ruler realizes this, he will then produce too little G. In general, $dP_g/dG = U_G/U_Q + \partial I/\partial G$.

48. Partridge, pp. 21-24.

49. Lane (pp. 416-17) applies the traditional approach when he defines the state's monopoly profit or "tribute" in terms of a difference between production costs and "the highest prices the traffic would bear."

50. The argument is not exact because $U_2$ on the left-hand side of Equation (8) is being evaluated at a different point than $U_2$ on the right-hand side. Here the difference is neglected. Later we make something of it.

51. Moore, pp. 474-75.


## CHAPTER 6

1. Lipset defines modern or "liberal" democracy as a "political system which supplies regular constitutional opportunities for changing the governing officials. It is a social mechanism for the resolution of the problem of societal decision making among conflicting interest groups which permits the largest part of the population to influence the decisions through their ability to choose among alternative contenders for political office. In large measure . . . this definition implies a number of specific conditions: (a) a 'political formula,' a system of beliefs, legitimizing the democratic system and specifying the institutions — parties, a free press, and so forth — which are legitimized, i.e., accepted as proper by all; (b) one set of political leaders in office; and (c) one or more sets of leaders, out of office, who act as a legitimate opposition attempting to gain office (p. 71)." Or as MacIver puts it: "Democracy is not a way of governing . . . but primarily a way of determining who shall govern and, broadly, to what ends . . . . The people . . . do not and cannot govern; they control the government (p. 59)." Mayo agrees and adds that "Political systems can be classified as more or less democratic according to a number of criteria (periodic mass elections, equal voting, political freedom) associated with popular control and designed to make it effective; only if a particular system meets the tests of a substantial number of these criteria do we . . . call it democratic" (p. 60). See also Rostow and Schumpeter, pp. 269-73.

2. Data available from Auster on request.

3. See the discussion of the reasons for this in Auster (May 1977).

4. As does the artifice of allowing the League of Women Voters to ignore any minor candidates in their TV debates.

5. Let us belabor the obvious. Traditionally, the theory of the firm speaks of the owners of the firm, but little thought is given to the meaning of the verb "to own." It would seem that the person or group of persons who decide the distribution of net revenues of the firm are its true owners. Of necessity, those individuals who make the firm's other decisions control the distribution of the firm's net revenues. Even when the income of such indi-

viduals is in the form of contractual payments they remain owners of the firm. Over time the contract will adjust to absorb any permanent increase in profits; in the short run fluctuations in the profit level will be absorbed by retained earnings. It makes little or no sense to speak of a separation of ownership from control. Control is ownership. The stockholders are the owners of the stock of the firm, a bundle of vague rights including a residual claim to the firm's capital and the collective right to replace the board of directors. The firm is not its capital, just as it is not its labor. It is a decision mechanism and is necessarily owned by the people who make the decisions.

6. This and the public nature of the product may in part explain the generally greater interest in national elections than in stockholders' meetings [see also Silver (1973)]. It would be interesting, however, to see if there were any relationship between participation by categories in stockholders' meetings, including the sending in of proxies, and voting participation (say by sex or race or some other category).

7. At some points, however, it becomes unclear whether the citizen owns the state or the state the citizen. Laws which entirely regulate personal conduct, for example, suggest that the citizen does not even own his own body. Such policies, however, are sometimes attempts by the ruler to lower his cost of producing order by transforming the population into a more culturally homogeneous group (Wallenstein, pp. 147-57) which is, of course, easier to exploit.

8. It is not clear whether or not this disintegration of the order producing industry is good or bad. Silver (1977) has stressed that this represents more competition since those are substitute ways of producing order. Auster feels however, that the judiciary and police, for example, may also be viewed as complementary factors in the production of order. As early as Cournot it was shown that it is better to have perfect complements produced by a single monopolist than by competing monopolists. The issue would appear to depend on the elasticity of demand for order and the elasticities of substitution among the various factors which produce order.

9. When the profit-maximizing level of profits is negative, the optimal level of public good is zero.

10. Even in the limit of this overproduction, citizens would not be indifferent to having no state and their present situation. That would only be true if public and private goods had identical factor intensities.

11. See Appendix III.

12. See Quigley, pp. 49-59, for a variety of examples. Perfect identification exists when the individual's utility function depends directly on social aggregates as opposed to personal levels.

13. Again, see Appendix III.

14. See Downs (1957).

15. Actually there is some reason to believe that public goods will be de-emphasized by representative democracies relative to private goods. Aranson and Ordeshook have provided some theoretical basis for this apparent tendency in the U.S. There are no doubt many inefficiencies produced by our current system which are not fully discussed here.

16. May we assume that no one would argue that it did not succeed in doing so immediately. Stalin's power clearly exceeded that of even FDR.

17. The limit on exploitation is determined by the overall distribution of goods in the sense of the ratio of property owned by the political ruling class to those held by the rest of society—one could make this even more continuous and more complicated. But there doesn't seem to be much point in doing so in our present context.

18. Auster as opposed to Silver.

19. Silver has a taste for democracy.

20. Pages 49–51.

21. Auster-Silver "Comparative Statics of the Utility Maximizing Firm," SEJ, (April 1976).

22. The demand curve is $Q = A \cdot P^B$, $B < 0$.

23. Similarly, the greater the size of the elasticity of demand the more likely is backward bendingness. There is also a possibility of instability; however, we do not consider that issue here.

24. An earlier version of the remainder of this chapter was published by Auster in Leiter and Sirkin (eds.).

25. There is also variation in the levels of characteristics across civil service jobs. The position of policeman has considerable status and power relative to that of garbage collector. One possible test of the theory presented here would be to see if there was a positive relationship between the way in which various ethnic groups ranked jobs in terms of status and their composition *ceteris paribus* in these jobs.

26. Admittedly, some jobs may have zero levels of some characteristics.

27. The length of the list is unimportant and perhaps indeterminate. The relative importance, quantitatively, of the various factors is, however, an interesting issue. We do not propose to address it.

28. On the other hand, the hiring process may attempt to take account of the possibility that people with characteristics incompatible with the job exist and try to screen them out. More will be said on screening in Chapter 8.

29. Our work, apparently, relates in part to that of Downs (1966) and Niskanen who distinguish various "bureaucratic types"; however, our list is somewhat different and was derived in a different fashion essentially independently of their work. Niskanen's belief that leisure is not an important argument of the individual's utility function is incorrect in our opinion. This belief, although prevalent, is entirely unsupported by any evidence and indeed flies in the face of such evidence as the dramatic decrease in hours worked over the last 70 years, to cite one example. He now appears to have modified his position on this.

30. Of course returns which are negligible for others may not be so for those who are relatively satiated with other forms of gratification, e.g., the ultra-rich, who may also like to gamble.

31. Downs' (1966) "Statesmen" are presumably such people; his "Zealots" comprise some of the people distinguished in the preceding paragraphs.

32. Silver, Appendix II, cites the example of the resistance of the Warsaw ghetto as an example of political participation in the face of certainty of defeat, an illustration of patriotism at work.

33. Both of these tendencies are now apparent.

34. Recognizing this, some police departments now attempt to discover which of their applicants would commit crimes by administering lie-detector tests, etc. Whether such programs in fact work is probably open to debate. Apparently Chicago used to use them and no longer does, but is considering using them again.

35. According to Lester Thurow, in private conversation, in any case.

36. This paragraph is drawn from R. S. Ahlbrandt, Jr., "Demand and Supply Considerations in the Delivery of Public Goods and Services." Mimeo. His conclusions are based on other published studies cited in that work.

37. *New York Times,* April 25, 1970, pp. 1, 18.

38. Ibid, p. 18.

39. Silver does not wish to be associated with this paragraph.

40. Silver has had only good experiences with the police.

41. Auster.

42. Hart.

43. This aspect of the inefficiency of the U.S. Armed Services may, however, be attributable to another factor, which is somewhat less directly tied to the exploitation of the population. The army of a democracy has a tremendous incentive to distort the way in which it fights so as to produce a good public image of war (e.g. by means of low casualty rates). What better way to do this than to have lots of people in the service, but very few people fighting? In that case, most people's war stories will be relatively idyllic tales about pot and women, jokes and fun times, fostering the cult of militarism.

44. See Gordon Tullock's insightful "The Transitional Gains Trap" for a discussion of this same phenomenon in a somewhat broader context. Of course, in Chapter 8 Auster suggests a possible way out of the trap.


## CHAPTER 7

1. An earlier version of this material was published by Silver in Leiter and Sirkin (eds.).

2. See note 1 of Chapter 6 for the working definition of "democracy."

3. Cahill, Trevelyan, Wood. Report on Knapp Commission Study, *New York Times*, December 28, 1972.

4. Deane.

5. Deane.

6. F.B. Smith, Trevelyan, Wood.

7. Reischauer (1964).

8. Lockwood, p. 39.

9. Lockwood, p. 144.

10. Reischauer (1964).

11. Lipson (1948), pp. 19–26.

12. Condliffe, pp. 31–37.

13. Germani, Scobie, pp. 196–204.

14. Board, pp. 30–31.

15. Board, p. 31.

16. K. Samuelson, pp. 187, 199, 210–11.

17. McCord, pp. 255–56; Miller, pp. 30–36.

18. Hammond, pp. 164–68.

19. Lipson (1964), pp. 78–79.

20. Zimmern, pp. 140–41.

21. See Forrest, pp. 35–66; Huxley, pp. 40–41.

22. Frank, pp. 48–50.

23. Brunt, p. 55.

24. Brunt, pp. 57–58; Frank, pp. 49–50.

25. Hay, pp. 32–35.

26. Brucker, pp. 149–50, 380; Hay, p. 119.

27. Cheyney, pp. 129–30.

28. Thompson, p. 403.

29. Hodgett, pp. 209–11.

30. Ferguson, pp. 137–39, 266–67.

31. Page 75.

32. Moore, p. 465.

33. Ferguson, p. 4; Franz, p. 4; Koenigsberger, pp. 85–86.

34. Rising prosperity of the French peasantry prior to 1789 (Moore, pp. 471–72) may have contributed to the revolution, but we have placed greater stress upon declines in the expected cost of revolution caused by the monarchy's attempt to reform from above (see Appendix II).

35. Page 255.

36. (1964), pp. 245–46.

37. Page 83.

38. Page 101.

39. Page 566.

40. Although the arguments are quite different, we sympathize with the conclusions reached by David M. Potter. According to this historian, "the principles of democracy are not universal truths, ignored during centuries of intellectual darkness . . . but rather . . . democracy is the foremost by far of the many advantages which our economic affluence has brought us" (pp. 117–18). Alvin Marty called our attention to a similar statement of J. R. Hicks that increases in wealth facilitate the demand for "liberal democratic goods."

41. Pages 260–69.

42. For a more complete discussion and references to the literature see Silver (1973). Most studies report a positive correlation between the income of individuals and their political participation (see the useful exchange in *Public Choice* among Fraser, Frey, and Russell).

43. Key, p. 17.

44. See Chapter 2.

45. Page 108.

46. Hammond, pp. 37–45.

47. Thapar, p. 51.

48. Brunt, pp. 8–9, 29, 246–77.

49. It seems doubtful that among historical states active consent ever took the form of "direct" democracy without any meaningful trace of "representation." Even in ancient Athens the elected 10 "generals" and the elected Council of 500 may have represented the citizens. "The Council carried on all negotiations with foreign states and received ambassadors; it directed foreign policy. In internal affairs, too, almost everything was under its care; the officials had to report to it; it had supreme authority over all financial matters. Finally, its judicial functions had not entirely gone . . . (and) the Council had a certain right of punishment, especially over officials (Ehrenberg, p. 64)." Moreover, since the Council (or its committee) prepared and guided the affairs of the popular assembly, it was certainly able to make important negative decisions (Hermens, pp. 28, 46). See also Chamberlain's discussion of Rousseau (pp. 112–16). A more fundamental question is raised by the absence of women in the Athenian popular assembly. See Kitto, p. 225, for an interesting discussion.

50. See Chapter 6.

51. The anthropologist Hoebel observes that hereditary monarchy "is so common among advanced primitive societies that we must conclude that the need for centralized control outweighs the urge for democratic freedom at this level of social development. The resurgence of democracy comes later (p. 527)." See also Burling, pp. 46–47.

52. The former is suggested by Taviss (p. 15). See also the closing remedy in Chapter 8.

53. To the extent that democratic selection of the state results in a more nearly optimal

provision of state services and/or reduces the exploitative component of the rulers' incomes (neither of which seems likely—see Chapter 6) which might be particularly important to persons whose incomes had risen above a subsistence level, the argument in the text requires that these benefits to the population would be more than offset by the additional cost of establishing and maintaining democracy. For a lucid attempt to construct a general theory of choice between "open" and "closed" political systems at the individual level, see Groth and Curry.

54. In the perspective of the present work H.B. Mayo's assertion that democracy in Athens did not depend on slavery but that the "financial returns (only) enabled Athens to live at a higher standard, and to erect the Parthenon and other magnificent public buildings (p. 43)" is of dubious validity.

55. Knutson, p. 21.

56. Knutson, p. 23.

57. Knutson, p. 27.

## CHAPTER 8

1. This chapter was written entirely by Auster.

2. If, however, there are fixed costs to the formation of new jurisdictions and to changing the level of public good, then as the work of M. Spence suggests, some non-optimality will still be present.

3. See Chapter 3. May we note that the Romans then ruled the Mediterranean world, most of the Middle East, and parts of Asia and Africa.

4. The Chinese used to pay doctors when they were well and stop payment when they were ill.

5. A plan similar to the above, but designed for the hospital sector has been proposed by Jerry Gordon and myself. Currently we are seeing if a sufficient number of volunteer health systems can be found to induce SSA to fund a field experiment.

6. N. Georgescu-Roegen provides an excellent discussion of why in general a number, or vector of numbers, will be unable to perfectly represent the qualities of something, or more basically the fullness of what is. There is always a "qualitative residual" beyond our grasp. We are pointing out that in some circumstances there is a law of the increasing importance of that residual.

7. This individual then becomes the residual income recipient or "pseudo-entrepreneur," at least to some degree. The issue of the appropriate level of risk-sharing complicates matters. In the presence of risk the full incentive of every dollar saved being the property of the "pseudo-entrepreneur" is generally not optimal. This rather technical issue need not be discussed here; however, I am indebted to my colleague J. Cox for bringing it to my attention.

8. We might recall that at the time of the Viet Nam War, Sonny Barger (leader of the Hell's Angels) was ready to go over and see what his boys could do. I suspect that they could have done more than General Westmoreland whose defenders could only cite in his defense his "logistical genius," the fact that he could relax every day by playing an hour or two of tennis and his lifelong association with the Boy Scouts.

9. Whatever those were. Clearly, objectives might have to be sufficiently broad so that the enemy would not be given free strategic information.

10. Apparently the Army discovered during World War II that it took longer to get National Guard units combat ready than it took to ready raw recruits.

11. In the limit we can at least suggest the possibility of open war games with big prizes. Perhaps, as was the case with the British privateers, the heavy equipment could be supplied by the government.

12. The reader might consult Auster (1977). Papers by Ellickson and Pauly raise the issue that such an equilibrium might not exist. As Ellickson points out, however, the result obtains because of the so-called "indivisibility" of individuals, i.e., that no individual can actually live in more than one jurisdiction at a time. This is true, but only if we wish to use the same notion of time that creates difficulties such as Zeno's paradox, of the arrow in flight that wasn't moving, i.e., "points in time." If we consider periods of time, then multiple dwellings are allowed. I for one maintain residence in both Arizona and New Mexico. I was born in Brooklyn. Ellickson went to school in Cambridge, Massachusetts, and now lives in L.A. Remove this "indivisibility" and their result would appear to vanish as well. Thus, it would not hold in a multiperiod perfect foresight context, which is closer to the context we have in mind.

13. States are overgovernments for counties, for example.

14. "Consolidation and Voter Choice: The Public School System in Transition." A.T. Denzau, R.J. Mackay, R.J. Staaf, presented at Public Choice Meetings 1975.

15. One might suppose that potential competition might be effective, perhaps it is. Clearly, however, it is currently not enough. Moreover, the effectiveness of potential competition would be increased by these proposals. Large states are very difficult to overthrow.

16. These amendments, like constitutions themselves, would operate by changing the structure of opinion so as to render the use of the central states' superior power of coercion unlikely. Use of this power by the rulers automatically decreases "legitimacy" which would cause them problems (revolt, general revolt) and, if they are rational, prevents them from doing so.

17. William Niskanen informs us that similar proposals (the Virginia and Kentucky resolutions) were covertly supported by Thomas Jefferson. In the original, states were only to be allowed to nullify laws in areas not specifically assigned to the Federal government. The problem with this version, however, is that given the reality of supreme court judges, it is not clear that any nullification would, in the long run, ever be possible.

18. Interestingly, there was some movement in that city to secede from the Union itself at the time of the Civil War.

19. See also my discussion in "The GPITPC . . . " Appendix III.

20. "Renting the Streets" and "Variants of Compensating Elections, an Approach to the Gambling Problem" in *American Re-evolution,* (Auster and Sears eds.).

21. An interesting alternative would be to divide the surplus up among all participants in the election. Then everyone would have a positive incentive to see correct changes made. See our discussion of the alternative forms of CE's in "Variants of Compensating Elections, an Approach to the Gambling Problem," in *American Re-evolution. ibid.*

22. Those familiar with the so-called Coase theorem will recognize the optimality of such decisions and their approximate ability to solve the free-rider problem. The mechanism is essentially a type of "two-price auction," which as Smith shows, necessarily causes people to have incentives to reveal their true preferences even in public goods situations. Gaming might be a problem but it always is—even with private goods. Again Smith's work is invaluable.

23. Further, if gambling in general were legalized, the size of *this* gambling could be reduced.

24. Peter Aranson, for example, has suggested that laws which only passed by $X\%$ or less be open to nullification.

25. See the brief discussion of this point in Auster-Silver (1973).

26. This solution is essentially what the antitrust literature refers to as vertical disintegration. Many of M. Friedman's excellent suggestions for the reform of our government are essentially examples of this type of approach.

27. See V. Smith's paper, "Mechanisms for the Optimal Provision of Public Goods," in Auster and Sears, eds., *American Re-evolution,* Tucson (1976). This discussion is heavily influenced by discussions with Smith; however, only I am responsible for any continued misunderstandings.

28. Vernon Smith, JAI Press (1978). If the induced utility functions have a zero income elasticity of demand for public good, then exact optimality occurs. When that elasticity is positive an over allocation of about 10% is typical.

29. See the discussion in "An Experimental Market for Public Goods: the PBS Station Program Cooperative," J.A. Ferejohn and R.G. Noll, CIT, Social Science Working Paper No. 106, January 1976.

30. One simply induces individual valuations which have a majority slightly preferring one alternative, while the minority intensely favors another. For a discussion of how one induces preferences see Smith (AER).

31. This is not to deny, however, that for some of us, some parts of the services the state provides are bad.


## APPENDIX I

1. Milton Friedman, *Price Theory: A Provisional Text* (Chicago: Aldine Publishing Co., 1962).

2. J. De. V. Graaff, "Income Effects and the Theory of the Firm," *Review of Economic Studies* 18 (1950–51): 79–86.

3. N. Kaldor, "The Equilibrium of the Firm," *Economic Journal* 44 (March 1934): 60–76.

4. Earl O. Heady, *Economics of Agricultural Production and Resource Use* (New York: Prentice-Hall, Inc., 1952), pp. 536–37.

5. J. Fred Weston, "The Profit Concept and Theory: A Restatement," *Journal of Political Economy* 62 (April 1954): 152–70.

6. Friedman, p. 105.

7. Ibid, p. 93.

8. Ibid, p. 94.

9. Ibid, p. 94. Friedman does not answer the question, but he states that "such differences . . . will arise, not only as differences arising from market imperfections or momentary disequilibrium, but also as permanent differences consistent with 'stable' equilibrium" (p. 94).

10. According to Alfred Marshall, "It is true even when a man is working for hire he often finds pleasure in his work; but he generally gets so far tired before it is done that he is glad when the hour of stopping arrives . . . The unwillingness of anyone already in an occupation to increase his exertions depends, under ordinary circumstances, on fundamental principles of human nature which economists have to accept as ultimate facts" [*Principles of Economics,* 8th ed. [New York: Macmillan Co., 1948), p. 141].

11. To obtain an idea of the magnitude of the theft problem in the presence of enforcement, consider that "white collar employees . . . in the U.S. are stealing about four million

dollars in cash and property from the employers each working day" [Norman Jaspar, *The Thief in the White Collar* (New York: J.B. Lippincott Co., 1960), p. 11].

12. Armen A. Alchian terms the resulting expenditures "the costs of enforcing contracts" and points out that they are absent in the owner operated enterprise ["The Basis of Some Recent Advances in the Theory of Management of the Firm," *Journal of Industrial Economics* (November 1965), p. 34].

13. R.H. Coase ["The Nature of the Firm," in *Readings in Price Theory* (Chicago: Richard D. Irwin, Inc., for the American Economic Association, 1952), pp. 331–51] places such costs at the center of his explanation of the existence of contractual income recipients. In our opinion, the advantage of "central planning" within the firm as compared to the use of the market is that the use of the market would involve many individuals acquiring the same information; this duplication would raise the costs of a given volume of output.

14. For a more complete exposition of these points in the context of share and cash renting in agriculture, see D. Gale Johnson, "Resource Allocation under Share Contracts," *Journal of Political Economy* 58 (April 1950): 111–23.

15. For simplicity we can think of the entrepreneur's available time as a physical maximum – there are only twenty-four hours in a day. The analysis could be made more sophisticated by deriving the available time from a money income-leisure indifference map (see Graaff, n. 2 above).

16. In most studies devoted to limits on firm size, the factor we have selected for emphasis is labeled "routine" and then ignored. However, it is worth noting that limits derived from factors such as external capital rationing and imperfect knowledge of the future on the part of entrepreneurs fit much less readily into the standard treatments of microeconomics than does a limit derived from the need to enforce contracts with hired labor. In a recent article, Oliver E. Williamson ["Hierarchical Control and Optimum Firm Size," *Journal of Political Economy* 75 (April 1967): 123–38] argues that a limit on firm size under "quasi-static" conditions is provided by a "loss in the quality of the data provided to the peak coordinator and in the quality of the instructions supplied to the operating units made necessary by the expansion [of the firm]" (p. 127). Williamson goes on to say that this alleged "control loss" will exist "even if the objectives of the subordinates are perfectly consonant with those of their superiors" (p. 127). Our point is that the fundamental source of limits on firm size is precisely the divergence of interest between the "peak coordinator" and his "subordinates." Another theory that may fit the standard treatment of microeconomics has been developed by R.H. Coase. This student suggests that limits on firm size might be due to the fact that "as a firm gets larger there may be decreasing returns to the entrepreneur function, that is, the costs of organizing additional transactions within the firm may rise. Naturally, a point must be reached where the costs of organizing an extra transaction within the firm are equal to the costs involved in carrying out the transaction in the open market" (Coase, p. 340). Unfortunately, it is not clear to us why the "costs of organizing transactions within the firm" should rise.

On this point, see also George J. Stigler, *The Theory of Price*, 3d ed. (New York: Macmillan Co., 1966), pp. 170–71.

17. Marshall lists among the advantages of the small firm that "the master's eye is everywhere; there is no shirking by his foremen or workmen . . . " and claims that "the gain from this source is of very great importance in trades which use the more valuable metals and other expensive materials" (p. 284). Also, Marshall maintains that one of the problems in establishing large-scale agriculture is the "difficulty of concentrating a great deal of labour in any one place" (p. 290).

## APPENDIX II

1. I find Lubasz's [26, p. 4] distinction between "overt opposition directed at particular laws, practices, or individuals" (rebellion) and "demand for general and fundamental change" (revolution) to be vague and intractable. Tanter and Midlarsky [40, pp. 264–67] present a useful survey of the various meanings scholars have given to revolution and offer a scheme for classifying revolutions.

2. Equation (4) is approximate because it ignores the typically slight influence an individual believes his participation will have on the likelihood of revolutionary success.

3. In view of the wide variety of factors reflected in $E$ it is probably misleading to call it, as Tullock does, the "entertainment value" of participation.

4. See Gottschalk [10] for a penetrating discussion of the various causes of revolution.

5. Military defeats at the hands of the Japanese also played a role in stimulating revolutionary activity [see part (2)].

6. The case of the Emperor Wang Mang sometimes called "the first Socialist on the throne of China" is interesting, but the facts are obscure. Wang Mang surrounded himself with Confucian scholars and in A.D. 9 promulgated reforms calling for the abolition of slavery and the distribution of land to peasants. It is not clear whether these reforms were carried out and (apparently) they were repealed in A.D. 12. It is clear that Wang Mang's reign was plagued by revolutions and disturbances until he was killed in A.D. 23 (see [24, pp. 88–109]). For additional examples and an insightful discussion of the role of reform the reader should consult Huntington [18, Chap. 6] and Hagopian [14, pp. 156–63], which unfortunately came to my attention only when this revision was in its final stages.

7. Current events provide many smaller scale examples. (1) Representative Floyd V. Hicks (Democrat, Washington) suspects that "permissiveness" in the Navy may have sparked racial clashes aboard Navy ships (New York Times, November 21, 1972, p. 7). According to the New York Times (November 22, 1972, p. 1) many Navy officers believe that the erosion of the command structure flows from Admiral Zumwalt's reforms beginning in 1970 relaxing dress and hair styles and appointing "minority affairs assistants" to counsel commanders on race relations. (2) In a discussion of illegal student demonstrations in Egypt the New York Times (January 7, 1973, Section 4, p. 3 and February 11, 1973, Section 4, p. 4) suggests that President Sadat who has been subjected to a personal attack by students "started in office more than two years ago with a series of liberalizing steps. For example, he removed the police from university campuses, where they had been assigned for surveillance – even in the classrooms – since the 1967 Arab-Israeli war. But in relaxing controls somewhat, he has whetted greater appetites for freedom than he dare satisfy". (3) With respect to prison riots I suspect that despite the protestations of the prison reformers, empirical studies would demonstrate that reforms precede prison riots rather than preventing them. According to Starr [38, p. 35] in the months before the Attica prison riot in 1971 "visitation privileges were greatly broadened; due process was afforded to men returned to prison for alleged parole violation; mail and book censorship were lifted almost entirely; limits were placed on the segregation of those accused of breaking prison rules and due process of a sort was provided to replace the discretion of the Deputy Superintendent in the imposition of punishment."

8. I have examined the related literature but have not found a plausible explanation of why reforms should cause "expectations" (or "aspirations") to increase at a more rapid rate than "achievement".

9. The Kennedy-Johnson "War on Poverty" provided jobs and incomes for a variety of revolutionaries including Huey Newton and Bobby Seale, the founders of the Black Panthers [3, pp. 178–79].

10. Under these circumstances "appeasement policies"—i.e., the buying off of "hard-core" revolutionaries (see Brennan [4, pp. 59–65]) are likely to be "misunderstood" by the bribed revolutionaries. In addition, such a policy will be ineffective to the extent that the government reforms initiate a *mass* revolutionary movement. Obviously the larger the number of potential revolutionaries to be bribed, the higher the cost of appeasement relative to repression.

11. A good illustration is provided by the repeal of most of Joseph's reforms under Leopold II [32, V.I., p. 396].

12. The historical importance of "demonstration" effects is illustrated by the scholarly controversy concerning "The Eighteenth Century Revolution: French or Western?" [1]. See also [11, pp. 116–18].

13. Available data suggests that the Russian Communist Party grew very rapidly in the months immediately preceding the October Revolution [36, pp. 172–73].

14. But see also footnote 17 and the discussion of type (4) revolutions.

15. Obviously Tullock's Equation (5) applies in this case since the individual's participation makes a large difference in the likelihood of success of the revolution.

16. The level of banditry may have been increased by floods which sent many peasants wandering. The floods in turn were at least in part caused by failure of the Manchu state to properly maintain dikes and systems of river control [27, p. 214].

17. This aspect may also play an important role in some type (2) revolutions. The 1868 overthrow of the Tokugawa Shogunate in Japan not very long after the appearance of Commodore Perry's ships comes immediately to mind as an example.

18. The role of economic affluence is considered in Chapter 7. Briefly, it is suggested that increases in income increase the demand for political democracy, or more broadly, personal freedom. Thus, government reforms increasing the incomes of the oppressed poor may precipitate both type (1) and type (4) revolutions.

19. Edwards' "four wishes of Thomas" are (1) the wish for new experience, (2) the wish for security, (3) the wish for recognition, (4) the wish for response [9, pp. 2–3].

20. The perceptive Max Nomad notes that "Russia's top stratum after the victorious Bolshevik Revolution consisted of the former revolutionary conspirators . . . Though calling themselves Communists, they took it for granted that they were to have the cream of all the good things that were still left after all the turmoil of war and revolution" [19, p. 28]. In some cases the private reward element is open and explicit as when Li Tzu-ch'eng promised all who helped him overthrow the Ming state that they would be released from the obligation to pay the land tax [16, p. 43].

21. This may help explain the popularity of college "open-admissions" policies, see [4, pp. 69–65].

22. The blindspot of Marxist theory with respect to the question of who will become a revolutionary is certainly related to its inability "to make a distinction between the interests of the manual workers and those of the rising new middle class of intellectual workers" [29, p. 88]. The latter group has been described as "the impecunious owners of an invisible capital that they had no opportunity to invest profitably" [29, p. 151].

23. Brennan [4] has shown that risk-loving persons who are poor have a relatively high probability of becoming revolutionaries.

## APPENDIX III

1. In some instances, e.g., Lindsay campaigns in the fashionable eastside of New York, participation may itself be a good, e.g., increased social contacts. In these cases the return does not depend on the outcome of the political system, but may depend purely on whom else is supporting the policy (candidate), and how many other supporters there are. We include these also.

2. It is interesting to note that whenever one of the major parties has from the beginning seemed doomed to defeat in the Presidential election (e.g., Republicans in 1964, Democrats in 1972), then they have had unusual difficulties raising funds. It might be interesting to see exactly what a rigorous analysis of contribution data along GPITPC lines would reveal.

3. For a discussion of thresholds in economics see Devletoglou [3].

4. If we dropped Assumption 1 then this would read, "the individual *believed* he was important to the outcome." We observe that political rhetoric often attempts to convince individuals, in the face of real evidence to the contrary, that they are important to the outcome.

5. From the point of view of predicting which policies will be supported by the individual, the key distinction is between those returns which are action dependent and those which are not. The returns which result purely from the adoption of the policy are, by definition, action independent unless (1), (2), or (3) holds. If a greater probability of being promoted in an expanding army depends on whether or not one has supported the expansion, then this return is part of the $P_{pi}$. This does not deny, however, that in some circumstances some individuals will derive satisfaction from acting in the public interest itself, that is, in favor of the policy with the higher $C_i$. This return is also part of the $P_{pi}$. Such individuals are called "patriots" when the institution is a government, and are said to "identify with the firm" when it is a firm; they are extremely valuable to any institution, but only to the extent that they correctly perceive which is the "best" policy. It seems to be generally accepted that "patriotism" is no longer fashionable—it is not clear whether or not "identifying with the firm" ever was. If in fact there has been a decline in these, then GPITPC would predict a corresponding decline in the quality of political system's choices for all institutions in society. It may be that "patriotism" is naturally high in the initial flush following the establishment of an institution, but then declines as the founders, who more closely "identify," die out. This would reinforce the tendency for institutional entropy of §2. The process by which "patriotism" (etc.) is produced is not clear. We do not consider it a first order motivation for most public actions at this stage in history.

6. The present paper was precipitated by a reading of that paper at the suggestion of M. Silver.

7. New York City street rumor has it that this is not an unknown practice in that institution. For a discussion of the shirking-enforcement problem in theory of the firm itself, see Silver and Auster [7]. It might be argued, however, that in long-run equilibrium wages will be lower in those industries where the opportunity for theft is higher and that, therefore, in long-run equilibrium, costs will not be higher. But such an equilibrium is unlikely to be reached. For one, information about theft opportunities is unlikely to be widely disseminated—for obvious reasons. Long-run equilibrium is a useful concept. It must, however, be recognized that some adjustment processes are very slow. In the second place, wages would only fully adjust to the amount of theft if there were no psychic costs to stealing—which there are (although for some individuals these may be negative; i.e., psychic benefits). Finally, one wonders whether in fact such an equilibrium is stable. Will not workers with

above average abilities to steal drive out those with below average abilities in those industries where the opportunity for theft is large (e.g., stevedores)? The problem is precisely Acker-lof's "lemon problem" [1], the generalization of Gresham's Law.

8. See, for example, Richelson's recent discussion [4]. Observe also the implicit use of "Theorem" there.

9. Ombudsmen are one type of institutionalized muckraker, but only when they actually perform their intended function. "Think and Suggest" programs is another example. The Chinese use group discussion centered around the teachings of Mao. This could be viewed as a variant of 2. An attempt to convince the person that his "selfish interest" is not "his" interest.

10. Because of this, a blind move towards "efficiency" would itself be "inequitable." In practice this will generally be the case when one tries to eliminate inefficiency, and this represents another argument for compensation mechanisms.

# INDEXES

## SELECTED AUTHORS

Acton, Lord 83
Adelman, I. 92, 93
Arrow, K. 45, 128, 155

Bakunin 61
Bradley, O. 88
Breton, A. 26, 61, 71, 159, 160
Breton, R. 61
Brundage, B. C. 18, 35
Buchanan, J. M. 63, 150, 154
Bucharin, N. 61

Carniero, R. L. 21, 22, 156
Claiborne, R. 61, 156, 159
Cobban, A. 91
Cohen, C. 94
Coulborn, R. 34, 156, 157
Cutright, P. 92

Dahrendorf, R. 24
Downs, A. 53, 162, 163
Durkheim, E. 7, 51, 153

Engels, F. 23, 25, 152

Fallers, L. A. 16
Forquin, G. 39, 157
Frazer, J. 23
Frech, T. E. 84
Fried, M. H. 25, 26, 152
Friedman, D. 26, 31, 155
Frölich, N. 26, 159
Fustel de Coulanges 23

Galbraith, J. K. 62, 77
Gluckman, M. 30, 60, 159
Goody, J. 17, 154
Greaves, H. R. G. 21

174

Hagen, E. F. 92, 93
Hintze, O. 39
Hirschman, A. O. 58
Hobbes, T. 8, 9
Hoebel, E. A. 57, 152, 153, 159, 165

Keith, R. G. 21, 156
Krader, L. 8, 18, 22, 154, 160

Lane, F. C. 20, 159, 161
Langer, L. N. 36, 156
Lanning, E. P. 21, 156
Lenin, V. 24
Linton, R. 17
Lippitt, R. K. 93
Lipset, S. M. 92, 93, 161
Lipson, L. 92, 154, 164
Locke, J. 65

McKenzie, R. B. 60, 160
Martin, P. T. 60, 160
Marx, K. 23, 60, 152, 155
Maslow, A. 95
Miller, J. C. 18
Monsen, J. 53
Morgenthau, H. 77
Morris, C. T. 92, 93
Morris, R. 72
Mosca, G. 24, 155

Niskanen, W. A. 40, 160, 163, 167
North, D. C. 26, 31, 61, 153, 159
Nozick, R. 21, 154

Oates, W. E. 37, 158
Olson, M. 26, 116, 123, 153, 157
Oppenheimer, A. 26, 159
Orzechowski, W. V. 54, 158

Price, B. 18, 153
Puller, L. B. 88

Riker, W. H. 12, 157
Rogers, C. 95
Russell, J. B. 22

Samuelson, P. A. 106
Sartori, G. 30
Schapera, I. 18, 151, 159
Schwartz, R. D. 18
Scott, T. 71
Simpson, R. 92
Smith, A. K. 92
Smith, V. L. 109, 167, 168
Stevenson, R. F. 18
Szasz, T. S. 7

Thomas, R. P. 26, 31, 153, 159
Tiebout, C. M. 97, 160
de Tocqueville, A. 104, 118, 120
Tucker, R. C. 24
Tullock, G. 9, 12, 23, 116, 130, 150, 151,
    152, 156, 158, 160, 164, 171
Turner, F. J. 58

Vicensvives, J. 91

Weber, M. 21
Wertenbaker, T. J. 20
Wesson, R. G. 62, 156
White, R. K. 93
Wittfogel, K. A. 20, 21, 152, 154
Wittman, P. 9, 151
Wolf, C. 92
Wolfe, R. 41

Yamane, T. 85
Young, D. R. 26, 159

## SELECTED HISTORICAL EVIDENCE

Africa 9, 17, 18, 30, 58, 60
Alexander 32
American colonies 40
Arabian caliphate 32
Argentina 90
Athens 40, 90

Australia 13
Aztec 19

Bantu 9, 18
Berlin Wall 59
Bismarck 41

Black Death 30, 91
Bushman 18

Caesar, Julius 31
Caligula 62
Capone 60
Carolingian Empire 14, 40
China 20, 35, 52
Crassus 76

Dakota 19
Darius 38
Diocletian 30, 62
Dnieper 19, 20, 33

East Africa 22
Egypt 34, 36
England 58, 89
Eskimos 19

Frederic William of Brandenburg 18
French assembly 76

George III 32
German tribes 13, 32
Germany 39
Greece 13, 19, 23, 35

Han Empire 32, 33
Hanseatic League 20, 40
Hebrew 13, 18
Hittites 61
Hottentots 18
Hundred Years War 22, 59

Inca 35
India 58
Italy 20, 23, 39

Japan 18, 35
Johnson, Lyndon 59

Kamakura 40
Kiev 22
Khan, Genghis 32
Korea 32

Lithuania 18

Malay 60
Medes 22
Meiji 18
Mengamok 60
Mesoamerica 18, 19, 20
Mesopotamia 18, 20
Mexico 36
Middle Ages, 13, 14
Muscovy 38, 59
Mycenean cities 33

New Zealand 90

Order of Teutonic Knights 20
Ottoman, 39, 59

Pax Britannica 58
Persian Empire 38
Peru 21, 35
Portugal 20
Post-neolithic Societies 13
Prussia 33, 58

Rome 13, 91, 14 (Empire), 33
Russia 24, 36, 58, 59

Sargon of Akhad 34
Sioux 19
Serbs 59
Southeast Asia 102
Spain 20, 102 (Armada)
Sparta 90

## SELECTED SUBJECTS

Arrow Impossibility Theorem 45

Backward-bending supply curve of state
  services 78, 79
Blood feuds 57
Buchanan's Theorem 63

Campaign Reform Act of 1974, 71
Capital 2, 13, 47, 54
Central planning 23
Civil service 73, 82
Class 24, 76, 13 (working)
Compensation 13, 105, 106 (elections)

Community indiffence curves 50
Contract enforcement 28, 29, 38, 41
Corporal punishment 14
Criminal act 6-7 (defined), 7 (vs. punish-
    ment), 8 (as negative externality), 11 (in-
    ternal vs. external), 17
Crowding 44

Decision making 42, 56, 72-73, 161 (fn 1)
Democracy 4, 5, 70 (and competition for
    public approval), 69ff, 85-88 (and equity-
    efficiency problem), 29, 30, 75 (and shirk-
    ing problem), 4, 89ff (as consumer good),
    2, 71, 72, 77 (as form of ownership), 94
    (cost of), 161 (fn 1) (defined), 51, 70
    (median voter model), 69 (representative)
Discipline of continuous dealings 9
Divine right 62
Division of labor 16, 26 (and limits on mar-
    ket), 25-26 (and social conflict)
Domino effects 121

Efficiency 54, 69
Emigration restrictions 59
Enforcement 9
Entry 28, 56, 60, 61, 67
Envy 69
Equity 5, 55, 69, 70
Evidence, quantitative vs. qualitative 3
Exclusivity 53
Externalities 8 (defined), 83, 114
External threats 37

Factor intensities, 63
Federalism 4, 35, 38, 39
Feudalism 4, 39
Feuds 57
Firm, defined 1-2, 161-162 (fn 5)
Franchising 37, 39, 40
Free rider problem 17, 40, 56
Frontier 58
Full line forcing problem 103

General private interest theory of public
    choice (GPITPC), 75, 81, 94, 127ff
Growth 47
Guilt 10, 17, 50, 52

Imperialism 77
Incentive compatible mechanisms 108

Income 53
Information 66
Institutional entropy 74-76, 131
Institutional invisible hand 42
Irrigation systems 21

Labor 2
Land 2, 47
Language 15
Legitimacy 10, 12, 26, 39, 50
Limit price theory 60
Love 10, 50, 52

Marginal entry 67
Markets 15 (vs. societies), 55 (structure)
Median voter 70
Metaphysical 17, 43, 49-52, 54 (basis for
    order)
Monopolistic competition 2, monopoly 16,
    21, 55, 56 (natural)

Nationalism 52
New approach to consumer behavior 43
Nullification 104

Optimality assumption 2, 42
Order 12 (and income redistribution), 6, 44
    as public good, 10-11 (fn 21), p. 151,
    158 (fn 13) (defined and determinants
    of), 50, 54 (metaphysical basis of), 60
    (price of), 50-52 (resources and produce)
Ownership 2

Police 2, 26, 80
Policy 4
Political concentration 27 (defined), 33,
    35, 37-42, 55-57, 60
Political structure 1, 3, 98
Politician 82
Population 2, 16, 53, 18, 28 (growth of)
Potential competition 60
Power 82
Price discrimination 66-67
Protection, 2, 6, 11 (defined), 12 (public
    vs. private), 16, 17, 19, 44, 56
Public goods 6 (and avoidance cost), 41-42
    (and industrial concentration), 81 (and
    public workers), 56 (and market mechan-
    ism), 2, 56, 62-63 (and monopoly), 30,
    75 (and shirking problem), 44-49 (com-

parative statics of), 6, 44 (defined), 155
(fn 6) (impure, crowded, and mixed), 44,
56 (intensities)
Public workers 79-80
Punishment 14 (and affluence), 14 (as advertisement), 12 (as public good) 7-10
(as retribution), 7 (as treatment), 13-14
(corporal vs. monetary), 7 (defined), 17
(demand for), 12-13 (deterrent effect),
11, 17 (physical vs. psychic), 16, 67 (private vs. state), 9-10, 13 (rationalist view)

Red bureaucracy 51
Representative consumer 70
Residual income recipient 38-39, 74-75,
78, 112*ff*
Revolution 4, 21, 58-61, 63-66, 76, 94,
117 (defined), Appendix II
Rich 83
Risk 80, 82 (aversion)
Rulers 24 (and class rule), 30, 72-73 (and
control of production), 16 (defined), 31-
32, 59-61, 63-67, 69-73, 77*ff*, 123 (in-
come of), 79*ff* (personal characteristics
of), 60-61 (supply of)
Running amuck 60

Schooling 5, 62
Serfdom 22, 39, 58
Shirking problem 37 (and internal vs. external protection), Appendix I (and limits
on firm size), 80, 84 (and occupational
choice), 32, 54 (and passage of time), 33
(and population compactness), 53-54, 78
(and resource use), 41, 54 (and technological progress), 29-30 (defined)
Slaves 13, 14
Social cohesiveness 53
Socialism 23
Specialization 16, 17

State 21, 62 (advertising by), 23-24 (as
distinct from society), 19-20, 33-36,
39-41 (and compaction or urbanization
of population), 17-18, 25, 40 (and external threats), 8-9 (and externalities), 18,
20, 28, 37, 39-41, 53-54 (and size of
population, 25-26 (and stratification),
1-2, 16, 24, 26, 27, 30, 37, 55, 57, 68,
76, 78-79, 84, 98 (as firm), 16, 56, 68 (as
natural monopoly), 5-7, 68, 74, 84 (as
producer), 37 (central vs. local), 61-62
(communist), 16 (defined), 4, 31, 55, 57-
61, 64, 65-68, 70, 73 (exploitation by),
40 (federations of), 2, 73-74, 77-78
(forms of ownership), 2, 28-30, 55-57,
60, 76 (in industrial systems), 23-26
(Marxian view), 26 (public choice approach to), 21 (traditional view), 2, 8,
27-28, 30-33, 41, 52-54, 57 (sizes of),
21-23, 25, 31, 32, 64-68 (social contract
or consent vs. conquest), 73-74 (world),
21, 23 (idealist theory of)
Stockholders 72
Stratification 25, 26
Supplanting entry 60

Taxation 17 (and free riding), 26 (as price),
26 (as unique power of state), 57-61
(resistance to), 66-67
Tax farming 38
Theocracy 23
Tiebout forces 97
Time 47
Transport cost 33

Utility maximizing firm 78
Utility possibility curve 45

Vertical structure 37-40
Voters 70